Published by

ATLANTIC

PUBLISHERS & DISTRIBUTORS (P) LTD

7/22, Ansari Road, Darya Ganj, New Delhi-110002
Phones : +91-11-40775252, 40775214, 23273880, 23275880
Fax : +91-11-23285873
Web : www.atlanticbooks.com
E-mail : orders@atlanticbooks.com

Branch Office: Chennai
Phones : +91-44-48531784, 28291383
E-mail : chennai@atlanticbooks.com

Disclaimer

- The author and the publisher have taken every effort to the maximum of their skill, expertise and knowledge to provide correct material in the book. Even then if some mistakes persist in the content of the book, the publisher does not take responsibility for the same. The publisher shall have no liability to any person or entity with respect to any loss or damage caused, or alleged to have been caused directly or indirectly, by the information contained in this book.
- The author has fully tried to follow the copyright law. However, if any work is found to be similar, it is unintentional and the same should not be used as defamatory or to file legal suit against the author.
- If the readers find any mistakes, we shall be grateful to them for pointing out those to us so that these can be corrected in the next edition.
- All disputes are subject to the jurisdiction of Delhi courts only.

Printed & bound in India by Atlantic Print Services

Preface

The Gricean Cooperative Principle (CP) is a milestone in the domain of Pragmatics. A philosopher of language, Herbert Paul Grice (1913-1988) argues in his seminal paper "Logic and Conversation" (1975) that conversation is a cooperative endeavour between a speaker and a hearer. They engage in conversation with the assumption of a tacit norm or guiding principle of cooperation. Grice calls this Cooperative Principle. He defines Cooperative Principle saying: "Make your conversational contribution such as is required, at the stage it occurs, by the accepted purpose or direction of the talk exchange in which you are engaged".

This Cooperative Principle comprises four maxims:

1. Quantity maxim: Give required amount of information—neither more nor less.
2. Quality maxim: Do not say what you believe to be false.
3. Relation maxim: Be relevant.
4. Manner maxim: Avoid ambiguity, vagueness and be brief and clear.

Grice further argues that a speaker may fail to follow a maxim. When the speaker blatantly deviates from a maxim, it leads the hearer to infer an unstated meaning called 'implicature'. Experts in the field like Fraser (1990), Peter Grundy (2000), Jacob Mey (2001), and Elizabeth Black (2006) claim that it is the deviation from a maxim which signals speaker's communicative intention and, hence, is significant for utterance interpretation.

Another dominant pragmatic principle is Politeness Principle. A sociolinguist R. Lakoff (1973), social scientist S. Levinson, and an anthropological linguist P. Brown (1978/1987) propose that being linguistically polite means avoiding offence to the hearer and trying to preserve his 'face', a person's sense of self-esteem. G.N. Leech (1983) defines politeness as minimising the expression of beliefs which are unfavourable to the hearer and maximising the expression of beliefs which are favourable to the hearer. Leech's model of politeness comprises six maxims: Tact, Generosity, Approbation, Modesty, Sympathy, and Agreement. Pragmaticists and experts in the field claim that very often the CP is sacrificed for the sake of PP.

This book aims at showing how the application of Gricean framework enriches the interpretation of novelistic discourse. The book analyses conversations in the five Indian novels in English in which characters deviate from the four maxims of CP. The book also analyses the conversations in which the characters face the conflict between following CP and PP. The focus is on examining why and how the characters deviate from the maxims of CP and pinpointing the significance of maxim-deviations in the interpretation of fictional discourse. Though the focus of analysis is on these five novels, conversations from novels/short stories by the well-known writers like Henry Fielding, Charles Dickens, D.H. Lawrence, Raja Rao, R.K. Narayan, Khushwant Singh, Chaman Nahal, Rama Mehta, O. Henry, H.G. Wells, and Premchand have also been analysed from the point of view of Gricean Cooperative Principle and Politeness Principle.

The book is based on genuine research carried out by me. The theoretical insights have been drawn from Philosophy of language, Sociology, Social Psychology, Sociolinguistics, Anthropology, and Pragmatics, which make the book multidisciplinary in nature. The piecemeal and in-depth analysis of conversations shows that in the study of deviations from Gricean maxims lies God's plenty.

The book will be immensely useful to philosophers of language, social psychologists, sociologists, sociolinguists, pragmaticists, teachers, and students of English literature and budding researchers in Pragmatics.

I am grateful to my friend Late Prof. D.K. Binnar (Pune), Prof. Z.N. Patil (EFLU, Hyderabad), and Prof. Ashok Thorat

(IASE, Pune) for igniting my interest in the exciting field of Pragmatics. I am deeply indebted to my motivating, competent, and enthusiastic supervisor Prof. (Dr.) Jyoti S. Rane, Principal, Pratap College, Amalner. My thanks also go to my wife Mrs. Ranjana and my sons Gaurav and Sameer for letting me concentrate on this work. I wish to thank my colleague Prof. Sanjay Pate for technical support during the publication of this book. Finally, I thank Atlantic Publishers and Distributors Pvt. Ltd. for bringing out this book expeditiously and in an elegant design.

Chalisgaon (M.S.) **Shivaji D. Mahajan**

Contents

1
Theoretical Framework

1.0. Preliminaries

This chapter aims at explicating language as a socio-cultural phenomenon and then explicating the basic pragmatic concepts like Cooperative Principle and Politeness Principle on which the present study hinges. The Cooperative Principle and Politeness Principle constitute their maxims. These maxims are followed or flouted in the process of verbal interaction universally. But the operation of these principles and their maxims is constrained by the vital factors like society and culture. These factors govern the conversation of the participants in casual as well as in fictional discourse. This study focuses on the operation of these pragmatic principles in fictional discourse. Five Indian novels in English have been selected for this study. These five novels are as follows:

1. *Temporary Answers* (1974) by Jai Nimbkar
2. *Heat and Dust* (1975) by Ruth Prawer Jhabvala
3. *Cry, the Peacock* (1980) by Anita Desai
4. *Socialite Evenings* (1989) by Shobha De
5. *The Binding Vine* (1993) by Shashi Deshpande

Though the main focus of analysis is on these five novels, conversations from the novels/short stories by the well-known writers like Henry Fielding, Charles Dickens, D.H. Lawrence, Raja Rao, R.K. Narayan, Khushwant Singh, Chaman Nahal, Rama Mehta, H.G. Wells, O'Henry and Premchand have also been analysed from the Gricean framework and Politeness Principle point of view.

By way of prolegomenon it could be said that language is an integral part of individual's life. The existence of an individual in general without language is utterly unthinkable. One of the most significant purposes for which an individual in any society uses language is communication. He uses language also for expressing his thoughts, feelings, desires and attitudes. The basic aspect of individual's life is his urge to establish and reinforce relations with his fellow beings through language. This function of language is called 'phatic communion' in linguistic parlance. It stands that language becomes a powerful tool in his hands. In using language he empowers himself and also influences others. Kelkar (1993: 3) emphasizes "It is certainly the power we have been looking for in language. Language use is the manifestation of this power to activate the bond between words and meanings."

This point of language use as a powerful vehicle can be explained with an illustration from a novel *Hard Times* by Dickens. In this novel a character named Slackbridge is a leader of factory workers Union-United Aggregate Tribunal. He addresses the Union members about a worker named Stephen Blackpool's refusal to join the Union. It would not be unfit to quote here how Slackbridge wins the workers' applause through his address. This is how he begins his address:

> Oh, my friends, the downtrodden operatives of Cocktown! Oh, my friends and fellow countrymen, the slaves of an iron-handed and a grinding despotism! Oh, my friends and fellow sufferers and fellow workmen and fellow men! I tell you that the hour is come when we must rally round one another as one united power and crumble into dust the oppressors that too long have battened upon the plunder of our families, upon the sweat of our brows, upon the labour of our hands, upon the strength of our sinews, upon the God-created glorious rights of Humanity and upon the holy and eternal privileges of Brotherhood! (138)

Thus, Slackbridge proceeds to pour his venom on Blackpool and turns him out to be a traitor. Slackbridge's pungent use of terms like 'oppressors', 'plunder' and 'sweat' almost bewitches the ears of the fellow-workers. He so sways the audience by his oratory and fiery address that Blackpool is ultimately excommunicated. This powerful tool called language does not exist in isolation. It is an integral part of a society in which it is used. The next section discusses how language use is controlled by societal speech norms.

1.1. Language, Society and Speech Norms

Language is the most powerful and most important tool of human interaction. It is available to all humans in their daily exchange of thoughts, feelings and messages. It is clear from this that language is something special to human species. As a powerful means of communication it cannot be isolated from the society that uses it. A society is a group of people who share common traditions, interests and values. The existence of a group of people without language is unthinkable. Emphasizing the relation among society, language and individuals Hudson (1980: 10) remarks—"Society consists of individuals and both sociologists and sociolinguists would agree that it is essential to keep individuals firmly in the center of interest." A society is not just a group of people or individuals. It is a network of relationships among individuals. These relationships are established and strengthened through a system called language. This network of relationships among individuals is complex. It grows and lives through verbal interaction. The relation between language and society has been proven by Sociolinguists, Sociology, Social Psychology, Pragmatics and researchers. Thorat (2000: 30) remarks that "A language is a reflection of the society in which it is used. The fabric and the texture of that society gets mirrored in its code." Trudgill (1983: 32) says that "Language is very much a social phenomenon. A study of language without reference to social context inevitably leads to the omission of some of the more complex and interesting aspects of language and to the loss of opportunities for further theoretical progress."

The foregoing remarks imply that language is a very crucial phenomenon in the web of relationships among human beings. These human beings are the users of language. The use of language in society implies a host of factors that influence and constrain the ways people talk in their social context. Weisler and Milekic (2000: 16) observe that "The use of language is sensitive to a variety of social and contextual variables and can be analyzed at many different levels of description."

It is pertinent to ask in this context what these factors or variables are that influence language use. There are a host of factors that warrant consideration. These factors include participants, their relationship with each other, social class, education, age, sex, setting and purpose behind engaging in verbal interaction. The use of language is governed by these social factors. Language is used with a variety of purposes. For example we use language for addressing people, for greeting them and for complimenting them. We also use language for admiring and respecting people. The choice of linguistic form used for addressing a person reflects whether our relationship with the person is formal or informal, friendly or distant. The use of a word 'Sir' shows that one is addressing a superior and showing respect for him. In English the master and the servant are seen addressing each other by using the same pronoun 'You'. Corresponding to the English pronoun 'You' Hindi has three pronouns—'tuu', 'tum' and 'aap' to be used depending upon who one is talking to and how one views the other. This illustration points out that there is a lot of non-linguistic information conveyed through language use. Holmes (1997: 4) opines that "The choice of one linguistic form rather than another is a useful clue to non-linguistic information. Linguistic variation can provide social information." For Coates (1986: 12) "Linguistic variation is not random but structured. Structured linguistic variation is a direct consequence of the structured social variation in the speech community."

While considering the relationship between language and society one vital aspect which cannot be lost sight of is culture. The word 'culture' implies a set of values, customs and modes of behavior acquired by an individual as a member of a society. It also signifies knowledge, belief, and morals acquired in the process of socialization. There are various forms which reflect this knowledge, set of values and modes of behavior. These forms are dance, painting, music and literature. The most dynamic medium through which this knowledge is acquired is language. Put it in other words, language is the medium through which culture is acquired, preserved and transmitted. There is correlation between the structure of language and the structure of culture. Hence, Lyons (2002: 324) remarks "Full understanding of the several kinds of meaning that are encoded in the grammar and vocabulary of a language comes only with a full understanding of the culture or cultures in which it operates."

The parameter of culture acquires a great significance not only in terms of language but also in terms of the study of literature. Hence, Z.N. Patil (1994: 14) emphasizes that "Any discussion of language and literature without properly contextualizing them in the matrix of the various aspects of the culture of their production and use is bound to be incomplete."

These observations could be illustrated with an example or two. It is a fact that greetings are integral part of any society and culture. In a sense greetings are a universal activity. Greetings, though a part of routine life, are culture-dependent and culture-specific. Basically they show concern for the addressee's well being. As culture-specific phenomenon they may indicate different concerns. The Arabic greeting "Salaam" literally means "Peace." The English greeting "Hello" is derived from "Healthy be thou". The point one notices is that the Arabic greeting shows spiritual concern whereas the English greeting indicates the other person's physical well-being. Underlying these greetings are the two cultural concerns—the spiritual and the physical respectively.

The other example will show how words carry cultural overtones. Let us take a look at the last two lines from A.K. Ramanujan's (1995) famous poem *Obituary*:

> And he left us
> a changed mother. (112)

In this poem the poet mourns his father's demise. He also enlists the legacy left behind by his father-debts, daughters and a grandson. The poem reaches its crescendo in the two lines quoted. The semantic import of the noun phrase 'a changed mother' could be understood to its desired effect only with reference to the Hindu patriarchal socio-cultural context. "A changed mother" first implies she is no longer someone's wife. As a widow she will have no vermillion-mark on her forehead. Bangles round her wrist will be broken. More than this she will be doomed to suffer humiliation in the Hindu society. Thus, 'a changed mother' connotes a pronounced change not only in her physical appearance but also in her socio-cultural importance. It is these cultural connotations which underlie language use in society. Hence Krishnaswamy, Verma and Nagarajan (1992: 15) comment "Language is looked at not just as a set of sentences but as a system of forms interacting with socio-cultural systems." Wierzbicka (1985: 176) also suggests that "It is very important to try to link language specific norms of interaction with specific cultural values."

Language, thus, is a socio-cultural phenomenon which operates according to society and culture-specific norms. A norm is a rule or a principle which serves to guide and control acceptable behavior. Every society has its own established norms. Language users as social beings adhere to these norms. Some of the norms are derived from the conduct and thoughts of great individuals and famous personalities. Generally every individual behaves according to the society's norms. He tries to avoid any conduct which may be labeled bad or indecent by his society. In a socio-cultural set up like Indian most of the individuals conform to social norms or norms for fear of being excommunicated from their caste or society. We rarely come across any brave behavior violating an established social norm.

The norms that are established by society relate to our physical as well as verbal behavior. The norms related to verbal behavior may, in other words, be called speech norms. These speech norms vary from society to society and culture to culture. A simple act of giving a telephone call exhibits diversity of norms in different cultures and countries. French people view the act of giving a telephone call as an intrusion whereas Americans take it as an act of politeness. Similarly, there are norms about introduction across cultures. In America when two strangers meet in the company of a mutual friend, introduction is a requirement. In Sweden, on the other hand, Swedes do not think it necessary to wait to be introduced by a third party on the occasion of a party. The Swedes just go around the room. They shake hands with everyone and introduce themselves to those people whom they haven't met before. Society and culture control linguistic interaction. Hence Yule (1996: 59) observes "Much of what we say and a great deal of what we communicate is determined by our social relationships. A linguistic interaction is necessarily a social interaction."

Every society provides a set of norms for verbal interaction. Language users learn to follow or flout such norms. Society also provides motivation to adhere to such speech norms. One such motivation is "face a person's sense of self esteem." The motivation behind engaging in interaction is trying to save our face as well as that of our fellow being. Philosophers of language, sociologists and pragmaticists have tried to get deeper insights into speech norms and motivation in adhering to such speech norms. In Pragmatics, these speech norms are termed 'Principles'. These are the principles like Cooperative Principle and Politeness Principle. The manipulation of these Principles constitutes the language user's pragmatic competence.

1.2. Gricean Pragmatics

Human beings spend most of the time of their life in communication. A lot of this process of communication depends on assumption. The speaker assumes that the hearer wishes to understand him. The hearer assumes that the speaker has communicative intention—he intends to communicate something. One asks a question, the other answers it. One makes an offer, the other either accepts it or rejects it. If this were not the case, the very foundation of linguistic communication will collapse. It is because of this assumption that the verbal exchanges run smoothly. Let us take an example of a short piece of conversation taking place between a clerk and a student at a college counter:

Student: Good morning, sir.
Clerk: Good morning. What can I do for you?
Student: I want an application form for admission.
Clerk: Which class?
Student: First year. How much is it?
Clerk: Ten rupees.
Student: Here is the amount.
Clerk: Please, take this form.
Student: Thank you.
Clerk: It's all right.

The interlocutors here give right amount of information. Their verbal contributions are relevant, truthful and clear. One questions and the other answers it. This makes their conversation run smoothly and successfully. They identify purpose in engaging in conversation. To achieve their purpose they follow an unspoken and a tact principle. Herbert Paul Grice—the late British/American philosopher—labels this 'Cooperative Principle'. In his seminal paper "Logic and Conversation" Grice (1975: 45) proposes "Make your conversational contribution such as is required at the stage at which it occurs by the accepted purpose or direction of the talk exchange in which you are engaged."

This is a kind of imperative that conversational partners are expected to observe. The verbal interactants are rational beings. They care about the goals which are central to their engaging in conversation. They assume that to make their conversation profitable they conduct the conversation according to some norm. The Cooperative Principle is such a norm that controls their verbal interaction.

Language users are rational agents as well as social beings. As members of society they are engaged in solving problems and achieving some individual or collective ends. In so doing they influence each other. This influence is reciprocal or mutual—a pivotal part of social interaction. This social interaction is impossible without cooperation. Cooperation is a process in which two or more persons combine and make efforts to achieve their ends. They engage in a team work. This cooperation is physical or verbal. Cooperation is an integral part of language users as social beings. Hence Sharma and Sharma (1997: 232-33) emphasize "The physiological, mental and even the spiritual needs of the individual remain unsatisfied if he does not agree to cooperate with his fellow members of society."

Grice (1975: 45-46) proposes the following four maxims constituting the Cooperative Principle:

1. "The Maxim of Quantity:
   - Make your contribution as informative as it is required (for the current purposes of the exchange).
   - Do not make your contribution more informative than is required.
2. The Maxim of Quality:
   - Do not say what you believe to be false.
   - Do not say that for which you lack adequate evidence.
3. The Maxim of Relation:
   - Be relevant.
4. The Maxim of Manner:
   - Avoid obscurity of expression.
   - Avoid ambiguity.
   - Be brief (Avoid unnecessary prolixity).
   - Be orderly."

Let us take an example of the following conversation from R.K. Narayan's *The Bachelor of Arts*:

He asked, "Mother, do you like the girl?"

"Yes, she is good looking."

"Is her voice all right? Does she talk all right?"

"She talks quite well."

"Does she talk intelligently?"

"Oh, yes. But she spoke very little before me. She was shy before her future mother-in-law."

"What class is she reading in, mother?"

"Sixth form."

"Is she a good student?"

"Her mother says that she is very good in her class."

> "Her father says that she plays very well on the veena. It seems she can also sing very well.... Mother, her name is? He knew it very well but loved to hear it again.
> "Susila," mother said. (162)

This is a conversation between Chandran—the hero and his mother. This conversation is conducted prototypically according to the Gricean proposal. The partners in the conversation provide required quantity of information. Their contributions are truthful. Each of them makes relevant contribution in clear and brief manner. In other words, the conversation takes place according to the framework of the Maxims of Cooperative Principle.

Conversation is a goal directed and goal controlled activity. The goals vary from situation to situation. Conversational partners are rational beings. They engage in verbal interaction with goal of providing or receiving information. They intend to influence others or be influenced by their fellow beings. Their purpose may be to compliment, to direct or to congratulate others. Hence, it is expected that they conduct their conversation according to a norm of giving information. They are supposed to give information neither more nor less than what is required. For example, in normal circumstance if A asks B his/her name, B is expected to say "I am XYZ" or "My name is XYZ". In other words, he/she is expected to adhere to the Quantity maxim.

The maxim of Quality, on the other hand, accounts for the fact that in conversation we assume that our partner is not being untruthful. He/she is not misleading or deceiving us. He/she is saying something which is true. Unless we assume this, it would be difficult to engage in conversation with our co-locutor. The Relation maxim dictates that we make contribution relevant to the ongoing context. In other words, the conversational partners are supposed to stick to the topic of their current conversation. The Manner maxim proposes that the conversational partners avoid ambiguity. They are clear and brief. They avoid prolixity and indirectness. Also they adhere to the norm of presenting events in their chronological order. Pointing out the significance of verbal cooperation Finegan and Besnier (1989: 332) state

"Unless speakers cooperate in the endeavour to communicate reliably and efficiently, the communication process will break down to the detriment of everyone."

It is flagrant that these maxims serve as guidelines for conduct of talk exchanges. Conversational partners are rational individuals. Their conversations are goal-directed. Even in using the norm of greeting existing in their culture and society, they aim to reinforce their relationship with their fellow beings. They take recourse to these norms to facilitate conveying of information and message efficiently. Chilton (1987: 222) says "Cooperation will mean acceptance of prevailing norms and communication will often be deemed not to have occurred if these norms are not observed."

These maxims are, thus, not arbitrary. They lubricate the process of conversation and make it a cooperative endeavour. For Fraser (1990: 222) "These conversational maxims are guidelines for the rational use of language in conversation." A significant point to be noted here is that these maxims differ from 'rules' of language. If one says, "They are speaking, isn't it?", one is said to break the rule of tag question. Breaking of tag question rule renders the sentence ungrammatical. On the other hand, breaking a maxim does not mean that one fails in using the language. As Fraser (1990: 222) remarks "Violation of conversational maxims may be accepted as signaling certain speaker intentions."

These maxims of conversational cooperation have a distinct nature. Leech (1983: 8) characterizes the maxims/principles of conversation as follows:

(a) Principles/Maxims apply variably to different contexts of language used.

(b) Principles/maxims apply to variable degrees rather than in all-or-nothing way.

(c) Principles/maxims can conflict with one another.

(d) Principles/maxims can be contravened without abnegation of the kind of activity which they conduct.

This characterization suggests that the application of these maxims in verbal interaction is not so smooth as it appears.

Their application is context-dependent. The term 'context' includes participants, their relationship with each other, their shared knowledge, their socio-cultural background and above all the time and place of occurrence of conversation. Pointing out the significance of context Grice (1971: 59) says "In cases where there is doubt, say about which of the two or more things an utterer intends to convey, we tend to refer to the context (linguistic or otherwise) of the utterance."

If one of the conversational partners has imperfect command of language, he fails to observe a maxim i.e. to use the appropriate term, he 'infringes' a maxim. Due to his imperfect command of language he fails to understand what the other partner intends to say. He fails to communicate relevantly. Take for example a look at the following conversation between a client (C) and a waiter (W) in a hotel:

C: Waiter, is there the soup on the menu?

W: No, I have just wiped it off.

The client intends to ask whether the food item 'soup' is mentioned in the menu. The waiter takes it literally meaning if the soup has fallen on the menu. Hence he replies that he has cleaned off the soup. In other words the waiter fails to work out the 'intention uptake' of the client. He replies irrelevantly. The situation is rendered ludicrous.

It also happens that when two maxims conflict with each other, a speaker or a hearer upholds one maxim at the expense of the other. This could be illustrated with the help of following exchange:

A: When did Mulk Raj Anand die?

B: Sometime in September 2004.

Here B does not give the right amount of information for A's needs i.e. he gives less information than A needs. He apparently does not follow the maxim of Quantity. But this is not random. He does not know the exact date/day of Anand's death. Thus, he does not tell a lie. His is an attempt to uphold the maxim of Quality.

The foregoing discussion explicates that not all conversation is prototypically conducted as per the norm of verbal cooperation. On many an occasion there are deliberate omissions, misleading statements, digressions and uninformative remarks. Put it in other words, conversational partners do not follow/observe these maxims. There is non-observance of a maxim/of maxims. Grice (1975:49) first refers to three ways of non-observance of the conversational maxims:

1. Violating a maxim
2. Opting out of a maxim
3. Flouting a maxim.

It is pertinent to briefly explicate what these cases of non-observance mean. A speaker flouts a maxim when he wants to lead the hearer to look for a meaning which differs from the literal meaning of his utterance. He flouts a maxim means that he deliberately fails to adhere to the maxim. For Grundy (2000: 78) "Flouting a maxim is a particularly salient way of getting an addressee to draw an inference." A violation of a maxim occurs when a speaker will be liable to mislead. When a speaker indicates his unwillingness for one reason or the other, to behave as required by a maxim, he is said to be opting out of a maxim.

Later Grice refers to other ways of non-observance of a maxim and that are infringement and suspension of a maxim. In this case a participant has no deliberate intention of misleading or deceiving his hearer. This happens when he has no perfect command of language or when his communication ability is impaired by his very physical constitution or by way of drunkenness or nervousness. When it is not expected of a conversational partner that he will follow a maxim, it is a case of suspending a maxim.

A couple of examples are necessary to pinpoint the non-observance of maxim. Here is an example from R.K. Narayan's *The Bachelor of Arts*. The novel tells us the story of a young man Chandran. He is the final year student. Natesan is the Secretary of the College Union. The following talk takes place between Chandran and Natesan:

> "You cannot deny that Brown is a fine Principal. He has never turned down any request to preside at meetings."
> "That's all you seem to care for in a man. Presiding over meetings! It proves nothing."
> "He is a humbug, take it from me," said Chandran. "He gets his thousand a month and no wonder he is pleasant. Remember that he is a scoundrel at heart." (8)

This colloquy takes place after a debate organized by the College Union is over. Chandran was a Prime mover in the debate on the subject "Historians should be slaughtered first." Chandran hoped Natesan to say something about his speech. Natesan began talking about his studies and his election expenses. Chandran was interested in hearing Natesan's compliment on his argument. Natesan showed only the superficial interest in Chandran's speech. This excited Chandran and he began naming Brown—their Principal who presided over the debate.

As Natesan made no reference to Chandran's speech, Chandran got disappointed and angry. This forced him to be cynical about Brown calling him a humbug and scoundrel. This was his attempt to mislead Natesan about Brown. This becomes clear a couple of minutes later. Natesan grips Chandran's hand and says that Chandran's speech was wonderful, fine and eloquent. It was praised by the Principal also. At this moment Chandran's real opinion about Brown is revealed. This is how he apologizes:

> Said Chandran, "Don't for a moment think that I dislike Brown. I agree with you entirely when you say that he is a man with a pleasant manner. He has a first rate sense of humour. He is a great scholar. It is really a treat to be taught Drama by him. I was only trying to suggest that people saw humour even where he was serious. So, please, don't mistake me" (9). This is a case of violation of Quality maxim by Chandran.

An infringement of a maxim occurs when a participant lacks perfect command of language or when there is some weakness in his physical constitution. Deafness is one such weakness in physical constitution. Let us illustrate this with an anecdote or two. There was a woman. The woman had given birth to four children at a time. She wanted to give the news for publicity. She contacted the local newspaper reporter. She gave him the news telephonically about her giving birth to four children. This is how the conversation proceeded:

> "Sir, I have begotten four children at a time," the woman reported.
>
> "Would you repeat that, madam?" the reporter asked.
>
> The woman replied, "No I cannot bear that. That is a very painful experience."

The reporter was deaf. He requested for repetition of her news as he failed to hear her. He used the deictical term 'that' for 'news'. He asked "Would you repeat that, madam?" The woman understood 'that' meaning 'giving birth to four children at a time'. Thus, both the partners got caught into the knot of a deictical term 'that'. The result was that the woman did not recognize the other's intention rightly. This could have been avoided by the reporter by replacing 'that' with something like "Would you repeat your statement/news, madam?" There was unclarity on the part of the reporter. That led the woman to reply irrelevantly. One's failure to hear and to be clear led to other's being irrelevant in her talk exchange. Talking in Gricean terms, one infringed the maxim of Manner while the other the maxim of Relation.

> A similar infringement occurs in a conversation between a child and a visitor. The visitor comes and asks the child, "Beta, what is your name?"
>
> "Uncle, my name is Pappu," the child replies.
>
> "That is surely your nickname. School ka naam kya hai."(intended to ask—what is your name in school?).
>
> "Pillai Public School," replies the child.
>
> Here, too, the child fails to interpret the intended question about his name in school due to his lack of command of language. This leads him not to relate his name in school but his school's name. He infringes the Relation maxim.

When in spite of knowing something a speaker does not wish to divulge the information, he is said to opt out of a maxim.

A general observation shows us that politicians very often opt out of a maxim. They do not want to divulge their strategy to the opponent/rival party. The following exchange takes place between a news channel correspondent and a leader of a political party after results of Assembly elections in an Indian State are declared:

> Correspondent: "Sir, the results for all seats have been declared. No party has the majority of seats. Would you like to join hands with the NDA (National Democratic Alliance)?"
>
> Political leader: "A meeting of our party activists is taking place this evening. They will decide what to do. No more comments."

Being the President of his party he must have some well thought out strategy regarding the formation of the government in the State. In the circumstance of election results just declared, he does not wish to divulge his move/strategy. Hence, he does not provide the information as required by the correspondent. He has opted out of the maxim of giving required amount of information.

In some circumstances it is not expected that the speaker will behave as required by the maxim. On some occasion it could be observed that people are not expected to be clear and direct. They structure their conversational contribution in such a way as to hide something. They could be said to suspend a maxim. In an Indian social context, for example, conversational partners are not expected to be clear and direct when dealing with delicate and sensitive topic such as rape.

In Shashi Deshpande's novel *The Binding Vine* Shakuntala's daughter Kalpana is raped. She is admitted into hospital and examined by Dr. Bhaskar Jain. When Shakuntala moans over this incident, cries and sobs, Vanaa—the narrator Urmila's childhood friend—tries to console Shakuntala by being indirect/oblique. This is how Vanaa comforts Shakuntala:

> "Your daughter has been--------." Vanaa hesitates, searching for the Marathi word, gives up. "Someone has wronged her." (58)

Even the doctor is being indirect. He says:

> Look, tell her it is already in the records. I have put it down after examining her. How the Chap in casualty could have missed it, I can't imagine. (58)

The doctor and Vanaa are not expected to be direct and use the word—'rape'. Vanaa substitutes this word with 'someone has wronged her.' The doctor refers to it by using the deictical term 'It'. They suspend the Manner maxim.

A striking thing one notices about the non-observances of conversational maxims is that the flout of a maxim significantly differs from violation, suspension, infringement and opting out of a maxim. A speaker flouts a maxim with a deliberate intention of prompting the hearer look for a meaning which differs from the stated or literal meaning. In the case of the other kinds of non-observance a speaker has no such intention of making the hearer look for meaning rather than the expressed or stated meaning.

After discussing Grice's assumption about human verbal communication, his proposal of Cooperative Principle, its maxims, their application in verbal interaction and the five ways conversers deal with these maxims, the discussion of his concept of implicature is in order. Human verbal interaction has an important side to it. Human beings convey a lot indirectly through what they say literally. Put it in other words, human verbal conversation is characterized by difference between 'saying and meaning'. It means that we convey more than what we say through linguistic expressions. This could be illustrated with the following sets of sentence—A and B:

Set A: 1. A: What is your name?
2. A: My daughter is making progress.
3. A: I have consulted some classic books on Pragmatics.
4. A: I saw a car.
5. A: He is an Englishman. He is, therefore, brave.

Set B: 1. A: Will you have a slice of cake?
B: I am on fast.
2. A: Are you joining the party tonight?

3. A: Do you like tea?
   B: Does the sun rise in the east?

In Set A in the first sentence the speaker indirectly suggests that he does not know addressee's (A) name and hence he has reason for wanting to know addressee's name. In the second sentence the speaker indirectly conveys that his daughter has not done brilliantly. The third sentence hints at the fact that the utterer has consulted 'not all' classics on Pragmatics. The fourth sentence implicates that the speaker saw one car/the car does not belong to him. While in the last sentence the speaker suggests that the person's being brave is a result of his being an Englishman.

In Set B in the first example the addressee says one thing and conveys another thing indirectly. In order to interpret B's response A has to ask what the connection there is between his offer of cake and the addressee being on fast. A would have to infer that B's being on fast hints that he does not want a slice of cake. In the second example B has apparently not adhered to the maxim of Quantity. The question by A expects the response 'yes' or 'no.' B's response that he has an examination the next day leads A to infer that B is having examination means studying tonight and studying tonight means B would not join the party. B implicates by his contribution and A infers via maxims of Quantity and Relation that B would not join the party.

In the third example the addressee flouts the maxims of Quantity, Relation and Manner. He makes the speaker bring his geographical knowledge into play—the sun rises in the east. If the speaker's answer to addressee's question is 'yes', then the addressee's answer to speaker's question is 'yes'. Thus, the addressee indirectly conveys (implicates) that he likes tea.

Analyzing these sentences one could state that they state one thing and indirectly convey another thing. That is, there is an extra/added meaning conveyed. This is the meaning inferred by an interlocutor. Such an inferred meaning is called an 'implicature'. For Grundy (2000: 73) "Implicature is any meaning that is implied i.e. conveyed indirectly or through hints and understood explicitly without ever being explicitly stated." For Forrester (1996: 51) implicature is "The force associated with the recognition (by the listener) of the intention (speaker's) to communicate." All the sentences in the above examples thus convey implicatures.

For Grice (1975) there are two types of implicature—'Conventional' and 'Conversational'. A significant difference between conventional and conversational implicature is that for conventional implicature no special contextual knowledge is required. For working out conversational implicature, on the other hand, some special background knowledge (socio-cultural, participants, their mutual knowledge, their relationship with each other etc.) is required. Hence conversational implicature is also termed 'particularized implicature.' The implicatures as in the first set of examples are of the former category while those in the second set belong to the latter. For a conversational implicature to be worked out it is to be assumed that the interlocutor is cooperative at some deeper level. Conventional implicature holds the same on all occasions.

In his seminal paper "Logic and Conversation" Grice (1975: 50) specifies that to calculate an implicature the hearer will rely on the following data:

1. The conventional meaning of the words used together with the identity of any references that may be involved.
2. The Cooperative Principle and its maxims.
3. The context—linguistic or otherwise—of the utterance.
4. Other items of background knowledge.
5. The fact (or supposed fact) that all relevant items falling under the previous headings are available to both the participants and both participants know or assume this to be the case.

Implicature is, thus, a meaning inferred by an addressee with preserving the assumption of cooperation. What is significant in working out this 'inferred meaning'/'implicature' is the speaker's/utterer's intention—what the speaker or utterer intends to convey. Grice (1971: 58) formalizes the conveyance of this speaker-meaning as implicature—"A meant NN something by X" is (roughly) equivalent to—"A intended the utterence of X to produce some effect in an audience by means of the recognition of this intention."

In this formalization "A" refers to speaker, "X" refers to utterance and meant NN refers to speaker's intended meaning which is the non-natural meaning—the meaning different from natural/conventional meaning of the utterance X produced. This formalization suggests that if an audience fails to recognize what the speaker's intention is to communicate in producing an utterance, he cannot work out/calculate the 'implicature'. Hence Akmajian et al. (2001: 352) propose "Linguistic communication is successful if the hearer recognizes the speaker's communicative intention. Linguistic communication works because the speaker and the hearer share a system of inferential strategies leading from the utterances of the speaker's communicative intent." Walker (1975: 154) also observes "Generally an utterance carries conversational implicatures because the speaker (or the writer et cetera) intended it to."

Another significant concept which is a part of calculating an implicature is mutual and shared knowledge. An addressee is able to work out/infer the intended meaning on the basis of contextual knowledge shared with his conversational partner. Gibbs (1987: 565) defines this mutual and shared knowledge as "A speaker S and an addressee A mutually know a proposition P if and only if:

> S knows that P
>
> A knows that P
>
> S knows that A knows that P
>
> A knows that S knows that A knows that P
>
> ------ and so on *ad infinitem*."

This implies that the concept of mutual knowledge plays a very vital role in getting at conversational inference/implicature. Hence Gibbs (1987: 577) proposes that "Knowledge of the context and knowledge of the speaker are not always sufficient for successful for comprehension. Instead, making conversational inferences must invoke knowledge and beliefs that listeners and speakers mutually share."

The above explanation of the notion of conversational implicature could be illustrated with respect to the factors like Gricean Cooperative Principle, speaker-intention and mutual/ shared knowledge with an example from Rama Mehta' *Inside the Haveli.*" In this novel Bhagwat Singhji's wife is the old lady of the haveli in Udaipur. Her husband-Bhagwat Singhji has died. In this context, she blesses her daughter-in-law: Geeta. The old lady says:

> "God bless you, May you always wear red. May gold always shine on your hands." (256)

What does the old lady intend to implicate? How does Geeta work out her mother-in-law's intended meaning? A whole gamut of their mutual knowledge and beliefs in Indian socio-cultural context is called for. In Indian culture a woman believes it is her fortune to die before her husband dies. After the death of her husband no woman is supposed to wear ornaments like bangles, marriage necklace (of gold) and wear a *bindi* on her forehead. Through her blessing the old lady implicates that she herself has become a widow. Her daughter-in-law Geeta—should not experience such misfortune. Both her daughter-in-law and her son should live a long life. Her sincere desire that her son and daughter-in-law should live a long life is conveyed in an indirect (a circumlocutory) manner. She generates an implicature through the flout of Manner maxim. This blessing serves duel functions. It serves to comfort her daughter-in-law and also expresses the wish for the longevity of her daughter-in-law and her son.

Put it in the Gricean framework, Geeta has to assume that her mother-in-law is being cooperative, that through this blessing her mother-in-law intends to wish indirectly for Geeta and her husband's longevity and intends to comfort her. To infer her mother-in-law's intention in producing the utterance Geeta has also to take into account what significance 'wearing red' and 'gold shining on hands' have in Indian context. Her mother-in-law has also to assume that Geeta is capable of reasoning and getting at her intended meaning. As Grice (1997: 71) asserts:

> "One cannot have intentions to achieve results which one sees no chance of achieving and the success of intentions of the kind involved in communication requires those to whom communications are addressed to be capable in the circumstances of having certain thoughts and drawing certain conclusions."

Simply put, a speaker intends to convey something to an addressee on the assumption that the addressee has reasoning ability and will work out what has been intended to be conveyed through an utterance. This happens between Moorthy and Madanna's wife and between Moorthy and Satanna's wife in Raja Rao's novel *Kanthapura*. This is how their talk proceeds:

> He says, "I ask you: will you spin a hundred yards of yarn per day?"
>
> But Madanna's wife says, "I am going to have a child."
>
> Satanna's wife says, "I'm going for my brother's marriage." (103)

Moorthy wants to start a Congress group in Kanthapura. He is on the campaign to convince the people in the village how they can fight unitedly against the Red-Man's Government. Starting a Congress group is a medium of uniting people. In order to be members of Congress he proposes them to fulfil some conditions. The one willing to be a member of Congress has to pay four annas or spin two thousand yards of yarn per year. He has to speak truth and practice Ahinsa. He must wear only the khadi cloth. Moorthy reaches Rachanna's verandah and the women and children of pariah quarter encircle him. He takes the chance to solicit the women to be Congress member. He questions Madanna's wife and Satanna's wife if they would spin a hundred yards of yarn per day. Madanna's wife's reply that she is going to have a child drives her point home. Moorthy reasons that she won't be a member of Congress. What she intends to convey indirectly is worked out by Moorthy. The same reasoning process applies to Satanna's wife's reply.

To sum up, it would suffice to state that people engage in conversation with an unspoken agreement of cooperation. They normally believe that their interlocutors do not mislead them or tell them lies. They provide information needed for current purpose of communication. They try to be clear, brief and relevant. They conduct their conversation according to set of rules or principles. Cooperative Principle is one such principle or rule of conversation. This constitutes its maxims like maxim of quantity, quality, relation and manner. These are rules that guide conversation. It, however, does not imply that these maxims are literally adhered to. They are very often contravened. To put it in Gricean parlance, they are violated, flouted, infringed, suspended and opted out. The most intriguing but equally interesting case of non-observance is a flout. This is a blatant non-observance of a maxim which leads the hearer to look for an indirect meaning called implicature. This speaker-meaning is worked out by an addressee with the assumption that the speaker is being cooperative and on the basis of the literal/stated meaning of an utterance. This literal meaning serves as a base for inferring implicated meaning. Hence, Grice (1982: 232) puts "Natural meaning is in some specifiable way the ancestor of non-natural meaning."

The calculation of implicature is possible due to mutual knowledge of addresser and addressee, knowledge of language and knowledge of the use of language. This knowledge includes participants' assumption, beliefs, their relationship with each other, history of the talk-exchange (who has been referred to before/what is the topic of talk) and conventions of communicating. Cooperativeness is one such convention of communicating. Briefly put, conversers are able to interpret utterances with their linguistic and pragmatic competence. The role of Cooperative Principle and its maxims is undoubtedly significant in that as Schiffrin (1995: 194) points "The CP and its attendant maxims allow speakers to lead their hearers to interpretations of communicative intent (speaker-meaning) that go beyond the logical meaning of what they say."

It could be argued that without assumption of cooperation and without pragmatic competence there could be many a slip between a cup of tea and lip in verbal interactions. As has been stated earlier human verbal communication is conducted as per principles. The principle of cooperation is one. The other is 'Politeness Principle'. The following section discusses the concept and models of politeness.

1.3. Models of Politeness

It is pertinent to say a few things about politeness-linguistic politeness before discussing the theories and models of politeness. Language is an integral part of individual's life. It is a group of individuals that constitutes society or community. But society is not merely a group of individuals. It is a network of relationships. These relationships are established and strengthened through verbal interaction. This verbal interaction is a delicate weapon. It can make or mar our relationships. For making and maintaining our relationships one usual means is of greetings. In English, for example, we have such expressions like 'Hello', 'Hi', 'Good morning', 'Dad', 'Dear', etc. In Indian context the greetings are 'Namaste', 'Namaskar', 'Ram Ram', 'Sat Sri Akal', 'Jai Bhim' and 'Salaam'. Meaningless they may seem, they help us nevertheless to consolidate relationships with our fellow beings. They work as adhesives which help link people together. Thorat (2000: 119) points out the significance of greetings by observing "Two interactants are like two cogs in the network of social relationships. If there were no greetings, the cogs would grind to a halt. In order for the cogs to latch onto each other and to rotate smoothly we require some sort of lubricant and greetings function as this lubricant."

In order to carry on our social bonding we move a step further. Through linguistic communication, we compliment, congratulate, bless, persuade, advise and request our fellow beings. We use words and expressions that sound pleasant to them. In order to be pleasant to others we show consideration for others. We try to make others feel easy and comfortable. The verbal interaction we engage in reveals our attributes like respect, appreciation, humility and consideration for others.

The language we use for interaction with others provides us choices/forms to select from. The choice of one form rather than another shows how we are viewing our interlocutor. Asking someone time is a very simple act. For this we choose to employ particular linguistic form in English. We have various such forms available as the following:

(a) Tell me the time.

(b) What is the time?

(c) Would you tell me the time, please?

(d) Could you be kind enough to tell me the time?

The two forms (a) and (b) obviously would sound unpleasant, dry and clinical. The last two forms (c) and (d) would reveal our concern and civility towards the other. Put it in other words, the other would feel pleasant to listen to such forms. The form "Tell me the time" is an imperative or imposition. Impositions as it is commonly agreed are inherently impolite. Observation shows us that generally nobody likes to be ordered/commanded. Hence this form would be unpleasant to the other. To put briefly, to be polite means to be considerate, respectful and caring for others. To be polite means to make others comfortable and easy. To be considerate, to be polite towards others involves deployment of various strategies. These politeness strategies are revealed in various models of politeness. The models of politeness we are going to discuss are by the following sociologists, pragmaticists and experts in the field of Pragmatics:

1. Robin Lakoff (1973)
2. G.N. Leech (1983)
3. Brown and Levinson (1978/1987)
4. Bruce Fraser (1990)
5. R. Pandharipande (1992)

1. Lakoff (1973) in her trend-setting paper claims that only syntactic rules are not enough for determining acceptability of sentences. We have to take into account the pragmatic factors and rules to determine their acceptability. The pragmatic factors are—speaker's assumptions about his addressee, his feelings about his status relative to his addressee, the real-world situation and the effect he wishes to achieve on his addressee. The rules of pragmatic competence are:

1. Be clear and
2. Be polite.

The rule of clarity has been formulated in Grice's Cooperative Principle along with its attendant maxims. These maxims are applied when the communicator's aim in conversation is to convey information maximally and efficiently. On the other hand, if he wishes to reaffirm and consolidate relationship, he will follow the second rule-Be polite. Lakoff (1973: 298) lists the following three rules of politeness:

"Don't impose
Give options
Make A (addressee) feel good-be easy."

Rule 1—'Don't impose' accounts for the fact that one should not infringe into other's business. One should remain aloof. The strategies to follow this rule are the use of passive, impersonal constructions and use of technical terms to avoid mentioning the unmentionable. Using an impersonal construction is a strategy and it implies that the addresser does not want to infringe on the addressee. In passive construction the agent is deleted because it frees the agent from personal responsibility of the action described. In other words, passive and impersonal constructions avoid mentioning a person. The purpose is not to impinge on the addressee. Asking question about personal things like one's name, place and possessions is prefaced by asking permission to ask the question. The following is an illustration from *The Bachelor of Arts*:

"May we know where our master is coming from?" Somebody asked. (109)

Chandran's dress, appearance, his shaven head and the ochre loincloth make the villagers in Koopal take him as a sanyasi, as an ascetic. They are the innocent, simple and unsophisticated people. They see him in the pose of meditation and with his eyes shut. It would have been impolite on their part, had they baldly asked—"Where are you from?" Hence their question with the construction—"May we know--------?"

Keenan (1976) gives a wonderful example of the practice of Malagasy speakers to avoid making reference to individuals by their names in their utterance. They believe that referring a person by his name would invite the attention of someone in the world of living or dead. Something unpleasant would befall the person referred to. Referring to a person by his name would make some malevolent ancestral force to take the person away from the living. They use the second name given to a person. This second name is an unpleasant item like "Dung Heap", "Dog Face" or "Garbage Girl". There is also a strategy of referring to an individual using generalized animate noun like 'boy, girl, person'. A wife refers to her husband using the noun 'person' and asks "Is the person still sleeping?" She may even use an agent noun like "Cow watcher, house builder or teacher". It is not unusual for a wife referring to her husband by saying 'the cow watcher is hungry'. In Lakoffian parlance Malagasy speakers use strategies like referring to a person by generalized animate noun or an agent noun for the sake of politeness. It would be impolite in their society to identify an individual by his personal/first name.

Rule 2—"Give options". This rule of politeness means that a speaker leaves option open for hearer. The speaker should leave the hearer make his own decisions. The strategies used for making the hearer make his own decisions are 'hedges' and 'euphemism'. 'Hedges' are cautious notes or glosses like—"You know, sort of, kind of, I suppose". They are used to suggest that the speaker does not assert himself about something as that would offend the hearer—that would leave no option to the hearer as to the truth of the sentence uttered. The hearer would be buffaloed or bewildered. This rule operates in the following conversation in Anita Desai's novel *Bye Bye Blackbird*:

> Mrs. Miller, looking drier and more brittle every minute, rises and says, "I suppose, I had better make you some tea. You would like some tea, I suppose, Mrs. Sen?" (78)

Mrs. Miller is Adit Sen's former landlady living in Harrow. He visits the landlady with his wife Sarah Sen one Saturday afternoon. They are courteously led into a parlour by Mrs. Miller. Mrs. Miller offers to make tea for them. She is their hostess. It would be impolite on her part not to offer them tea. She could just say, "I had better make you some tea", "You would like some tea." But her offer is coupled with a hedge/gloss "I suppose...". What is striking is that the hedge is repeatedly used, first initially and then sentence finally. Even if she is a hostess, her offer of tea is hedged. Her glossing to her offer is oriented to leave option to Mrs. Sen whether to accept the offer or to refuse it. Put it in other words the offer is glossed with "I suppose" for being polite to the guest.

Euphemistic expressions are inoffensive and agreeable expressions used for unpleasant and offensive things and actions. They are used to dispel the unpleasant effect and suggest the addressee that he need not interpret what is being said literally. He is given the option of interpreting the euphemistic expression according to his socio-cultural encyclopaedia and beliefs. The euphemistic expressions refer generally to sex, bodily functions, death, rape and prostitution. They are marked by indirectness and substitution. There is a danger in being euphemistic unless the addressee is linguistically competent. It may lead the addressee to misinterpret the phrase/sentence uttered. Unless the hearer knows, for example, what the phrase "kicking the bucket" means, he may take it literally and misconstrue the speaker's intention. To interpret the unpleasant sense 'dying' the hearer has to take it that way.

Rulc 3—"Make A (addressee) feel good and friendly". This implies that the speaker tries to create a feeling of camaraderie or friendship with the hearer. For this purpose he needs to employ strategies like complimenting, congratulating, blessing and showing concern for the hearer. He may also employ expressions of agreement and nickname or diminutive of the hearer's name. Even making offers and giving gifts are geared to make the addressee feel comfortable and friendly. The following two conversations will illustrate some of these strategies used by the conversers. The first is from *The Bachelor of Arts*:

> At this they begged him to say, "Master, our village is so unlucky that few come this way. Bless us with your holy presence for some more days, we beg of you." Chandran shook his head but they would not let him go. "Master,

> your very presence will bless our village, we rarely see men here. We beg of you to stay for some days more...". (109-10)

The villagers in Koopal have taken Chandran to be an ascetic. He has decided to leave the village. His sitting cross-legged, his closing of eyes and the pose of meditation force them take him as a sanyasi. They compliment him calling him 'Master' and his presence 'the holy presence' and request him to bless them. A striking thing in this compliment is that the villagers elevate Chandran and at the same time they denigrate themselves as belonging to a village which is unlucky. The compliment is very touching. Chandran has decided to leave Koopal. But the compliment makes him feel that he is being treated here with consideration. His presence is being highly valued. Resultantly, he goes back to the bunyan tree and stays for a few more days.

The second example is from the celebrated story *The Gift of the Magi* by O' Henry included in an anthology edited by Jawale and others (13-17). The conversation between the two characters runs as follows:

> "Give me your watch. I want to see how it looks on it."
>
> Instead of obeying, Jim tumbled on the couch and put his hands under the back of his head and smiled "Dell," said he, "Let's put our Christmas presents away and keep them awhile. They are too nice to use at present. I sold the watch to get the money to buy your combs." (17)

This is the conversation between Della and her husband Jim. Della wanted to buy a nice and rare Christmas gift for her husband. Falling short of money she sold her golden hair out and bought a platinum fob chain for Jim's gold watch. When he comes home back in the evening, she is eager to see if the chain befits his gold watch. He has shocking and surprising news for her—he has sold his gold watch for buying a set of combs for her hair—combs for which she has craved for so long. Before he breaks the news to her, he tries to establish rapport and create a feeling of camaraderie with his wife. He resorts to using a diminutive 'Dell' instead of 'Della'. In other words his is an attempt to make her feel good and comfortable.

> Thus, for Lakoff politeness seems to be the avoidance of offence. Lakoff (1973: 297-98) puts "It is considered more important in a conversation to avoid offence than to achieve clarity."

Her paper is oriented to show that it is more important in conversation to avoid offence (to be polite) than to aim clarity. The rules of politeness may differ in their applicability but their basic form is the same universally, i.e. these rules are universal. These rules apply not only to linguistic but also to non-linguistic or non-verbal behaviour.

2. Leech (1983) proposes an elaborate and a rich system of maxims in his model. He views politeness as minimizing the expression of impolite beliefs and maximizing the expression of polite beliefs. Put it in other words, being polite would mean minimizing the expression of beliefs which are unfavourable to the hearer and maximizing the expression of beliefs which are favourable to the hearer. To do so would involve an operation of various maxims. Leech (1983: 132) proposes the following six maxims:

1. Tact Maxim:
   (a) minimize cost to other
   (b) maximize benefit to other
2. Generosity Maxim:
   (a) minimize benefit to self
   (b) maximize cost to self
3. Approbation Maxim:
   (a) minimize dispraise of other
   (b) maximize praise of other
4. Modesty Maxim:
   (a) minimize praise of self
   (b) maximize dispraise of self
5. Agreement Maxim:
   (a) minimize disagreement between self and other
   (b) maximize agreement between self and other

6. Sympathy Maxim:
   (a) minimize antipathy between self and other
   (b) maximize sympathy between self and other.

A moment's reflection would show that Generosity and Modesty maxims are 'self-centered' whereas Tact and Approbation maxims are 'other-related'. These four maxims have bipolar—cost-benefit scales and praise—dispraise scales. The last two maxims have unipolar scale-agreement and sympathy. The label 'other' applies not only to addressee/hearer but also to third party person/people. Leech (1983: 131) claims that "These maxims are necessary to explain the relation between sense and force in human conversation. That is—they help us to explain why indirectness is used in human verbal interaction."

There are certain illocutionary acts/speech acts which relate to the social goal of establishing and maintaining comity. For example, ordering, begging, demanding and asking are acts that compete with social goal of comity. Giving an order is inherently competitive because it imposes on the addressee, decreases comity and hence is tactless. The following is a simple imperative:

S: Give me your pen.

This expresses speaker's intention to make hearer do something. It overtly gives no option/freedom to the hearer to say 'yes or no.' It expresses cost to hearer and benefit to speaker and is thus violation of Tact maxim. The speaker would then need to mitigate the imposition by using form/s like the following:

S: Will you give me your pen?

S: Would you be kind enough to give me your pen?

S: Could you possibly give me your pen?

These forms give the hearer freedom of response and also put the hearer in the deferential role. Hence they are tactful. The speaker may also use the minimizers like 'just' or 'a bit' to reduce the implied cost to the hearer in verbal interaction.

The Generosity maxim is adhered to through convivial acts like offering, inviting, greeting, thanking and congratulating. Offer and invitation, in particular, are polite because they imply cost to speaker and benefit to hearer. Gu (1990: 244) gives an example of deceptively simple conversation between A and B:

A: I can drop you in town if you like.

B: It is very kind of you, but it will cause you some inconvenience, won't it?

A: No, not at all. I am going in that direction.

B: Thank you very much.

A offers B lift which is at A's cost and B's benefit. By the Tact maxim A is polite. By saying "No, not at all, I am going in that direction" A minimizes cost to himself. This is against Generosity maxim: "maximize cost to self". But at the deeper level despite B's mention that the lift will cause inconvenience to A, A persists in making the offer. In his saying that "I am going in that direction" A is maximizing benefit to B and minimizing the debt B owes to A. He is implying his sincerity in making the offer. In Chinese culture if A offers B something, A will usually minimize by means of speech the cost which the offer will incur to him. B on the other hand, will maximize by means of speech the benefit from A's offer. Taken in the context of Chinese culture both A and B are generous—polite.

The Approbation maxim dictates us to minimize dispraise and maximize praise of other. It asks us to avoid saying unpleasant things about hearer/third party. Complimenting the hearer/third party would mean following this maxim. Compliment is an utterance which refers to something valued positively by conversers and it is attributed to the hearer/third party. According to Holmes (1988: 455) there are four broad topics of complimenting: "i. Appearance, ii. Ability or performance, iii. Possessions and iv. Some aspect of personality or friendliness." An example would help elucidate the point. The following compliment occurs in Anita Desai's *Bye Bye Blackbird*:

> Here I am in such wise, wonderful people like the Swami Binodanand of Hampstead and it is a challenge to me to make, to create a meeting place where these great wise people can come and lecture to us lesser beings, us little ones. (43)

The compliment occurs in the course of conversation between Mrs. Sarah Sen and her former landlady Miss Emma Moffit. Moffit is going to start a little Indian club. An Indian Swami Binodanand who presently lives in Hampstead has written to Miss Moffit that he would give Yoga lessons free on Wednesday. She lavishes her praise for the Swami. Two things are striking here. One is that the compliment is attributed to third party—Swami Binodadand. The other thing is that the complimentizer Miss Moffit minimizes praise of herself by saying "us lesser beings, us lesser ones." Analyzed on the touchstone of Leech's maxims—the complimentizer is polite by upholding the Approbation maxim-maximizing other's praise and the Modesty maxim—the maxim of minimizing self-praise. One observes that when someone cannot praise other, he either sidelines the issue or gives minimal response like 'well' or prefers to remain silent.

An observation of human conversation shows us that people agree as well disagree with their conversational partner. They try to be direct in the agreement but indirect in their disagreement. A counter-argument is prefaced by 'yes' or 'but'. The following conversation taking place between a professor of English and a student validates this argument:

P: "A Suitable Boy" by Vikram Seth is an immensely readable novel.

S: Yes, but it is too lengthy.

The student partially disagrees with the Professor. He tries to mitigate his disagreement. In most circumstances a partial disagreement is preferred to complete disagreement. It is considered rude or impolite to directly disagree with the other. Agreeing and disagreeing are a matter of being favourable and unfavourable respectively to the other. Hence Leech introduces a separate agreement maxim in his proposal. Last but not the least important maxim is Sympathy maxim. Certain illocutionary acts like condolences and congratulations are expressions of sympathy for misfortune and fortune as to the addressee. Hence they are considered polite speech acts. Agreement with and sympathy for the addressee are the strategies that go a long way to establish rapport and common ground with other. They are integral parts of polite linguistic behaviour.

3. Brown and Levinson (1978 and 1987) have proposed the best known and most influential approach to politeness. Their approach to politeness stems from Goffman's (1967) notion of 'face'. For Goffman (1967: 5) face is "The positive social value a person effectively claims himself by the line others assume he has taken during a particular contact." Goffman's focus is on social interaction and he believes that to maintain and enhance 'face' is an important goal of human conversation. An individual has to earn this value/face in his interaction with others in society. For this he has to perform 'face work' (12). This is the action that signals two points of view—a defensive orientation towards saving his own face and a protective orientation saving other's face. Face work includes face saving practices—"defensive practices (saving one's own face) and protective practices (saving other's face)." These defensive and protective practices establish and maintain social order and solidarity.

Goffman's notion of face is the fountain head of Brown and Levinson's approach to politeness. They (1978: 66) claim that: "All adult competent members of the society have (know each other to have) 'face'—the public self image that every member claims for himself, consisting of two related aspects: (A) Negative face: the basic claim to territories, personal preserves, rights to non-distractions i.e. freedom of action and freedom from imposition. (B) Positive face: the positive consistent self image/personality (crucially including the desire that this self image be appreciated and approved of) claimed by interactants."

In human verbal interaction this face is often damaged or threatened. There is a certain degree of friction in human interaction. There are various communicative acts like ordering, advising, criticizing, begging, asking, disagreeing and requesting that are intrinsically face-threatening (face threatening acts). Individuals try to defend their face. They assume that it is in their best interest to maintain each other's face. Hence they try to redress the threat to face. As Brown and Levinson (1987:

24) put: "Some facts are intrinsically threatening to face and thus require softening."

To redress the threat to face they develop Politeness principle/strategies. By using these strategies individuals communicate their messages, their intention to be polite and reduce the face-loss. There are three super ordinate strategies. These could be diagrammatically shown as follows:

Strategies

Do the face threatening act

1. On-record
   (a) Baldly (Without redress)
   (b) With redress (Positive politeness, negative politeness)
2. Off-record (Litotes, hyperbole, irony etc.)
3. Don't do the face threatening act

Doing the act on-record would mean performing the act without attempting to hide what we are doing. In fact, there are three subordinate on-record strategies:

(a) Perform the act without redress.

(b) Perform the act with the positive politeness redress.

This includes strategies like complimenting, offering, seeking agreement, avoiding disagreement, promising, gifting, exaggerating interest in addressee and attending to his wants.

(c) Performing the act with negative politeness redress.

This includes strategies like minimizing imposition, apologizing, questioning, hedging, impersonalizing and being indirect.

Doing the act off-record means performing the act in such a way as to pretend to hide it. This involves strategies like Litotes, hyperbole, tautology, hints, presupposition, ambiguity, irony, rhetorical questions etc. In order to play down the face loss we may prefer not to perform/do the act at all.

If, for example, I want to ask someone time and I say "Tell me the time", it is a threat to his negative face because it imposes doing something on his part. It gives him no freedom to reply 'yes/no'. Put it in other words I am being impolite. If, on the other hand, I say "Got the time mate" I am treating the addressee as a friend/as an equal as I am using the informal term 'mate'. I am being positively polite. Still it is possible to perform the same act in the following way:

> "Could you tell me the time, please?"
>
> I am playing down the imposition by leaving an option of saying 'yes/no' to him. I am hedging the act with—"Could you tell------?" and also using the transparent politeness marker 'please'.

In other words, I am orienting to save the addressee's negative face. This would be an example of negative politeness. In this model by Brown and Levinson the term 'politeness' has not been explicitly defined. It could be stated that for Brown and Levinson politeness is "the use of redressive language designed to compensate for face threatening behavior." Though their model derives from Goffman's notion of face, it differs from Goffman's notion in that for Goffman 'face' is a public property that an individual can attain only through verbal interaction. Brown and Levinson claim that face is a private property which is bestowed on a person and every competent adult member of society possesses it.

4. Fraser (1990) provides four perspectives on politeness: 'the social-norm view', 'the conversational-maxim view', 'the face-saving view' and 'the conversational-contract view'. The social-norm view to politeness is based on the assumption that every society has a set of norms. These norms prescribe a certain action or a state of affair in a given context. If an action is in consonance with a prescribed norm, it is viewed as polite/politeness. If an action is contrary to the norm, the action is impolite/rude.

For example, India is a multi-religious country. There are numerous places of worship like temples, mosques, Gurudwaras, Buddhvihars and churches. There is an equally big variety of religious customs and rituals. In Hindu temples, those who conduct ceremonies are to be referred to as "Pujaris or Pandits". One who has renounced worldly life, who wears white, yellow or saffron clothes should be addressed "Swamiji". The head of a sect is to be addressed "Mahantji". Addressing them, thus, according to their position would be an act of politeness. The manuals of etiquette in a society reveal this assumption of politeness.

The 'conversational-maxims view' views politeness in terms of maxims/rules of conversation. These maxims are guidelines that control human conversation. A verbal behavior in accord with one or more of these maxims is viewed as polite behavior. Lakoff's (1973) and Leech's (1983) maxims we have discussed earlier are examples of this approach to politeness. 'The face-saving view' is associated with Brown and Levinson (1978/1987). This is an elaborate and influential current approach to politeness. 'The conversational-contract view' has been proposed by Fraser and Nolen (1981). For them being linguistically polite means entering into a conversation with an understanding of terms and conditions of conversational contract. Every speaker has certain rights and obligations imposed by social institutions. He has obligations like taking turns, using mutually intelligible language and speaking sufficiently loudly for the hearer. Not adhering to these obligations would mean violating conversational contract and being verbally impolite.

5. Pandharipande (1992) discusses the politeness phenomenon with reference to address/reference terms in Indian English. She defines politeness as "a mode of expression which results when an utterance abides by the conventions of appropriateness" (243). From her framework it derives that an utterance is polite if it meets the constraints of appropriateness (Maryada). For her Indian/Indianized terms of address are the exponents of underlying Indian conventions of Maryada. For example in Marathi a third person plural pronoun 'tumhi' is polite when a granddaughter uses it to address her grandfather. When the grandfather uses it for his granddaughter, the use of the same pronoun is impolite. Her argument is that address/reference terms are one of the constituents of the conventions of appropriateness in the Indian socio-cultural context and thus reflect the Indian social reality.

Thus, we have discussed the concept of politeness and various models of and perspectives on politeness. The proposals and models of politeness show one that politeness has been the hub of pragmatic literature since the trend-setting paper by Lakoff. The Politeness Principle does not operate in human conversation in an exclusive way. It overlaps with other pragmatic principles as well as with speech acts. The present study is not concerned with speech acts. The next section discusses the trade-off between Cooperative Principle and Politeness Principle.

1.4. Cooperative Principle and Politeness Principle

Sociolinguists, semanticists and ethnomethodologists talk about the interdependence of language and society or culture. They also characterize at least five functions of language in society namely—informative (conveying information), expressive (expressing speaker's or even a writer's feelings/emotions), directive (directing or influencing the behavior of others), aesthetic (creating an artistic effect) and the last but not the least important-phatic (maintaining social bonds/cohesion). It is the phatic function that concerns us in this study. This is the function of language to maintain social equilibrium. To achieve this equilibrium we indulge in so-called 'small talk' or 'sweet-nothings'. Greetings, farewells and routine formulae like "How are you?" are inevitable and integral parts of such 'small talk'. "Hi", "Hello", "See you next" are empty of meaning if only taken at face value. What one says through these formulaic expressions matters little. The intention behind them to be friendly and to consolidate our relationships counts. The point that emerges from this is that however 'small talks' they may be they are employed to attain our intentions or goals: to be friendly, to strengthen our relationships and to maintain social equilibrium.

Basically the talk-exchange or conversation we engage in is directed by a number of goals. In order to achieve these goals we design and structure our utterances. Some of the goals are just illocutionary such as giving a warning or making a request or getting something done by someone or getting warm. Given that I want someone to give me his pen, I would design/structure my utterance which would help me attain my goal. For example, I would say, "Give me your pen". Conversation is not just about achieving the illocutionary goal/s just referred to. It also consists of using and choosing conversational strategies and achieving the goals—observing the conversational principle of cooperation (giving required amount of information, being truthful, relevant, clear and brief) and the principle of politeness (being generous, modest, tactful and agreeable). Observing such conversational principles is by no means arbitrary. It is motivated by desire/purpose. The desire in adhering to principle of cooperativeness is as Grice (1975: 47) puts "A maximally effective exchange of information".

The motivation in observing politeness norm is as Leech (1983: 82) says "To maintain the social equilibrium and the friendly relations which enable us to assume that our interlocutors are being cooperative in the first place". Leech claims grounds for his proposal of these conversational or theoretical principles alongside the rules of grammar. The rules of grammar if followed, render a sentence grammatical if not followed render it an ungrammatical sentence. These rules are exclusive. The conversational principles and their attendant maxims can conflict with one another and can be contravened without abnegation of the kind of activity they conduct.

A converser faces a problem when two or more of the principles/maxims conflict with each other. This is a problem of choosing between Scylla and Charybdis. This is where the converser has to navigate to deal with the situation. Very rarely is it possible for him to be both cooperative and polite. Returning to the earlier example I face a problem in which goals conflict with one another—the illocutionary goal-asking someone to give me his pen—observing the Cooperative Principle—being informative, truthful, relevant and clear and brief and Politeness Principle—maintain social equilibrium and friendly relations—being tactful, generous, modest and agreeable. How do I solve the problem? Of course by designing and structuring my utterance to that end. In uttering "Give me your pen" I am brief, clear and direct i.e. I am being cooperative via Manner maxim. But in producing this utterance I have issued a command. It gives the addressee no option of saying 'yes or no'. I am also being costly to the addressee via Tact maxim. Asking him to give me his pen is costly to him and beneficial to me. That is I am structuring my utterance to achieve my illocutionary goal without being polite. I face, then, another problem-by so structuring my utterance can I maintain good social and friendly relations? In structuring my utterance I am imposing-imposing my will on the addressee. This runs counter to the Principle of Politeness. In this situation then I would choose an utterance like:

"Would you give me your pen?" or

"Could you lend me your pen?" or

"I left my pen at home".

In the first two I am avoiding the issuance of a command/ imposition and at the same time leaving an option to the addressee to say 'yes or no'. In the third I am being indirect. I am letting the addressee infer the action he should perform rather than the action be commanded of him. Put it in rhetorical terminology I am sacrificing Cooperative Principle via Manner maxim at the expense of being polite via Leech's tact maxim or Lakoff's rules: "Don't impose" and "Give options".

Let us illustrate the tug-of war between the Cooperative and Politeness Principles with an example from the story *Mr. Know All* by Somerset Maugham included in an anthology edited by M.A. Yadugiri and Barbra Naidu (1996: 47-55). The following is what the hero of the story Mr. Kelada says:

> "I was mistaken," he said, "It is a very good imitation, but of course as soon as I looked through my glass I saw that it wasn't real. I think eighteen dollars is just about as much as the damned thing's worth". (51-52)

The contextual background knowledge of the story is necessary to account for the interplay of being cooperative and being polite. Mr. and Mrs. Ramsay were travelling on a liner from San Francisco to Yokohama. The narrator and Mr. Know All (Max Kelada was his real name) were their co-passengers. Mr. Know All was going to Japan on pearls business. He knew all the best pearls in the world. Mrs. Ramsay was wearing a chain of pearls. He claimed that the pearls were real and must have cost about fifteen thousand dollars. When Mr. Ramsay was at Kobe in Japan, Mrs. Ramsay was living alone in New York. One of her admirers had given her the chain at the departmental stores for eighteen dollars. Mr. Ramsay bet that the pearls were imitation. Mr. Know All claimed that they were real. He was cock sure for he was in the pearl's business. He examined the chain with his magnifying glass. A smile of triumph spread over his face.

Mr. Know All was about to speak that the pearls were real. But he saw Mrs. Ramsay's face. It was turning white. She was going to faint. She stared at Mr. Know All with wide eyes. Her eyes had a desperate appeal. She was going to be exposed. Mr. Know All read her thoughts. He understood her difficulty. He pitied her. He accepted deliberately that the pearls were imitation and lost the bet of a hundred dollars to Mr. Ramsay. He handed a hundred dollar note to Mr. Ramsay.

Thus, in the sentence quoted Mr. Know All tells a lie to save Mrs. Ramsay from humiliation. He sacrifices the Cooperative Principle via maxim of Quality for being considerate to and making Mrs. Ramsay feel good or comfortable. He also incurs the cost of a hundred dollars to himself. Put it concisely he is uncooperative to be polite to her. Brown and Levinson (1978: 100) point out that "One powerful and pervasive motive for not talking maxim-wise is the desire to give some attention to face. Politeness is then a major source of deviation from such rational efficiency and is communicated precisely by that deviation".

However we do come across the situations in which both the Principles are contravened in preference to the illocutionary goal. This could be illustrated with an anecdote of a school boy in a cosmopolitan English medium school. The teacher was explaining to the students the Christian idea of Trinity. Her emphasis was on the life and teachings of Jesus Christ. She spoke for almost an hour and then asked the students "who is the greatest man on the earth?". An American boy stood up and answered "Abraham Lincoln". The teacher was shocked. An English boy said "Winston Churchill". A small boy who never raised his hand and answered any questions in the class, started waving his hand. The teacher asked him to answer the question. The boy replied that Jesus Christ is obviously the greatest man in the world.

All the Christian boys were with Abraham Lincoln, Winston Churchill, Karl Marx and Sigmund Freud. The boy who stood for Jesus Christ was a Jew. When the class was over, the teacher caught hold of the boy in the corridor and asked him if he was not a Jew. The boy replied that certainly he was a Jew. The teacher asked him why he stood for Jesus Christ. The boy silently said, "He is a Jew. In his heart of hearts he knows that Moses is the greatest man the earth has ever produced". He answered that Christ is the greatest man because this is the answer the teacher expected. But there was more to this. The teacher had declared a prize for answering her question. He stood for Jesus Christ for getting the prize. Explained in the rhetorical terminology the boy told a lie to his teacher. He broke the maxim of Quality (of truthfulness). He incurred the cost to the teacher who gave him the prize. His current goal in answering the question was getting the prize. To attain that goal he sacrificed the Cooperative and also the Politeness Principle via Quality maxim and Tact maxim respectively. The anecdote would show one that conversation is a goal-directed activity. Of course, it is difficult to identify set of goals that control human conversation. The goals just reveal themselves as the conversation proceeds. As Taylor and Deborah (1987: 91) claim it is "The illocutionary goals which vary from utterance to utterance".

There are a host of other rhetoric/pragmatic principles that could be accommodated in a model of language use. These are principles like Irony, Banter, Interest and Pollyanna Principle. Leech (1983: 82) states the Irony Principle as follows:

> If you must cause offence, at least do so in a way which does not overtly conflict with the PP, but allows the hearer to arrive at the offensive point of your remark indirectly, by way of implicature.

In simple words when a communicator intends to be offensive to the other but wants to appear polite, he is ironic. He conveys something opposite from what he literally states. He generates an implicature by flouting Quality maxim. Irony becomes a weapon less dangerous than being directly critical, threatening or insulting the other. One could observe how members on a staff in a college, school or an institute are being ironical. When a member is not on good terms with his colleague, he is very often ironical in referring to his colleague saying "S/He is a scholar". One is offensive but wants to appear polite and hence takes recourse to an ironic remark like the one above.

Bantering is an impolite way of being friendly or good with the other. In order to show our solidarity with the 'other' we say something which is apparently impolite and obviously untrue. But what we say is really polite to the other and is really true. This principle also manifests largely in human casual verbal behavior. A striking thing about bantering is that it is taken recourse to generally by interactants of equal rank or status and in very intimate relationship. One would very rarely come across a junior bantering with his boss or senior. Interest Principle proposes that we make our conversation interesting rather than boring. Elaborations and exaggeration are common ways of making conversation interesting. Pollyanna Principle states that in the course of conversation we should talk on pleasant topics and bright side of things instead of dark and unpleasant side. There are situations in which we have to mention the unmentionable things. To accomplish this task we are euphemistic. We prefer the positive proposition to the negative one. Let us take a simple example of a pair of sentences:

(a) The glass is half-empty.

(b) The glass is half-filled.

Saying (b) is following the Pollyanna principle as it expresses a positive proposition whereas (a) would be a violation of the principle.

Sociologists, ethnographers of communication, sociolinguists and discourse analysts have shown concern for how the factors like sex and discourse type exercise their control over the nature of linguistic behavior in social organization. Brown and Yule

(1983) for instance refer to two macro-functions of language—the transactional and the interactional. The former implies the expression of content and information through language whereas the latter implies language used in maintaining social cohesion, negotiating social relationships, expressing personal attitudes and showing solidarity. If the type of discourse is transactional, if one is concerned with just conveying of factual information, one would conduct the conversation in accord with the Cooperative Principle. He would be requiredly informative, truthful, relevant and clear. This type of discourse could be found in a doctor telling a nurse how to administer an injection/a medicine to a patient.

On the other hand, if one's aim is to establish and maintain relationship, a common ground with addressee, he could be said speaking with interactional purpose. That is he would be engaged in interactional discourse. Most of the every day human conversation is primarily interactional rather than transactional. Even the small-talks about weather and one's health are oriented towards reaffirming our social relationships. Put it in the words of Kasper (1990: 205): "In interactional discourse, therefore the Cooperative Principle is regularly overridden by the Politeness Principle in order to ensure that participants' face-wants are taken care of."

Participants very cleverly make use of linguistic facilities like address terms and phatic tokens to manipulate their relationships. These devices are available in their linguistic repertoire for negotiating their relationships. Some of the strategies evolve in the course of actual conversation. One readily remembers the phenomenon of accommodation as a cooperative as well as politeness strategy. Linguistic accommodation means the convergence of speech style. This includes the following features:

1. Altering the vowel quality towards each other.
2. Echoing words and phrases used by the conversational partner.
3. Simplifying vocabulary and grammatical patterns.
4. Translating complicated message in addressee's jargon.
5. Adapting the length of utterances.

It has been observed as Stockwell (2003: 25) puts "That in Britain men tend to accommodate more towards women, whereas in the U.S. women tend to move further towards the male norm." Taken sex-wise this reveals the difference in their being cooperative with and polite to the other.

Studies on linguistic sex-differences reveal that even a strategy of questioning is viewed differently by men and women. Women use questions as conversation-maintenance strategy. Men, on the other hand, interpret questions as request for information and thus take them at face-value. For women question means an act which requires an answer. Through questioning they ensure that a conversation continues. Women tend to promote continuity in their talk. Verbal aggression and interruptions are generally avoided in their conversation. Men take interruptions as opportunity to seize other's turn. Due to these features of men's and women's conversation Coates (1986: 154) concludes "Women tend to organize their talk cooperatively, while men tend to organize their talk competitively."

Human conversation underlies the operation of various personal, social, cultural and linguistic factors. It has two vital components—sense (literal meaning) and force (intended meaning). Accounting for sense is the domain of semantics whereas accounting for the relationship between sense and force requires a rhetorical model of language-use. Such a model includes a set of pragmatic/rhetorical principles. It is argued that these principles control human communicative behaviour. The model includes a host of principles like Cooperative Principle, Politeness Principle, Irony Principle, Banter Principle and so on. Human being's communication underlies values like relevance, clarity, brevity, tact and politeness. It is possible to account for these social values with a potential and viable framework. The principles of cooperation, politeness and Irony in particular, provide a means/framework for interpreting human conversation. The Principle of Cooperation and Politeness are so closely related to each other that Cutting (2000: 54) says "Politeness is a basic form of cooperation." They introduce communicative values like relevance, truthfulness and brevity that operate in human society.

Engaging in conversation is a purposeful activity. Through it human rational agents try to attain their goals. Their goals may be illocutionary—requesting, complimenting, begging, criticizing, promising and borrowing something from someone. Besides, they have to obey principles/norms of conversation like being requiredly informative, truthful, relevant, being polite and at times being ironic. Conversing is a linguistic juggling act. One has to keep and control simultaneously various balls in the air. There is a perpetual conflict or clash among the principles/norms of conversation-particularly being cooperative, polite and ironic. One weighs and prioritizes these norms in the course of ongoing conversation.

1.5. Conclusion

At the outset of this chapter we have discussed the interdependence of language and society. Every society has a number of values, traditions, interests and norms of behavior. These values and norms are reflected through language. The social factors like age, sex, class, education and attitudes of human beings towards one another control the process of face-to-face conversation. The social use of language for conversation reveals a lot of non-linguistic information. One of the important functions language performs in society is establishing, maintaining and negotiating human relationships. Even 'small-talks' about weather and health are geared towards this goal. As rational beings language-users conduct their verbal interactions according to the norms of speech prevailing in their respective society.

Language philosophers, sociologists, sociolinguists and ethnographers of communication have provided insights into the speech norms and motivations in adhering to them. Through communication which is a part of social interaction we try to solve our problem and achieve our goals. We co-operate one another physically as well as verbally. As far as verbal communication is concerned, we co-operate by giving required amount of information, by being truthful, relevant, brief and clear. This is the basic assumption of Grice (1975) in proposing the so called Cooperative Principle. This Principle comprises four maxims: Quantity, Quality, Relation and Manner. Grice also points out that very often these maxims are not observed by conversers for personal and socio-cultural reasons. By not adhering to one or more such maxims they intend to convey implied meanings called 'implicatures'. Thus, conversational partners are apparently uncooperative but it is assumed that they are cooperative at some deeper level. This triggers the search for intended messages.

Another powerful motivation and norm in communication is caring for other's 'face' (Goffman: 1987). This is a sense of self-esteem that every person possesses. When engaged in communication, communicators see that it is in their best interest to preserve their own as well as other's face. Avoiding 'loss of face' is equated with politeness (here linguistic politeness). For sociolinguists like Brown and Levinson (1978/87) there are two kinds of face—positive and negative. The former implies desire to admired, liked and treated as equals by others whereas the latter implies one's desire for freedom of action and freedom from imposition.

The concept of politeness has generated a spurt of literature since 1962. A number of approaches and models of this phenomenon have developed since then. We have introduced the models or approaches by Lakoff (1973), Brown and Levinson (1978/87), Leech (1983), Fraser (1990) and Pandharipande (1992). For Leech (1983) Tact—a maxim of politeness—is itself a kind of politeness. For Giddens (1989/1993: 93) "Tact is a sort of protective device which each party involved employs in the expectation that in return their own weakness will not be deliberately exposed to general view."

We have also attempted to show how human communication underlies conflict between/among the Principles of rhetorics—Cooperativeness, Politeness, Irony, Banter, Interest and Pollyanna. The present study analyzes how the first three Principles conflict or compliment one another in the five selected novels. The second chapter discusses how the characters in the five selected novels deal with the Quantity maxim and analyses the implicatures embedded in utterances and the politeness concern in the deviations of this maxim.

2

Quantity Maxim in the Five Novels

2.0. Preliminaries

"Many men, many minds" thus goes an English proverb. Not all men are exactly similar just as no two men speak exactly alike. One comes across a great variety of people with different physical constitutions, different habits, different predilections, likes and dislikes, different intentions and abilities. Their habits, likes, dislikes, intentions and abilities control their talking and are reflected through their talk itself. When they enter into talk or conversation, they carry on and conduct their conversation with some assumptions and expectations. As far as conversation is concerned, speakers expect their conversational partners to cooperate by giving the amount of information required for the purpose of ongoing conversation. This is a tacit norm of conversation. They assume that they will put themselves in peril of misunderstanding if they do not follow this norm of providing required information. If they have to interact with the people around them, they adhere to this norm of conversing. Following this norm is an integral part of their social interaction. In Gricean pragmatics, this is the norm/maxim of Quantity in human conversation. The following section discusses the Quantity maxim and conversation in fiction.

2.1. Quantity Maxim and Conversation in Fiction

Conversation is governed by norms or principles. These norms or principles of human conversation are diverse. They guide and control human talk. Communicators engage in conversation with or without the knowledge of these norms.

They assume that their interlocutors have something to tell them through conversation. If this something has to be conveyed, they expect each other to cooperate. They expect their interlocutors to supply information necessary for the purpose of ongoing conversation. This could be said to characterize casual and everyday conversation. If someone gives too much information, he is branded by society as 'never shutting up' type of person. If someone fails to provide required and enough information, he is labeled as 'sullen' and rather 'secretive'. There do exist some such individuals in almost every society. There are 'never shutting up' type as well as 'sullen' and 'secretive' type of people in society. In literature also we come across such types of people/characters. One readily remembers garrulous communicators like Dickens' Josiah Bounderby in *Hard Times* and Marlow in Conrad's *Lord Jim*. Bounderby has the habit of talking too much of things which others would prefer to withhold. He does not hesitate to tell us his life story. His garrulity projects him as "the bully of humanity". In *Lord Jim* it is Marlow who practically narrates the entire story of Jim except in the first four chapters of the novel. One also encounters the laconic figures like Datta in R.K. Laxman's story *The Gold Frame*. Datta, a frame maker, lets his customers do talking. He has the habit of giving laconic answers to the questions of his customers.

The writer, be he a novelist, a dramatist or a story writer, is a creator of characters. As Boulton (1975: 71) remarks "The creation of characters is probably the most remarkable achievement of most good novelists." A novelist creates various types of characters—some simple and some complex. Some characters are easily remembered while others are instantly forgotten. He delineates characters in several different ways. One major way is through conversation. Through conversation he throws light on characters and also carries the story forward. The outline of his story and characters are revealed through conversation. This conversation goes on and is tailored keeping in mind the social class/community that a character belongs to. It would have been strange had G.B. Shaw put Queen's English in the mouth of Eliza Doo Little at the outset of the play *Pygmalion*. Hence Fowler (1977: 80) points out "Novelistic design and its execution are made in the medium of language and a language is the propriety of social community, impregnated with the values of thought-patterns of that community."

Simply put, conversation proceeds within the socio-cultural orbit and milieu. It is conducted in accord with the beliefs, values, practices and thought-processes that exist in society. The novelist, the creator of characters, is himself a part and parcel of the society he delineates. He puts that language in the mouth of his creations which befits social setting in his work. It is also that conversation takes place in multitudes of social situations such as legal trials, arguments, parliament, classroom, journalistic investigation and telephonic talk. In all such contexts the norm/maxim of providing information is normally adhered to.

As far as the Quantity maxim is concerned, normal and casual conversation reflects its observance. Most of the novelistic conversation also reveals that characters follow this norm by giving neither more nor less information than required. However one can also observe that on many an occasion characters in novels deviate from this norm. Of course the reasons for deviating from this maxim are not stereotyped but are unpredictable. The characters contravene this maxim with different purposes that vary from situation to situation. A couple of examples would help show why characters do not observe this maxim.

The first is a conversation from R.K. Narayan's novel *The Guide*:

> Raju asked, "Where are you from?" dreading lest the other should turn round and ask the same question.
>
> The man replied, "I am from Mangal."
>
> "Where is Mangal?"

He waved his arm, indicating a direction across the river, beyond the high steep bank. "Not far from here" he added. The man volunteered further information about himself, "My daughter lives nearby. I had gone to visit her. I am now on my way home. I left her after food. She insisted that I should stay on to dinner, but I refused. It would have meant walking home at nearly midnight. I am not afraid of anything, but why should we walk when we ought to be sleeping in bed?" (5-6).

Raju has been released from the jail and has taken shelter in a temple. A man named Velan appears and sees Raju on the granite slab. On being asked where he came from Velan replies that he is from a village, Mangal. In answering the second question "Where is Mangal?" Velan supplies unsolicited information about himself and his visit to his daughter married to his sister's son and thus deviates from the maxim of Quantity. He seems to do this on purpose. He has a problem. His step-sister is marriageable. Her wedding has been fixed with his cousin's son. But the sister does not accept this plan and has run away from her wedding. She now sulks in a room all day. The place where Velan meets Raju makes Velan sense that Raju is a man of importance. He takes Raju to be a pontiff. He innocently hopes to be helped by Raju. His intention is to solicit advice from Raju about what to do with his sister and hence wants to hasten up the information about himself. He provides more information than needed by Raju.

Thus, the flout of the maxim of giving required information is intention-bound. It has double intentions. One is to get help from Raju for his personal/domestic problem. The other is to convey that he is a man of sensibility. Raju rightly works out his implicature because Raju remarks immediately after Velan has finished "You are very sensible." The talk by Velan appears to be rumbling but serves his intentions.

The other example of conversation is from Raja Rao's novel *Kanthapura*:

> "I didn't know you were such a learned lawyer too", laughed Bade Khan.
>
> "But a final word. Will you oblige me by procuring me a house or not?"'
>
> "No, police Sahib I tell you humbly I cannot. I am not the owner of the whole village. But if there is anyone who is ready to offer you a house, please take it and turn it into a palace. I can see no objection to that." (20)

Bade Khan is a Policeman sent by the Red man's Government to spy the activities of the villagers of Kanthapura. He needs a house to live in. Patel Range Gowda is the revenue collector of the Government. Patwari Nanjundia sends Bade Khan to Patel Range Gowda. When asked if he would help Bade Khan procure a house, Patel Gowda provides more information than required by the policeman. His answer "No, Police Sahib" would have sufficed Bade Khan's question. But he tells Bade Khan that he is not the owner of the village. If anybody offers him a house, he has no objection to that. He blatantly fails to adhere to the maxim of Quantity. He intends to generate the implicature that he is indifferent to Bade Khan. The fact is that Range Gowda is also the representative of the Government like Bade Khan. But he is of the community that the Sudras in his village belong to. He wants neither to stop anyone offer his house to Bade Khan nor wants to take Bade Khan's side. His over-informativeness flagrantly reveals his indifferent stance to Bade Khan. Range Gowda's indifference infuriates Bade Khan who spits and leaves Patel Gowda instantly.

More interesting than the above two is the following conversation from O' Henry's story *The Romance of A Busy Broker* included in the anthology edited by Jatin Mohanty. The conversation between a New York broker Mr. Harvey Maxwell and his lady Secretary Miss Leslie has been taken *in extenso* as follows:

> "Miss Leslie," he began hurriedly, "I have only a moment to spare. I want to say something in a moment. Will you be my wife? I haven't had to time to show my love to you in the ordinary way, but I really do love you. Talk quick, please, I am busy."
>
> "Oh, what are you talking about?" exclaimed the young lady. She rose to her feet and gazed upon him round-eyed.
>
> "Don't you understand?" said Maxwell, a little impatiently. "I want you to marry me. I love you, Miss Leslie. I wanted to tell you and I was able to take a minute when things had slowed down a bit. They are calling me to the phone now. Tell them to wait a minute, Pitcher. Won't you Miss Leslie?"

> The secretary acted very strangely. At first she seemed overcome with surprise, then tears flowed from her wondering eyes, then she smiled cheerfully through them and one of her arms slid tenderly about the broker's arm.
>
> "I know now," she said softly. "It is this old business that has driven everything else out of your head for the time. I was frightened at first. Don't you remember Harvey? We were married last evening at eight o' clock in the Little Church around the corner." (25-26)

This conversation takes place in the lunch-break hour in Maxwell's office in New York. It is seen that the broker and the Secretary are more informative than needs warrant. The broker could just have said to her "You are my wife. We are now free. Let's make love." He refrains from imposing his marriage on her. She could have just said, "We already got married last evening. You should remember that." In stead of asserting that they are husband and wife they intend to leave option to each other through their Yes/No questions: "Will you be my wife?", "Won't you Miss Leslie?" and "Don't you remember Harvey?". This is because assertions give no options to conversers and are treated impolite. To show their concern of politeness for each other Mr. Harvey and Leslie are more informative. Put it in pragmatic terminology they sacrifice the maxim of Quantity to be polite to each other and to care for each other's 'face'.

The above interactions show that characters like the real-life people very often break the maxim of Quantity. The motivations for deviating from this norm are contingent, situation-dependent and vary from context to context. As in the examples above Velan and Patel Gowda are more informative than the other demands for achieving their personal intentions. In the last conversation the broker and Miss Leslie's deviation from the maxim is 'alter-centred'. The non-observance of the maxim is 'other-centred' rather than 'self-centred'. In the latter the communicators contravene the maxim for the sake of politeness—for protecting other's face. The section that follows discusses how the characters in the five novels under study deal with the maxim of Quantity. In particular it discusses their non-observance of this maxim. It is concerned with how and why the characters deviate from this Gricean norm of conversation.

2.2. Quantity Maxim in the Five Novels

A novel is a slice of life and as such it presents to us a portion of the vast panorama of life. The novelist accomplishes this task through people/persons in the novel. These people for Forster (1995: 42) are "The actors in a story." They unravel the author's point of view and also the plot of a novel. The characters in a novel bear verisimilitude to the people in real life. Like the people around us they have habits, their likes, dislikes, particular way of behavior and speech. They are pitted by their creator in a particular setting/situation. This setting controls the way they talk/communicate with other characters. The specificities of their manner of speaking linger in our mind. We may not be able to recall and remember the plot of a novel but their mannerisms of speaking hold our attention and we remember them for the times to come.

We have such a gallery of character creations by Dickens. After reading *Great Expectations* it is impossible to forget Joe Gargery. He is a rich source of humour for his mannerisms in speech as well as his grammatical errors. He says, "Lookee" instead of "Look", "I meantersay" instead of "I mean to say" and "Thankee" instead of "Thank you". In his meeting with Miss Havisham she asks Joe if he is the husband of Pip's sister. He turns towards Pip and replies that he certainly did marry Pip's sister when he was a single man. In R.K. Narayan's *The Guide* we notice the opaqueness and obliquity of Raju's talk. A villager named Velan approaches Raju in a temple. Velan says that he has a problem. Raju pours the information to him with an air of pontificality:

> "If you show me a person without a problem, then I will show you the perfect world. Do you know what the great Buddha said?" Velan edged near. "A woman once went wailing to the Great Buddha, clasping her dead baby to her bosom. Thc Buddha said, "Go into every home in this city and find one where death is unknown. If you find such a

> place, fetch me a handful of mustard from there and I'll teach you how to conquer death." (14-15)

In fact when a speaker says to a hearer that he has a problem, the hearer is expected to ask what the problem is. This is what Raju does not seem to be doing. However through his example of Great Buddha Raju opaquely conveys to Velan that if he has a problem, there is nothing new in it. Everybody has some problem or the other and Velan is no exception to this.

The point these illustrations drive home is that the conversation of fictional characters reveals a number of things about them. The fictional characters deviate from the norm of pronunciation as well as from the need of precision and straightforwardness in verbal expression. General Science tells us that there is a great variety of substances in our surrounding. These substances are made from a finite number of constituents. These constituents are called elements or chemical elements. Elements are divided into two classes: metals and non-metals. Copper, iron and aluminium are metals. Oxygen, Carbon and Bromine are examples of non-metals. Metals have the properties like ductility, malleability and conductivity. The metals that can be drawn into wires have ductility e.g. gold, silver and copper. The metals that conduct heat and electricity have conductivity e.g. copper, iron and aluminium. The metals that can be beaten into sheets have a property called malleability. Aluminium and iron are malleable metals. Language is like metal. It does not have the properties like ductility and conductivity. But it does have malleability. Language is malleable. The characters in a novel like a creator of characters make language malleable. They adapt language. They shape it to serve their communicative purposes. Put it figuratively they 'bend it like Beckham'. They execute the achievement of their communicative goals either by adhering to the maxims of communication or by not observing them.

As far as the Quantity maxim is concerned, the characters in novels can deal with the maxim in six different ways. They can straightforwardly follow the maxim. They can provide the required amount of information to their co-locutors—neither more nor less. They can contravene the maxim in five ways: flouting, violating, suspending, infringing and opting out of the maxim. The least interesting of these is the first. The most interesting of the non-observances is the flout. This is because a flout is a flagrant and blatant attempt to deviate from the maxim. This is intentionally done by a character to prompt his/her conversational partner to look for an extra meaning called 'implicature'.

Before we illustrate the flout of this maxim by the characters in the five selected novels let us take an example or two of the flout of this maxim from other texts/situations. A telling example of a flout has been given by Jenny Thomas (1995: 65-66). The speaker is Rupert Allanson—an MP and an expert on the British Intelligence Services. Discussing the identity of the so-called Fifth Man he informs his addressee:

> "It was either Graham Mitchell or Roger Hollis and I don't believe it was Roger Hollis."

The derivation of an implicature by the addressee would involve the following reasoning:

1. Allanson has flouted the maxim by giving more information than required.
2. The addressee would assume that Allanson is being cooperative.
3. Allanson fails to observe the Quantity because he is confronted with a clash between the Quantity maxim and the Quality maxim. This is because he strongly believes that Mitchell was the spy (Fifth Man) but he does not have adequate evidence for this fact.

Thus, he sacrifices the Quantity maxim at the cost of Quality maxim. The implicature deduced is that 'he strongly believes that Mitchell was the spy but he has no sufficient evidence to assert this fact. Also that his belief may not be accurate'.

Thorat (2000: 182) also gives a beautiful illustration of the flout of Quantity maxim by a character Meet Singh in Khushwant Singh's novel *Train to Pakistan*:

> "Who is the Deputy Sahib?" asked Iqbal.

> "You don't know the Deputy?" Meet Singh was surprised. "It is Hukum Chand. He is staying at the Dak bungalow north of the bridge. Now Hukum Chand is a *nar admi*. He started as a foot constable and see where he is now! He always kept the Sahibs pleased and they gave him one promotion after another. The last one gave him his own place and made him Deputy. Yes, Meet Singhji, Hukum Chand is a *nar admi* and clever. He is true to his friends and always gets things done for them. He has had dozens of relatives given good jobs. He is one of a hundred. Nothing counterfeit about Hukum Chand."
>
> "Is he a friend of yours?"
>
> "Friend! No, no" protested Meet Singh. "I am a humble Bhai of the Gurudwara and he is an emperor. He is the government and we are his subjects." (38)

In this talk the Quantity maxim is blatantly flouted by Meet Singh. He does so by giving more information than required by the two questions asked by Iqbal. The first question is a wh-question. Meet Singh narrates the story of Hukum Chand's progress and promotion. He also mentions Hukum Chand's cleverness and loyalty to his friends. To the second question—a polar question—a single word "No" would have sufficed. But Meet Singh glorifies Hukum Chand as the emperor and the government and humbles himself as an ordinary Bhai of the Gurudwara. The implicature generated is that "Hukum Chand is a sycophant and can be accused of favouritism". The answer to the second question also reveals Meet Singh's purpose to deify Hukum Chand. He is being cooperative in that he answers both the questions asked by Iqbal but his answers generate implicatures through his flout of Quantity maxim.

In the five novels under investigation we come across various characters failing to observe the maxim on many an occasion. They deviate from the maxim in various ways: by providing more information, by giving less information and withholding information they possess. We will first consider the cases of flout because flouting is the non-observance which is semantically loaded. Let's take up the flout of Quantity maxim novel-wise as under:

(1) *Temporary Answers*

(2) *Heat and Dust*

(3) *Cry, the Peacock*

(4) *Socialite Evenings*

(5) *The Binding Vine*

Jai Nimbkar's *Temporary Answers* lays bare the threads that weave human relationships. The nucleus of the novel is Dr. Vineeta Sohani—a widow at thirty. She wades her way through memories of her husband Nagendra's sudden death, her relationship with her mother, her younger sister Madhuri, her childhood friend Dr. Vilas, her friend Kishori, Kishori's husband Madhu, Professor Abhijit Gokhale and the people at the Charity Health Centre. Dr. Vineeta successfully battles the complications in her relationship with a host of people around her. Though she is not deft initially in the art of conversation, she pulls up gradually and moulds a new life as an independent and working woman. This she accomplishes through her verbal interactions with the people around her. A close look at her conversations with others pinpoints how she and her interlocutors deal with the maxim of Quantity.

The following are instances of why the characters in the novel flout this maxim. Let us discuss them one by one as follows:

> "Were you studying here?"
>
> "No, I was married there."
>
> "Then you were here only for a visit?"
>
> Kishori had not told him anything about me.
>
> I said, "No, permanently. My husband died a few months ago and I'm now living with my parents." (4)

This is a conversation between the narrator-protagonist Dr. Vineeta Sohani and Professor Abhijit Gokhale. This maiden encounter takes place at a party at the flat of Kishori-Vineeta's friend. The questions are asked by Abhijit Gokhale and demand just "Yes/No" answer. But Vineeta is over-informative to his questions. On being asked if she was studying in Bombay she provides an additional bit of information about her marriage. On being asked whether she is in Pune for a visit she replies that her husband has died and she is now with her parents. By thus being over-informative she implicates to Abhijit that she is a widow and as such living with her parents. She provides unsolicited information about her private and domestic life. This she does due to her getting jittery. Even at thirty Vineeta could not sail smoothly into a conversation with a person she first met. Her conversational partner Abhijit is not only a professor but also a writer. A confirmed bachelor he has the capacity to make her feel that he is interested in her. In the very first meeting he wields confidence in Vineeta and makes her talk. This is also because he is the first man she has met and talked with after a long time. His uncanny capacity fascinates her and forces her to talk with him. This with the consequence that after their first parting she finds it impossible to sleep that night.

> "Wouldn't your parents have helped?"
>
> "My father had died that year and my mother had gone to live with her brother in Indore. In any case I don't think that she had a great deal of money. What ever she had she probably needed to live on. Of course Madhu could have chucked at all and got a job but he didn't want to. It would have made him more unhappy in the long run. I tried to find a job but it wasn't so easy, without even a degree at my name." (11)

This talk takes place between Vineeta and her friend Kishori. Kishori has started working at All India Radio. Her husband is running an advertising firm and they have been living a dreary and miserable life. Necessity has prompted her take on an odd-spot job at All India Radio. Hence Vineeta asks Kishori if her parents wouldn't have helped her a single-word reply "No" would have sufficed. But she pours in information about her father, her mother and her husband Madhu. By so doing she implicates that in no condition would her parents have helped her. Her intention in being more informative than required by Vineeta is not only to implicate but also to suggest how it was a matter of real necessity for her to try some job and help her husband in need. In this context her reply also insinuates how Kishori is an independent sort of woman who wouldn't like to coop up in the house with her brats for twenty-four hours.

> I said, "Are you going to set up a practice here?"
>
> I am seriously considering it. There are a lot of things in favour of me. My father's good will for one. Also the house on Bhandarkar Institute Road. It is a good location. I think the heart of the city is now saturated with doctors. It's time things moved out. The house can be converted, without any trouble, into consulting rooms, an operation theatre, a couple of convalescing rooms. And the first floor can be a flat for me. The ground floor is big enough for both of us and if I want to expand later, it will be no problem as the compound is big enough. (24)

In this talk there is a flagrant flout of the maxim by Vilas. He is a childhood friend of Vineeta and has just returned from England. When Vineeta asks him whether he would set up a practice as an ENT specialist in Pune, he replies how favourable the location is and the conditions are for him. The bits of information he supplies to Vineeta implicate that Vilas has done a lot of well-thought out and considered planning. In fact, he has come to offer her the partnership in his Clinic to be set up. His over-informativeness is a deliberate move on his part to persuade her to accept the partnership—a heaven—sent opportunity for her. As he has thought they would have offices in the same building—he as an ENT specialist and she as a paediatrician. As it turns out later his attempt to persuade and convince her do not go in vain. Vilas and Vineeta settle in a clinic as partners. His over-informativeness on this occasion goes a long way to play a vital role in their delicate and critical relationship.

> Vilas said, "Where did you meet him?" or was it an arranged marriage?"
>
> I smiled, "It does seem impossible that two people from such disparate backgrounds should meet, doesn't it? No, it was not an arranged marriage, though Mother was pleased

> that I proved smart enough to make such a good marriage. I met him at a wedding reception."
>
> "It was not the sort of wedding we would ordinarily have found ourselves attending, but the bridegroom's father was a friend of my father's and he had a special personal invitation. I would never have gone if I had known how rich the people were. The display of wealth at the wedding was something I had never seen before and I was miserable because we looked so out of place, so like poor country cousins. Someone introduced Nagendra to me. He talked to me with practiced ease, made me talk about myself and seemed impressed by the fact that I was a doctor. It gave me confidence and I began to enjoy talking to him. Before we left that day he asked me for my address. I gave him the address of a friend who was living in the hospital because I didn't want mother to know. He said he might come and see me if he was in Pune and drop me a line if he was coming. When I actually received a letter from him I was surprised. It was like an impossible dream come true. We wrote to each other regularly after that. And occasionally he came to see me. It still remained a little unreal. Until we were actually married, I couldn't quite believe that Nagendra, who had everything and could have his choice of the most beautiful and glamorous girls, wanted to marry me." (23-24)

In this talk between the narrator-protagonist Vineeta and Vilas—a friend from her childhood—the two questions initiated by Vilas are answered by Vineeta in two of the utterances—"It was not an arranged marriage" and "I met him at a wedding reception." All the other information she provides Vilas is geared to lay her soul bare to him. She refers to the genesis of the relationship between her and Nagendra—her husband. It implicates to Vilas that her marriage with Nagendra was an offshoot of her clandestine affair with him. It pinpoints how blindly she felt gravitated towards him and how Nagendra was intent on seeing her and getting her hands in marriage. Put it in other words her marriage with Nagendra was a matter of dream coming true as it was quite unbelievable for her.

Ruth Prawer Jhabvala's *Heat and Dust* presents the so-called "East-West Encounter." The young narrator comes to India to unravel the mysteries of her grandmother, Olivia's life with her husband, Arthur Douglas Rivers of 1923. Olivia's loneliness and boredom in the bungalow in Satipur makes her receive invitation from the young prince, the Nawab of Khatm. She becomes a frequenter to the Nawab's palace in Douglas' absence. She is irresistibly drawn towards the Nawab and visits the shrine of Baba Firdaus with him. She develops intimacy with the Nawab and becomes pregnant from him. She approaches his mother, the Begum and gets the baby aborted. She never returns to Douglas and goes to the Nawab. He sends her to the hills near a town called X.

The young narrator comes to India in 1970s to unravel her grandmother's mysterious past. She finds a big room in the crowded locality of Satipur. Her landlord, Inder Lal, is a married man, but his wife Ritu is always ill. Inder Lal and the narrator develop a liaison. Like Olivia she also becomes pregnant at the shrine of Baba Firdaus from Inder Lal but unlike her grandmother she decides to have the child and thus goes to the same town called X to have her baby born.

These two stories—that of Olivia of 1923 and of the narrator, her grand daughter of 1970s—are related through the host of British characters and the Indian characters. The British characters are Olivia, Douglas Rivers, Mr. and Mrs. Saunders, the Crawfords, Major Minnies, Harry and Chidanand (Chid for short). The Indian characters include the Nawab of Khatm, his mother—the Begum, Inder Lal, Inder Lal's mother, his wife Ritu, Dr. Gopal and Maji. The cross-cultural encounters among these characters reveal their attitudes to one another and the British characters' attitude to India—the mystic land. But this is not the purpose and the special focus in the present study. We are concerned with how the characters exploit the strategy of conversational cooperation, particularly the maxim of Quantity.

Let's discuss why they flout the Quantity maxim. The following are a few instances:

> "What's happening in Khatm?" He did not answer but shut his eyes again. She said, "I hear there are some sort of riots." She insisted:
>
> "What's it all about? Tell me. No, you must."
>
> After a pause he said, quite fretfully "How should I know? After all I live in the palace and nothing like that happens there, does it?"
>
> "Nothing like what?"
>
> "How should I know," he repeated. "I stayed in my room all day yesterday and this morning. What else can you do in this hideous terrible heat? Have you looked outside? Have you seen what's it like? Once these dust storms start, they go on forever. No wonder everyone goes mad?" (71)

One morning Harry—the guest and the friend of the Nawab of Khatm, hurries to Olivia's bungalow in the Civil Lines. The English ladies—Mrs. Crawford and Mrs. Minnies—have just reassured Olivia that there is nothing to worry about Satipur, the State adjoining to Khatm. Here in Satipur the communal riots spread like forest fire. Olivia knew that this was the time of the Husband's Wedding Day (*Pati Ki Shaadi Day*)—a religious fair at the shrine of Baba Firdaus. The Muslim inhabitants manage to create communal disturbance on that day. Olivia is eager to know whether the riots would resurge this year too. In fact, she compels Harry to tell her what it is all about. The replies by Harry do not answer her questions. Harry withholds a chunk of information about the communal riots. His withholding the information that he possesses is deliberate. He knows that the Nawab is the protector of the gang of rioters—his Muslim fellowmen. The Nawab is eager to see them and hear what they have to say. He even embraces them as if they are his brothers. The rioters are the low-class ruffians allowed to walk in and out as if they own the Palace. Harry does not intend to divulge the Nawab's nexus with the rioters, the murderers and the dacoits. In fact, the Nawab and Harry have liaison with each other. He tells Olivia earlier, "He likes me, you see" (34). "I do want to do everything I can do to make him happier—I am here because I like him, not for any other reason" (35). Harry camouflages the Nawab's nexus with the rioters as he knows well the nature of the Nawab—"When he wants something, nothing must stand in his way—one does not say "no" to such a person" (34). The novelist does not explicitly discuss this relationship between Harry and Nawab and hence a critic Shahane (1976: 132) remarks "The relationship between Harry and the Nawab (homosexual tinge) is puzzling." Harry does not want to invite the fury of the Nawab by telling Olivia about his part in the riots. Harry's flout of the maxim suggests deeper relationship between the Nawab and Harry and between the Nawab and the rioters.

> I asked, "Does it happen very often?"
>
> "Of course. These people cannot read and the orderlies are not very careful. You see your problem. If she is dying," he said, "then don't bring her, there is not much we can do."
>
> "But then where should she die?"
>
> "You see your problem," he said again. "There has been no addition to the hospital for over twenty years. We don't have beds, we don't have staff or equipment." (111-12)

Once the young narrator saw an old beggar woman lying in the outskirts of the mounds of refuse. Moved by the harrowing condition of the woman, she rushed to the local hospital at the Civil Lines end of Satipur to enquire if she would bring the woman to the hospital. There she met the Medical Superintendent, Dr. Gopal. In Dr. Gopal's room came the two out-patients—Meher Chand and Bacchu Ram. Their prescriptions had got mixed up. Meher Chand suffering from piles was taking the medicines meant for gall-stones from which Bacchu Ram was suffering and *vice versa*. The narrator asked Dr. Gopal if the prescriptions often got mixed up. She also asked where the beggar woman, Leelavati, would die if not brought to the hospital. To the first question—Yes/No question, Dr. Gopal is over-informative. To the second question—the wh-question—he withholds the information.

The young Dr. Gopal thus flouts the maxim in two ways. A long list of difficulties he gives to the narrator implicates that: the best thing for Leelavati is to die where she is. His over-informativeness also results from his liking to talk to the narrator to practice his English and also to unburden himself. At the deeper level his information conveys as Bijawat R. (1997: 183) observes "Gruesome, repulsive and nauseating" condition of hospitals and doctors in India of 1975. One is reminded of Margaret in Jhabvala's another novel *A New Dominion* who is bitterly critical of Indian hospitals and doctors when she says, "Doctors don't know a thing" (146). In this novel Margaret dies pathetically in the storeroom of the small hospital in Maupur.

> Olivia said, "Where is he?"
>
> "In Indore. Yesterday he heard from Simla—they are threatening an enquiry and he sat up all night composing telegrams and this morning he drove off to Indore to consult his lawyers."
>
> "Is it true Harry? Is he involved with them?"
>
> "Goodness knows. As far as I am concerned, he's always right and they are wrong. I hate them. They are the sort of people who have made life hell for me ever since I can remember. At school and everywhere. Well, as long as they stick to bullying me—but when I saw them doing to *him* and *here*—no that's unbearable. And he won't bear it. They'll find out. You should have heard last night. "Wait till my son is born" he said, 'then they will laugh from the other side of their mouths." (161)

After getting pregnant from the Nawab, Olivia is in mental conflict—whether to have a baby born or to get it aborted. She is dying to know where the Nawab is. Harry replies that the Nawab is in Indore. This suffices her question. But all that Harry informs her thereafter is geared to justify the Nawab's visit to Indore. The Cabobpurians—the family of the Nawab's wife, Sandy—are threatening to bring a case about Sandy's dowry against the Nawab. Hence he has gone to Indore to consult the lawyers on this issue. To the second question whether the Nawab is involved with the Cabobpurians, Harry supplies unsolicited information. It implicates that the Nawab and his in-laws are not on good terms. For them the Nawab is a little prince whom they compare to a gross swine. The Nawab fumes with fury for this. He is intent to avenge the in-laws by having a son born not from Sandy but from Olivia. Thus, Harry's over-informative reply to the first question is justificatory whereas to the second question pinpoints that Harry is on the Nawab's side.

> "Take the Nawab: I can't deny that he does fascinate me—as I am sure," he told Olivia, "as he does you."
>
> "Oh, gosh darling," Douglas laughed, "does he?"
>
> "Well," said Olivia laughingly back, "he is a fascinating man and terribly handsome."
>
> "Really?" Douglas asked, as if he had never seen him in that light.
>
> "Oh, absolutely," said the Major. "He is—a prince. No other word for him. The trouble is that his State is unfortunately not quite princely enough to satisfy either his ambition or indeed his need for money." (149)

At the dinner in Douglas' bungalow the discussion among Douglas Rivers, Olivia and Major Minnies centers around the Nawab. For Douglas the Nawab is the worst type of ruler—the worst type of Indian. He is a menace to himself, to the British officials and to the inhabitants of his little State. For the Major he is a very fascinating person. Douglas is naturally curious to know if the Nawab is fascinating to his wife too. Olivia asserts (giving emphasis on "is") that he is fascinating and terribly handsome. Major Minnies also flouts by being over-informative thereby generating the implicature that the Nawab is, all said and done, a prince unfortunately in financial trouble. At the deeper level it implicates that the Major and Olivia, too, are on the Nawab's side. Douglas—the husband and Olivia—the wife—are at cross-purposes. Olivia is right because the Nawab is handsome and fascinating enough to make her pregnant. Perhaps Douglas fails to recover this implicature.

Cry, the Peacock by Anita Desai is a pen-portrait of a woman, Maya. She is brought up in opulence by her doting father but is married to a man of cold intellect, an advocate named Gautama. Maya and Gautama are the Poles apart. One is hungry for love the other is devoid of the emotion of love. For him love is a superfluity. Poetry gives her absolute joy. For him the couplets are a trifle too much of the last century. She believes in love as the sustaining force and also believes in attachment. Gautama is a staunch follower of detachment—the teaching of the Gita. Thus, differences in attitude create wide chasms and unbridgeable gulf between them. They intensify Maya's sense of isolation and lead to losing of her mental equilibrium. Gautama, a man of intellect, pursued "threads of logic to its end slowly and steadily as a meticulous tortoise" (208). Walking with her on the roof of their house, lost in argument and logic, he came between Maya and the Moon. She saw him "fall then, pass through an immensity of air, down to the very bottom" (208). As a noble character Maya holds herself responsible for his death. She loses her mental balance and dies grief-stricken. It makes a very interesting reading perusing the psychological jolts of a young sensitive woman who is possessed by a childhood prophecy made by an astrologer—"Death to one of you (30), four years after your marriage, so the stars prophesy" (31). The inner world of Maya contrasted with the dreary outer world of Gautama is laid bare through a weapon of linguistic interactions and nuances and the characters in the novel. Almost all the key characters in the novel deal with the maxims of cooperativeness in various ways. For the present let us stick to their flout of the Quantity maxim as follows:

> "Is there so much work to be done this summer? Couldn't you get away—just for a short holiday?"
>
> His cigarette calmed him. He blew spirals of blue smoke into the dimness of the shuttered room. "Unlikely", he said. "There is a lot of work" and he turned his head to look at me and I turned upon my side. (41)

A whole gamut of contextual threads is needed to interpret this small talk between Maya and Gautama. It is Spring time. Her pet-dog Toto has died. It is impossible for her to get rid of his memory. But Gautama has shown almost no emotional concern for either Maya or for Toto. She is reminded of her doting father's program to take her to Darjeeling or wherever she wanted. Gautama's lack of concern for her reminds her of her princess-like childhood. His indifference makes her suffer searing pains and a fierce headache. She is eager to know if, like her father, Gautama intends to take her out for holiday in Summer. To her two questions he should have said—"Yes" and "No" respectively. He implicates it but he also asserts that he has a lot of work to do. By so doing he is insinuating that her father could take wherever she wanted to go. Her father could but Gautama "can not". It is impossible that he can get her away just for a short holiday. Instead of saying merely "Yes", he makes an assertion and that too in a relaxed manner—blowing spirals of blue smoke into their shuttered room. His is the world in which money matters. In any case he would not spend it for going out. It is not in his nature to satisfy her appetite for the curious and the hills. He is even ready to leave her go alone and live himself without her. He says, "I daresay I can manage considering I did so for a great many years before I married you" (41). His six-worded assertion speaks volumes about Gautama—his coldness to the very idea of going out in Summer. One gathers that he does not reciprocate her feelings at all.

> "And Birla Mandir—I never thought you would go there, to pray. Did she tell you to?"
>
> "Yes, she says I must, if I want a son. I suppose she knows,"
>
> Pom mused, crumpling the petals in her hand. "She has four sons."
>
> Then she smiled. "Why? Does it seem funny to you that I should listen to my mother-in-law?"
>
> "You," I had replied. "Funny" and gazed out of the window at the yellow dust through which the car ploughed and now into the depths of an ocean with its quite colours." (63-64)

This talk had taken place between Maya and Pom, her friend, during a drive in the car in which Pom had taken Maya. Pom had ordered her driver to take them to Birla Mandir. When Maya asked her if her mother-in-law told her to go to Birla Mandir, Pom replied positively. But unsolicitedly she continued that according to her mother-in-law, Pom should pray to Vishnu in the Birla Mandir if she wanted to beget a son. This piece of advice from the mother-in-law is out of her mother-in-law's experience—"she has four sons." By being over-informative Pom generates the implicature that she and her mother-in-law are superstitious and selfish. Their faith in Vishnu is motivated. Pom was a fashionable girl who painted her mouth, the outlines of her black eyes and tied up her hair in pigtails with enormous ribbons. She did not even speak of fate—she wasn't fatalist. Maya could not see Pom honestly considering to pray and prostrate before the idol of Vishnu in the Birla Mandir. It seems strange and comical that Pom who never referred to family tradition and superstition before should now follow her mother-in-law meekly and reverently. Put it briefly Pom's flout conveys her superstition, her selfishness and her superficial obedience to her mother-in-law.

> "The letter—Arjuna's letter! What was it that disturbed you so violently when you received it?" The ruin of your confidence in your father? No, No, it wasn't that. Let me see now.... The long fingers would suddenly flash with illuminations. "I have it! It was Arjuna's reference to that horoscope—that strange fuss over the horoscope that was cast for you. You never did explain that to me. Why? Why?"
>
> "Stop screaming, for God's sake, Maya, Maya!" And there he was shaking me roughly by the arm. There was a fear on his face as he stared down at me, holding me fiercely. "God, what has happened to you, Maya?"
>
> I couldn't look into that face that reflected my own fear, for the first time. I flung away from him trembling. "Don't make me tell" I whispered, then turned swiftly to clutch at him, his garments. "Don't ask me Gautama—you can make me tell, you can talk me into anything. You can force me into anything you like if you just keep talking and questioning long enough. But don't drive me Gautama, don't drive me." (168-69)

This conversation between Gautama and Maya centers around the theme—the horoscope that her brother referred to in his letter. Gautama wants to know about the horoscope cast for her by the astrologer and mentioned by Arjuna in his letter to Maya. Maya withholds the information required by Gautama. By not explaining the reference to the horoscope she flouts the maxim. In fact, the horoscope is the solid fact of her life, remembered and known. It is not a figment of nightmare nor is it a hallucination. Albeit the information she provides conveys that she would talk with him about anything but the horoscope. She is intent on keeping it a secret. She knows that Gautama is an unsentimental utilitarian. She fears that if he knows of the prophecy in the horoscope, he might put her in peril of life. He must not know, not even guess about the prophecy. If he does, new dangers would arise like sudden fires out of the cracked earth. If he finds out, nobody would save her from danger—the danger that he would put her to death. Hence, she ruminates—"It must be kept a secret. The danger of it, the terrible danger" (153).

Shobha De's *Socialite Evenings* relates the tale of a yokel, Karuna. A gauche middle-class girl, Karuna aspires to enter into the beautiful and flashy world of Bollywood. Through her mentor, Anjali she is drawn into the world of the socialite—film stars, rich businessmen, directors/producers, and a whole lot of others. She is acquainted to Ritu, trampy Si and Abe, Krish, Girish Sridhar and finally a reporter Ranbir Roy. The background of glittering city of Bombay and the silvery world of Bollywood allure us to see how the socialites live their "evenings" and "outings."

The love-hate relationships, the tensions and the free talks about the three letter word "sex" and the four letter term "fuck" are all unleashed through as Monti, A. (2000: 32) remarks "A high-flown extravagance of language." The sordid affairs of the narrator-protagonist Karuna and the lifestyles of Anjali, Ritu, Charlie, Si, Abe, Kumar Bhandari, a German ad-film-maker, Varun—an editor and an inventor of gossips and Ranbir Roy are the hinges of the plot.

It does help to see how these socialites in the Muppyland make and consolidate their relationships and express hidden motives and that through the framework of linguistic cooperation. The verbal encounters reveal how they deal with the maxim of Quantity. First, let us see the flout of the maxim by them in *Socialite Evenings*:

> "Who are you?" I asked suspiciously.
>
> "So good to hear your voice and know you are in New York."
>
> My God, I thought, thousands of miles from Bombay and it was Him! The ad-film maker, who had driven off so abruptly after being so nice and who had prompted Anjali to sharpen her fangs on me.
>
> "I ran into Anjali the day I was leaving India—she told me you'd be in New York. I called her up later in the night to ask whether she knew your contact. And listen, babe, that should be explanation enough. Can I buy lunch today?" (51)

After landing in New York and starting to stay with a Sindhi friend, Karuna receives a call for her. She picks up the receiver and asks who is calling her. The reply from the ad-film maker does not answer her question. He abstains from telling her his name/identity and flouts the maxim. The implicature he generates is: "I know you and you know me, telling you my name does not hold important for me. I am on the hunt for you through your mentor, Anjali." The open-ended question, "Can I buy lunch today?" further implicates that he wants to be intimate to her. The preceding and following context in the novel tells one that the ad-film-man is a "seasoned man of affairs" with a good skill of persuasion. Even though Karuna wants to keep herself away from him, he goes to the extent of addressing her "babe" (51), "sweet-heart" (52), "baby" (53), and "love" (54). Later no sooner does she meet him than he plants a great kiss on her mouth.

> All that sounded fine. But the picture still remained fuzzy. "Where did you meet this fellow? Have you slept with him?"
>
> "You're awful. You don't have any romance in you. You just want to spoil everything by asking crude questions. But to answer your noisiness—Yes, I have slept with him.

> It was wonderful. I felt the earth move. Just like in those books. For the first time I felt something." (74)

This informal and free talk takes between Karuna and her mentor-friend Anjali at the Willingdon club. Anjali's marriage with Abe is on the verge of breakage. Before it does, she has already found another man—a high income-tax official. Karuna asks Anjali where she met this man and whether she has already slept with him. Anjali withholds answer to the first question and is over-informative to the second. Taken as a whole her flout implicates that the place where one meets a man is not significant. The way she confesses her experience with the official implies what type of a woman Anjali is. She is as if steeped in romancing as contrasted with Karuna not having interest in such beautiful and simple thing as being intimate with a man. In Subhash Chandra's (2000: 144) words "Marriage, in no way, puts any restraint on Anjali's and Abe's respective sexual orgies."

It takes one no time to twig that Anjali's flout of the maxim implicates her 'promiscuity'—one of the key themes of the novel. Anjali's reply typifies the concept of extra-marital relationship prevailing among the so-called socialites.

> "Is the upstairs one pink like your bedroom?" I enquired.
>
> "Are you being bitchy as always? The answer is "no." But in case you are interested, it has also been designed by me and everybody just loves it. Most of Kumar's friends prefer it to the other one, but they dare not say so. The basement bar has been done up by Kumar himself and he's very proud of it." (134)

A month after Anjali's marriage with Kumar Bhandari, Anjali invites Karuna and Si to her house for lunch. Anjali shows them her dining-room, bedroom, the puja room and the bars—one on the basement and the other upstairs. Karuna enquires whether the bar upstairs is pink like Anjali's bedroom. Where only 'no' would have sufficed, Anjali relates to them how her husband's friends just love the upstairs bar. The question—"Are you being bitchy as always?" is used by Anjali to pay Karuna in her own coin as Karuna intends Anjali to remind her of her affair with

Pierre-by using the word 'pink'. Her over-informativeness is geared to implicate that: she is a sort of an interior designer and her husband Kumar Bhandari is a very generous man to allow his third wife, Anjali, to spend on things as she likes it. It is easy to see that Anjali indulges in self-praise and the praise of her husband—Kumar Bhandari—a Punjabi businessman with a factory which imports machine tools. He is a homo and has kept Murthy—an orphan boy. Kumar has made up to Anjali by letting her to do the things as she wishes.

> "Hey! This is fantastic. How about a drink tonight? How does that sound?"
>
> "Sounds complicated. First I'll have to kill my husband. Then dope my lover. May be I'll drug my six kids and tie-up my mother-in-law while I am at it. After that I'll give my partners their evening meal and I shall be ready for the big date. How does that sound. Smart ass?" (299)

Here is an Indian reporter from America—Ranbir Roy. This is his just second encounter with Karuna. A married man having two kids he is there to screw Karuna up. He just wants to treat her in a kidding manner. He wants to offer her a drink tonight. Once again one finds that Karuna is over-informative. The information she provides to Roy is intended to refuse his offer of a drink. The flout she commits is meant by her to be justificatory for her refusal. The bluntness of her implied negative reply is revealed by her calling him 'ass'. In the context of the novel Karuna's implicated refusal presents her as the modern new woman. She has now made up her mind not to strike up any intimate relationship or marriage with wolfish males. As Walter (2000: 158) opines "Her breaking out of the bonds of matrimony and finding her feet into a profession of her choice were all of a piece with her character."

After illustrating how the characters in the four novels referred to so far deal with the maxim of Quantity, let's take a few examples of the flout of this maxim of verbal cooperation in the remaining one novel viz. *The Binding Vine*. Shashi Deshpande's *The Binding Vine* (1993) is a novel with distinction. The narrator—protagonist is Urmila (Urmi for short). As the novel begins, we find Urmi grieving over the death of her baby daughter—Anu. She finds it difficult to forget her daughter. Grief-stricken she receives the love of her mother Inni and her childhood friend Vanaa. As she wades through to overcome her grief, Urmi discovers her dead mother-in-law, Mira's poems and diaries. Going through them she gets the picture of Mira's life. The darkest side of Mira's life she finds is Mira raped in marriage. Trying to understand the tortures inflicted on Mira and her conflicts, Urmi comes across Kalpana's tragedy—a young girl brutally raped and now lying on death-bed. Kalpana's and her mother, Shakutai's, sufferings have a lot for Urmi to learn from. Urmi very daringly takes the issue and brings it into limelight. Ultimately the criminal/ rapist, Prabhakar, is exposed. He is the husband of Shakutai's sister Sulu. Towards the end of the novel Sulu commits suicide due to a sense of guilt.

The lives of Mira, Shakutai, Kalpana and Sulu make Urmi accept her life and be content. Shakutai's resoluteness despite Kalpana's tragedy helps her learn that "The main urge is always to survive" (203). Urmi determines to get Mira's long—written poems published. The distinction of the novel lies for Nityanandan I. (1995: 66) in "The introduction of female bonding, the desire of woman to help another less unfortunate one."

The dominant theme in the novel is human relationships that perpetuate through the vine of life—the spring of life. It is our concern to see how the characters in the novel negotiate their relationship through the maxim of Quantity. The following conversational situations would help do this:

> "Isn't there anyone who can be with you?" How many children do you have?"
>
> "Three. Kalpana is the eldest." (58)

This talk takes place between Urmi's sister-in-law—Vanaa and Shakuntala (Shakutai) in the hospital ward. Vanaa and the doctor are treating Shakutai's daughter, Kalpana—a rape victim. Vanaa asks Shakutai if there isn't anyone to escort her to home and how many children she has. Shakutai withholds the answer to the first question. For the second question "three" would have been the required reply. But Shakutai adds that of three children the rape-victim Kalpana is the eldest. She flouts the maxim by being over-informative. "The eldest unmarried daughter being raped" has a truckload of implications in the patriarchal Indian social set up. The eldest unmarried daughter being raped entails the ruin of the family's name and impairing the marriage prospects of not only Kalpana but also Shakutai's second daughter, Sandhya. This is clear when Shakutai pleads "I have another daughter, what will become of her?" (59) She heaps the blame straight on Kalpana saying "she has shamed us, we can never wipe off this blot" (147). Her telling Vanaa that "Kalpana is the eldest daughter" at a deeper level implicates her plea to the doctor and Vanaa not to divulge what has happened to Kalpana. She does in fact appeal to the doctor "Don't tell the police" (58). Shakutai's agony, fear and helplessness have been expressed in an apparently small utterance "Kalpana is the eldest." From this we get as Sharma (2005: 48) remarks, "Shakutai's traumatic state."

> "You're alone?" he asks.
>
> "Yes, my mother and Kartik have gone with Vanaa and Harish. I had work, corrections piled up."
>
> "Hmm, Your father?" he asks bending down to look at Papa's photograph, hands behind his back.
>
> "Yes. He died four years back." (85)

One day returning from the sea-shore Urmila happens to encounter Bhaskar Jain, the doctor. Bhaskar solicitously drops her home in his car. Willing to get rid of him she finds that Bhaskar is looking at her expectantly. Hence she is forced to invite him in. No sooner does he sit down than he asks Urmila if she is alone at home today. The plain "yes" was enough for his question. But she informs unsolicitedly that her mother Inni and son Kartik have also gone out with Vanaa and her husband Harish. This is a deliberate gesture on her part. She implicates "I am alone and even my son Kartik is also out, go on and say what you want to say." This implicature is calculated by Bhaskar. What follows in their conversation after this are two delicate issues: marriage and Kalpana's case. Bhaskar, who is against marriage of girls, learns that marriage is a necessity to women as it gives women the guarantee of safety and protection from other men. Very cleverly is Urmila able to unearth crucial information about Kalpana's case—that the police officer in Kalpana's case is not on Kalpana's side. This gives Urmi a zeal to bring the issue into the limelight and fight for justice for woman.

> "Whose fault is it then? Whom do I blame?"
>
> "The man—the man who did this to her. Don't you see, can't you see he's the wrong doer?"

She looks at me in silence, eyes wide and startled as if the thought of the man has never occurred to her, "The man" she says after a small silence, "What use is it blaming him?" Women like you will never understand what it is like for us. We have to keep to our places, we can never step out. There are always people waiting to throw stones at us, our own people first of all. "I warned Kalpana, but she would never listen to me. I'm not afraid of anyone, she used to say. That's why this happened to her. Women must know fear" (148).

On visiting Shakuntala's house this talk takes place between Urmi and Shakuntala. Centripetal to their talk is the topic—Kalpana's case. Shakuntala squarely puts the blame on Kalpana for her being brutally raped. When Urmi intends to solicit whether the rapist is to be blamed for the heinous act, Shakuntala's "No" would have been enough. But Shakuntala adds the information about Kalpana's misdemeanor. Her over information exonerates the rapist and she takes Kalpana to task. It implicates: "The man isn't to be blamed but Kalpana is to be blamed. She is stubborn and crossed the '*lakshmanrekha*' laid by the man-dominated society for a girl's or a woman's behavior. "Shakuntala knows perhaps that a rape-victim is a loser on two counts: First, she has been raped. Second, the society will look down upon such a victim as a *kulta*—a characterless woman. Put it in a nutshell—all the unsolicited bits of information added by Shakuntala project her as a 'typical Indian Middle-class woman in a society governed by Manu's laws.'

In the preceding pages the cases of the flout of the maxim of Quantity have been discussed. As stated earlier the characters in a literary work—a novel or a play or a story are seen to deal with the maxim in different ways. A point to be noted here is the difference between the grammatical rules and the maxims of conversation. Very rarely does one come across a character breaking a rule of grammar. When the rule of grammar is broken, the sentence produced is rendered ungrammatical. But this is not the case with the conversational maxims without being detrimental to the very act of conversation.

The non-observances of the maxims of cooperation fall into the following categories:

1. Flouting
2. Violating
3. Infringing
4. Opting out
5. Suspending

The cases of flout of this maxim in the novels under study have already been discussed. The observation of the fictional conversation shows that the characters also violate, infringe, opt out of and suspend the Quantity maxim. We will take a few cases of these types of non-observance in the order—violating, infringing, opting out of and suspending. A character is said to violate a maxim when he/she misleads i.e. his/her information provided leads to false implicature. Let's take a look at the following encounter from *Temporary Answers*:

"What train did you come on?"

"The Express."

"Doesn't that get in the morning?"

"Yes, but I was bushed. We hadn't got a berth and hadn't slept all night. Madhu went to the office but I just went to the flat and slept like the dead. Then I got up and washed my hair. My, was it filthy! Then Madhu came back and we came here to fetch the children." (76)

Vineeta's friend Kishori had left her children to the care of Vineeta and had gone to Hyderabad with her husband Madhu.

When Kishori and Madhu come to Vineeta to collect back their children—Smriti and Hemant, Vineeta asks Kishori why she did not come in the morning as soon as she got back. Asked whether the Express arrives in the morning Kishori's "yes" is enough. But she fails to observe the maxim by relating that she was very tired and needed help. Hence the delay in coming to fetch her children. This is a misleading implicature she generates and thus can be said to have violated the maxim. It transpires from the novelistic context that Kishori is a 'user' and is selfish. The guiding principle of her life is her own need. All other considerations are for her minor. She is happy-go-lucky sort of woman and wouldn't like the burden of her children with her on the outing. She fabricates the excuses for her delay in coming to fetch her children in the afternoon instead of in the morning. Abhijit makes Vineeta aware of Kishori's characters: "She (Kishori) is a completely selfish sort who doesn't care if she hurts others" (80).

The maxim is violated in *Cry, the Peacock* in the following interaction:

> "The masks they wear—you must have seen them? And their costumes. And the special kind of music. And it is all out in the open, at night by starlight and perhaps they have torches. Yes, I suppose they dance by the torchlight...." Gautama got up abruptly, having finished his cigarette and stretched "if that is your only reason for wanting to go all that way south, I suggest you wait till a Kathakali troupe comes to a performance in Delhi, as it is bound to sometime—perhaps in Winter. It will be less expensive." (43)

Maya desires that Gautama should take her out to South in Summer so that she will see the Kathakali dances—their masks, costumes and music. The response Gautama gives her implicates—"yes, he will take her to a Kathakali not in Cochin or Travancore but in Delhi." One deciphers from reading the novel that this is a misleading implicature. Never ever does Gautama fulfill this desire of hers to see and enjoy the Kathakali dances. He is insensible, indifferent to her emotions and is rigid. He like his whole family would talk on any topic under the sun but love, music and poetry. The implicature his reply generates turns out to be false. In Gricean parlance he violates the Quantity maxim.

In *The Binding Vine* too Priti seems to violate the maxim in the following conversation with Urmi:

> "Would you use your own mother's life?" I asked Priti.
>
> And she said, "Yes, one has got to be objective, one has to distance oneself." (40)

Urmi's America-returned friend Priti is fascinated by Mira's life revealed in her diaries and poems. Like a progressive modern girl Priti proposes to Urmi that Urmi should write a script on Mira's conflicts and tribulations and Priti will make a movie on this. Thinking that Mira is Kishori's mother (Urmi's mother-in-law) Urmi declines to do so because she knows that Mira desired to keep her poems and diaries secret. They were 'strictly private and confidential.' Urmi in return asks Priti if she would use her own mother's story for the movie. Priti replies in the positive but is over-informative by saying that one needs to take out the personal element in one's life and make the movie objectively. The implicature is that: 'she (Priti) will make movie on her mother's life and present her mother's story in objective manner.' As readers we come to know hereafter that Priti's mother had become a maniac, depressive and an alcoholic woman in America. Priti never makes a movie on her mother's life. Her implicature proves to be false.

Infringement of a maxim occurs when a communicator lacks perfect command over language or when he/she is in a particular physical state—fever, hunger, drunkenness, excitement, frustration/nervousness. The communicator is either over-informative or under-informative or just remains tongue-tied in this state.

The following few illustrations could be cited as infringements of the Quantity maxim. The first is from *Heat and Dust*:

> "What has he studied?" Inder Lal asked, he was now keenly interested.

> "What have you studied?" he probed. "Do you know the Puranas?"
>
> "What about the Brahmanas?"
>
> Child did not hear these questions, he was looking at me with pleading, fevered eyes. (62)

The narrator and Inder Lal come across a Sadhu in a royal tomb's corner. The Sadhu is an English boy, Chid (Chidanand). He was on the pilgrimage. But feeling ill he had returned to the town of Satipur. The narrator tells Inder Lal that he is a Sadhu. He has studied Hindu religion. Indifferent in the beginning Inder Lal feels interested in Chid and hence asks Chidanand if he knows the Puranas and the Brahmanas. Chidanand is feeling ill. He is hungry. He has a fever. He cannot move even when a dog sniffs at him. In this physical condition he is unable to hear Inder Lal's questions and resultantly fails to answer. In pragmatic terminology Chid infringes the Quantity maxim. He has no intention generate any implicature as such.

Maya in *Cry, the Peacock* infringes the maxim in the following conversation:

> "I sent it away to be cremated", he said. "It is all over. Come, won't you pour out my tea?"
>
> "Tea?" she cried, looking up. "But ...!" And she stopped still to see that as every other evening, the tea-tray had been brought to the table beside her. (6-7)

Before Gautama comes home Maya's pet-dog, Toto dies. The dead body lies rotting in the sunlight. She loves her Toto very dearly and his death comes to her as a great shock. In the state of mourning, sorrow and despair she thinks of nothing but Toto. Like childless women Maya has developed a frantic attachment to her pet-dog. Her husband Gautama comes back in the evening. He telephones to the Public Works Department. The scavenger's truck comes and takes the dead body away for cremation. Gautama asks her to pour out tea for him as if nothing has happened. In the state of grief, woes and misery Maya is unable to respond to Gautama. She thus infringes the maxim.

In *The Binding Vine* Urmila infringes the maxim in the following talk:

> "Then why are you crying?"
>
> "Ssh Mandira, don't jabber. Just hold this here—like this. Don't let go, mind. I'll get some Dettol."
>
> "No, Amrut, it is okay, there is no need to fuss. I'd like to lie down for a while." (16)

Urmila is grieving over the death of her baby daughter, Anu. The loss of a loved one is simply unbearable for her. It is even impossible for her to forget Anu. To forget the dead is to betray. In this critical state of mind Urmila gets an attack of asthma. She bangs her head against the wall and gets a bump on her forehead. Her brother, Amrut, her sister-in-law Vanaa and Vanaa's daughter Mandira—all crowd in the room. When a little girl Mandira asks why Urmi auntie is crying, Urmi fails to answer her question. Urmi, thus, infringes the maxim.

When a conversational partner refuses to provide the information, he is said to opt out of the Quantity maxim. He opts out of the maxim for legal or ethical reason. When he does not want to hurt the other party or put another person in danger, he refuses to relay the required information. In Gricean parlance he is said to opt out of this maxim. In the novels under investigation one observes that the characters in these novels time and again opt out of the maxim. Let it be stated that the character has no intention to generate any extra-meaning called implicature.

A few instances of this kind of non-observance may be given from the five novels. The first is from *Temporary Answers*:

> I had hoped to slip past unobserved, but she called to me, "You had better have your tea and then a bath quickly." She said.
>
> "What's the hurry?"
>
> "Don't you remember it's Milind's thread ceremony?"
>
> "Oh, my god."
>
> "What's the matter?"
>
> "Nothing." (9)

This colloquy is between Vineeta and her mother. The mother wants Vineeta to accompany and attend the thread ceremony of Milind, Vineeta's cousin. When Vineeta exclaims "my god", the mother is eager to know what the matter is with Vineeta. Vineeta opts out to answer. Vineeta has no roof of her own. She is a widow at thirty. She is dependent on her parents, as she has no career of her own. Moreover she thinks that the age-old thread ceremony is silly and pointless. Also that she does not like that all her relatives see her there as a widow. She is unwillingly to attend the ceremony. But she does not summarily tell her mother about her unwillingness. It would mean a sort of disobedience and would hurt her mother. She takes recourse to a word "nothing" and thus opts out of the Quantity maxim.

We have another instance of this maxim being opted out in *Cry, the Peacock*:

> "Are you going to work late?" I ventured, having at length studied his long, set face, the frown, which implied no greater problems than that with which the brain could deal, the thin and firm white lips, the nicotine stained hand upon which his chin rested. He did not reply. (165)

Maya and Gautama are the Poles apart. Her name 'Maya' indicates that she is attached to the world whereas Gautama, her lawyer husband, is a picture of detachment. She believes in love as a power, as a force whereas he ridicules love with the help of argument from 'The Gita.' She hungers for his love but he is rather unresponsive to her desire. His unemotional attitude makes him remain unaffected by the death of Maya's pet-dog, Toto. For him money is the most important thing in life. He is cold like snow and far from passions. He studies the cases of property and money very coolly. Maya is haunted by the childhood prophecy of an astrologer that one of them will die within the four years of their marriage. She is eager to be close to him and to talk to him about life and death. He has no time and no consideration for her. He is more concerned with his work than his wife. Hence, when she enquires if he would work late that night, he does not reply. In Gricean terminology, he opts out of the maxim.

The narrator-protagonist of *The Binding Vine* Urmila opts out of the maxim in the following talk:

> "Sometimes, Urmila, I think I was cruel to the girl, but I did it for her.
>
> I wanted her to have all that I never had—education, a good life, a good marriage, respect from others. Look at me. What am I? I don't want my children to be like me." And then the cry breaks out of her.
>
> "Did I do wrong, Urmila, was I cruel to her?" And again, "I did not want to be born, is that why she is dying now? Is this my punishment?"
>
> I listen to her with a strange feeling. (112)

Shakutai's daughter-Kalpana has been raped and admitted into a hospital. Urmila visits the Ward and tries to comfort Shakutai. Unable to see the contours of Shakutai's face Urmila brings her home as a guest. As Urmila engages in making tea, Shakutai bursts out her fears, pains and helplessness to Urmila. She relates how her sister Sulu has been kind enough to bring up not only Kalpana but also Shakutai's son Prakash and youngest daughter Sandhya. She explains how motherly she has been towards Kalpana. She questions Urmila whether it is her fault that she has been cruel to daughter and that this is the punishment meted out to her. Urmila looks at Shakutai's gestures—her bones pushing themselves against the dry skin, the deathly stillness about the body and her face almost like a rigid mask. Urmila only listens to her and does not respond to her questioning and revelations. Put it in other words Urmila opts out of the maxim. This need not be taken to implicate that she does not want to commiserate with her Shakutai.

Having considered the non-observance categories like violating, infringing and opting out of the maxim, it is now the time to investigate how the characters in the novels undertaken deal with the maxim in another way—suspending the maxim. One may observe that there are many an occasion when characters do not provide required quantity of information. They do not fulfill the maxim as directed by Grice. They have access to the necessary information, but do not provide that as required by their conversational partner in the given context. They are said to suspend the maxim. The suspension of a maxim is a case when it is not expected of a conversational partner to follow the maxim due to socio-cultural reasons. They suspend the maxim when to mention something/somebody is a taboo, when it is supposed to bring bad luck, when the observance of the maxim will incriminate the speaker/other or being requiredly informative will bring disgrace and bad name for him or the other party.

In pragmatic literature a glaring example of suspending the Quantity maxim is found in the Malagasy Republic. As Keenan (1976: 70) points out "The partners in talk-exchanges regularly provide less information that is required by their conversational partner, even though they have access to the necessary information." The reason is socio-cultural. The people in this community believe that providing the precise information will invite the attention of the evil spirit to them. One also comes across the acting community in England avoiding to name Shakespeare's play *Macbeth* by this very word because it is believed by them that to mention the name "Macbeth" will bring them bad luck. They refer to the play as *The Scottish Play* instead. Briefly said, the conversational partners on number of occasions suspend this maxim. Once again the intention is not to generate any implicature.

In the novels under study characters suspend the maxim time and again. The following are a few examples. The first is from Shobha De's *Socialite Evenings*:

> "Do you know that you have joined the rank of battered wives? It's horribly humiliating Ritu—this is awful. It's demeaning. Don't you have any dignity? Self-respect?"
>
> "Come on, you have got to be joking. He'd do the smallest thing I asked him to. And how can it be humiliating when it's me who's doing the asking? And between you and me these slugouts lead to terrific sex. It's the only time I feel I'm not in bed with his mother." (130)

This is the telephonic talk between Karuna and Ritu. Ritu's husband had an affair with a tartlet and Ritu scolded the tartlet and also her husband. She even threatened her husband to castrate him. She picked up his vase and flung it at him. This was too much for him to bear. He took out his leather belt and pulped Ritu. He hit her hard against her nose and her nose bled like a geyser. Her face was swollen and the eyes began to puff. Karuna asked her if it was not insulting on her part to be treated this way. The word "No" would have been the apt reply. But Ritu is over-informative. She thinks that her plain 'no' would have been taken a lie by Karuna and disgracing for her. She suspends the maxim by being evasive to Karuna's question and still being more informative. She, thus, attempts to save herself from disgrace or bad name.

> "I'm sure. So, What's it now—just-me-and-my-friendly vibrator."
>
> "I don't have to dignify that question with a reply. Let's have Lunch." (135)

After her marriage with Kumar Bhandari Anjali invites Karuna and Ritu to her house. When they reach Anjali's house, Anjali is extremely delighted and shows them her cupboards, bathrooms and her Beauty's boudoir. When they enter Kumar's bedroom, Karuna finds a video meant for the servants to keep them away from spying. She compliments Anjali for her smartness in suggesting her husband this trick. Anjali accepts the compliment and says that she is a good and chaste woman these days. Her eyes, skin and hair are dull—the result of her staying off sex. Karuna asks Anjali whether she uses a vibrator to satiate her physical need. (Her husband is a homo). Anjali withholds the reply. She is now a changed woman after having affairs. She has become a religious woman. She is so changed that she would not even utter the word 'sex'. It would be disgraceful on her part to talk about sex, the vibrator and the like-things. Hence she withholds to reply to Karuna's question. Her invitation to have lunch instead is an attempt to suspend giving the required reply.

In *Temporary Answers* Madan, a twelve-year-old son of Mrs. Bhingare suspends the maxim in the following talk:

> "Who did this, Madan?" I asked.
>
> He said nothing.
>
> ....
>
> "Did you Madan?" I said, putting some ointment on his back. "Why did you steal? You know it's wrong, don't you? Isn't that they teach you in school?"
>
> Madan refused to break his sullen silence. (44-45)

Mrs. Bhingare brings her son Madan to the Health Clinic where Vineeta offers her honorary services. Madan has stolen money from the counter of a shopkeeper, Ramusheth. Ramusheth has beaten Madan on his back and upper arms. There are some welts on his back and upper arms left. His mother has brought him for the treatment. Dr. Vineeta asks him who has beaten him. Madan refuses to answer. When she again asks him why he stole the money from Ramusheth's shop, Madan again withholds the answer. For him to admit the stealth he has committed would bring bad name not only for him but also for his family as a whole. To save his family and himself he refuses to relay the information. His suspension of the maxim, thus, is highly motivated.

Gautama in *Cry, the Peacock* does the same in the following interaction with Maya:

> "What is death, then?" I asked, dropping down one ear-ring after the other."
>
> Two red rubies. "What is death to you, Gautama? Do you believe it?"
>
> "Perhaps if you clarified what you mean by death, I could tell you whether I believe in it or not. Though why you should give thought to such a subject mystifies me—it is a definitely a new trend in you. You used to tell me you were far too immersed in your thoughts these days? You are much too young." (166-67)

Maya is haunted by the prophecy made by an astrologer that one of them would die (Maya/Gautama) within four years of their marriage. She passes through mental crisis whether she or Gautama die. She asks if she dies, would it disturb

Gautama or not. She is eager to talk to him about death and life after death. But Gautama evades to answer what death is. Certainly the questions about death and life after death are tricky questions. Nobody knows their answers for certain. One does not expect the other to define precisely what death is. Gautama is no exception to this. Moreover he is more concerned with his professional work than his wife's health. Hence when asked by Maya what death is, Gautama fails to provide the required information and thus suspends the maxim of giving required information.

The following conversation from *The Binding Vine* is another instance of dealing with the maxim in this way:

> I moved away, lifting the chair we overturned when we moved the woman. Vanaa and the doctor hide her from my view, but in a moment I hear her moaning.
>
> "Will you drink some water? Sit up, that's right."
>
> She drinks awkwardly, the water running down the sides of her mouth.
>
> "Do you feel better now?"
>
> The woman bursts into sobs, the painful sobs of one not used to crying.
>
> I can hear the words, "My daughter", "My Kalpana...." (57)

The woman referred to is Shakuntala. Her daughter, Kalpana, has been brutally raped and has been hospitalized. Urmila has come to the hospital to see her sister-in-law, Vanaa. When she reaches the hospital, she finds Vanaa and the doctor, Bhaskar Jain consoling Shakutai. Bringing a glass of water Dr. Jain asks Shakutai if she would have some water and after having some whether she feels better or not. Shakutai does not answer both the questions. Her eldest daughter Kalpana has been raped. The sky has collapsed on Shakutai. A young unmarried daughter being raped means ruin not only for the daughter but also her parents and the whole family. The prospects of her marriage have been meager and the family has been stigmatized. There is younger daughter, Sandhya, too. It is all a traumatic experience for Kalpana and her mother in the patriarchal society in India.

One does not expect a mother in this context to contribute to the conversation as expected by the Gricean maxim. Hence, the mother of a rape-victim suspends the maxim.

2.3. Quantity Maxim and the Other Maxims of Cooperative Principle

The maxims of conversation, particularly the maxims of Cooperative Principle, differ from the grammatical rules in various ways. The rules of grammar are all or nothing, the maxims are more or less. A rule of grammar is either in operation or it is not. Maxims, on the other hand, are more or less. As far as the Quantity maxim is concerned, one can give far too much information, slightly too much information or insufficient information. The rule of grammar either operates or it does not. For instance, there is a simple rule in English: if the subject of a sentence is singular, the verb is singular. If the subject is plural, the verb is plural. This rule operates in the following examples:

(a) *Orhan Pamuk* is a Nobel Prize Winner.

(b) *Kiran Desai* is the Winner of Man Booker Prize.

(c) *Hulabullo in Orchard* and *The Inheritance of Loss* are the novels by Kiran Desai.

(d) *My Name Is Red*, *Snow* and *Istanbul* are the novels by Pamuk.

In (a) and (b) the subject is singular and hence the verb 'is' is singular. In (c) and (d) the subject is plural and therefore the verb 'are' is plural. Grammatically put, the rule of Subject-Verb Concord operates in the four examples. The maxim of Quantity, on the other hand, is more or less: One may be more informative or less informative than required or may just prefer to be tongue-tied.

Further, grammatical rules are exclusive. When one rule occurs, the other cannot operate in its place. The maxims of verbal cooperation can co-occur. In the same verbal contribution one can observe one or more maxims. One can be requiredly informative, be truthful, relevant and clear. The maxims have another nature. They may compete with one another. Unlike the grammatical rules the maxims may clash or conflict with each other. The communicators may observe one maxim or more maxims in the same verbal interaction. They may fail to observe a maxim in order to uphold another maxim. They face a situation of what Burt (2000: 993) defines "Maxim-confluence—a situation in which two maxims enjoin the same linguistic behavior on the part of the speaker." The play of observance and non-observance is contingent and goal-directed. The conversers follow one maxim and violate, flout, suspend and opt out of another maxim according to the demand of situation and the immediate goal of their ongoing conversational activity. In this section our concern is to investigate how the characters in the selected novels deal with the quantity maxim in relation to the other maxims.

The following interactions from the novels illustrate this play of observance and non-observance. The first is from *Temporary Answers*:

> "Who did this, Madan?" I asked.
>
> He said nothing.
>
> His mother said, "Ramusheth, the shopkeeper, did it. Madan stole money that a customer had put down on the counter. Ramusheth saw him and caught him. He is lucky, he got away with just a beating and Ramusheth didn't turn over to the police. And this—this worm wouldn't say he was sorry. He laughed at me and said he would do it again. Ask him if he didn't do that". "Did you, Madan?" I said, putting some ointment on his back. "Why did you steal? You know, it's wrong, don't you? Isn't that what they teach you in school?" Madan refused to break his sullen silence. (44-45)

Madam is a son of a worker in a fabric-dyeing factory. His mother brings him to the Health Clinic of Dr. Vineeta. There are welts on his back and upper arms. In the course of her treatment Dr. Vineeta asks Madan who did this to him and why he stole money from Ramusheth. To both the questions Madan remains tongue-tied. It is his mother who relates the happening to Dr. Vineeta. If Madan himself does it, it would bring disgrace and defame for him and his family. He suspends the maxim by remaining silent. Further, if he says 'no' to what his mother relates, he would violate the Quality maxim. Put it in the Gricean fashion he suspends the Quantity maxim to uphold the Quality maxim.

One comes across another instance in the same novel in which the Quantity maxim is not followed for the sake of another maxim. This is the conversation:

> I said, "Her shortness of breath seems quite extreme and her fingers and toes have bluish nail beds."
>
> "What does that mean?"
>
> "I couldn't really say without examination. It's possible. I am only being an alarmist. I hope so. But the symptoms could point to something wrong. Nothing serious, there is no need to worry. But get her checked, just to be on the safe side." (145)

On her visit to the house of Vilas and her sister Madhuri, Dr. Vineeta sees a four-year-old daughter of Swati, the younger sister of Vilas. Vilas notices that Anupama, Swati's daughter, has some problems with breathing. When Vineeta refers to this shortness of breath, her sister Madhuri enquires what the shortness of breath and the bluish nail beds of Anupama's fingers and toes mean. Vineeta could have just said that, "something is wrong. Get it checked." But she does not inform Madhuri requiredly in this context. What she intends to suggest is to be supplemented with evidence. Only saying that Anupama has problem with pulmonary artery would have been the violation of Quality maxim. Dr. Vineeta describes the symptoms of the disease to evidence Anupama's problem. In other words, Dr. Vineeta opts out of the Quantity maxim to uphold the Quality maxim.

In *Heat and Dust*, Olivia flouts the Quantity maxim in the following talk with Mrs. Crawford:

> "Don't forget he's a Mohammedan too," they told her.
>
> "Yes, but he is not like *that,* not a fanatic. Good Heavens."

She laughed at the idea. But their faces remained grim. She argued:

> "He's such a modern person. Why—he's just like—almost like one of us in that way. I mean he is not superstitious or begotted at all. He's so entirely emancipated."
>
> "Do you really think so?" Mrs. Crawford said flatly.
>
> "Oh, I'm sure of it. I've heard the way he talked about the suttee, it was just like an English person talking. He was so disgusted. Barbaric, he said." (69-70)

One morning Mrs. Crawford and Mrs. Minnies visit Olivia. They want to reassure her that this year the riots in Satipur would not be worse as the previous year. The Nawab could control the riots if he so intends. But they still think that he is a Muslim and the rioters are also Muslims supported by him. Olivia cannot believe that the Nawab can be an accomplice in the criminal activity. When Mrs. Crowford plainly asks her if she really thinks that the Nawab is a person with modern and English thinking, Olivia's reply "Oh, I am sure of it" is enough for the question. But she gives more information. She relates how the Nawab is disgusted with the barbaric practice of suttee in India. Olivia flouts the maxim to implicate that "the Nawab is a person with a modern thinking and hence cannot be suspected to be having his hand in the communal riots." She sacrifices the maxim of giving required information to disambiguate the proform "so" in Mrs. Crawford's question. Olivia flouts the maxim for the sake of observing the Manner maxim.

In the following interaction in the same novel one notices a different case:

> "Who were those men?"
>
> He didn't answer at once, and when he did, it was with another question,
>
> "Who do you think they were?" He gave her one of his shrewd looks, then laughed: "I suppose you think they are bad men. You must have heard many stories, I think, isn't it, and you believe they are true." Again she felt she did not have to defend herself or answer him.

> "But if they are bad men." He went on "I think they can't be so very bad because look what they have come here for." He pointed to the mound in the shrine on which some fresh garlands had just been laid and sticks of incense were still smouldering. "You see, they didn't come for any bad purpose but to pay their devotions." (133-34)

Once the Nawab takes Olivia to the shrine of Baba Firdaus on the Husband's Wedding Day. After he offers his prayers to the shrine, he leads her to a grove near the shrine. Some men emerge from the shrine and stare at the Nawab and Olivia. The Nawab speaks to them in a familiar manner and they fall at his feet. Olivia recognizes from their humility and their desperado faces that they are looking mediaeval bandits. When she enquires the Nawab who they are, he tells her why they have come and that they are not so very bad men. The fact is that they are the robbers and the rioters protected by the Nawab. He also receives a rake-off from them for protecting them. In answering Olivia's question the Nawab, thus, violates not only the Quantity maxim but also the Quality maxim because his over-informativeness generates a false implicature that: "the men are religious and that he (the Nawab) has no nexus as such with them." Analysed on the touchstone of Gricean pragmatics the Nawab's reply is the violation of both the maxims: Quantity and Quality.

One observes a clash between these maxims in Anita Desai's *Cry, the Peacock* in the following talk:

> "What is death, then?" I asked, dropping down one ear-ring after the other. Two red rubies. "What is death to you, Gautama? Do you believe it?"
>
> "Perhaps if you clarified what you mean by death, I could tell you whether I believe in it or not. Though why you should give thought to such a subject mystifies me—it is definitely a new trend in you. You used to tell me you were far too immersed in your thoughts these days? You are much too young." (166-67)

This is a conversation between Maya and Gautama at a very crucial juncture of time in Maya's life. She recollects a prophecy made by an astrologer that "one of them (Maya or Gautama) would die within four years of their marriage." She wonders whether she would be the first to die. If she dies, would Gautama react to her death in a shocking way? She is eager to know what his view of death is. The reply he gives withholds the answer to her question. In fact questions about life and death are tricky questions. One does not expect anybody to answer such questions precisely and exactly in a required way. Nobody knows their answers for certain. By withholding to answer her question Gautama suspends the maxim of giving information. His deviation from this maxim is geared to observe the maxim of being truthful. The answer he would have given to her question would not have been universally true and acceptable. Put it briefly Gautama faces the clash between the two maxims and sacrifices one to uphold the other.

In some situations the maxim of Quantity and that of Relation clash with each other in the conversation of fictional characters. This happens in Shobha De's *Socialite Evenings*. The following is the conversation *in extenso:*

> "Did you aim for his crotch or for his head?"
>
> "I would have missed either—but what happened later was awful. He came at me like a maniac. First he pulled out his leather belt from the trouser and then he stood over me with his eyes blazing. Phatak—I felt the leather on my arm and I was so stunned I couldn't even scream. Before I could open my mouth, it landed on my arm again. I lost my balance—I was sitting on the edge of the carpet. He was still standing at the same spot with his arm raised. Suddenly I felt a sharp kick in my side. And another one. Then I heard him say. "Shit! There goes my Bally shoe." Can you believe it! Then he threw his belt away and started to slap me around. One hard hit cracked against my nose. Before I knew it, my favourite Anokhi dupatta was drenched in blood. My nose was like a geyser with blood gushing from it. May be it was the sight of all that blood that made him panic. He stopped and yanked my face up by the hair. "Shit! I'd better get a doctor. Is there

> ice in the fridge?" I was still on the floor with the dupatta stuck to my nose. Some of the blood fell on the carpet—the stains are still here. I walked to the kitchen slowly to get some ice. It was so unreal, the whole thing. When I went to the bathroom to wash my face, I was shocked out of my wrist. The whole thing was swollen—twice its size. My eyes were beginning to puff and one side of the face was turning purple where it had got badly bruised. There were thick welts across my arms. But, do you know something—I quite enjoyed the whole thing. You must think—I'm crazy. But really, it was thrilling in its own way. Not the pain—but the experience. He didn't look like a pipsqueak anymore. I thought of Marlon Brando in "*A Streetcar Named Desire*" have you seen the film? You must?" (129)

One day feeling despondent, the protagonist Karuna calls her friend Ritu on the phone. In the course of their telephonic talk Ritu tells her that her husband has an affair with a tart and has thus cheated her. When he comes home, Ritu grabs his vase and flings it at him. Karuna asks whether Ritu aimed for his crotch or his head. The reply she gives Karuna is a piecemeal narration of the beating she receives from her husband. When only the reply "his crotch/his head" is enough, Ritu pours in over information to Karuna. Thus, she flouts the maxim of giving required information. The implicature generated is that "she is shameless and for her thrashing from husband is thrilling." Referring to a film *A Streetcar Named Desire* based on Tennessee Williams' play *A Streetcar Named Desire* she also breaks the Relation maxim. Underlying her reply is a light thrown on the type of woman Ritu is. She loves thrashings from her husband because they lead to 'terrific orgasms.' For her orgasms seem to be the only things that matter in marriage. In other words, Ritu flouts the maxim of Quantity and that of Relation. What is implicated is that "she takes delight in being beaten, in thinking to belong to a rank of batterd wives." It is very interesting to observe that Ritu who threatens her husband to castrate him for bossing her surrenders so meekly to him once he pounces on her. In likening herself to the heroine of the play she admits that she is a whore-like wife steeped with carnal desire.

In the above verbal interactions one observes that the characters in these novels face the clash of the Quantity maxim with the maxims of truthfulness, relevance and clarity and brevity. They flout, suspend and violate the maxim of Quantity sometimes to uphold the Quality and the Manner maxim. On some occasions they sacrifice both—the Quantity and the Quality maxim, the Quantity maxim and the Relation maxim. The non-observance of the Quantity maxim and the other maxims is goal-directed. Just as there is a clash between one maxim and the other, there is also a clash between one principle and the other—particularly Cooperative and Politeness principles. They do not operate in isolation. The section that follows is concerned with the Quantity maxim of Cooperative Principle and the concern for being linguistically polite.

2.4. Quantity Maxim and the Politeness Concern in the Five Novels

Linguists argue that language is a rule-governed behavior. There are rules and rules in language. These rules are related to the primary categories—the Parts of Speech and the secondary categories—Person, Number, Gender, Case, Tense and Mood. A speaker of language produces grammatically correct/well-formed sentences when he/she follows these rules. If any of these rules is not followed when it is to be followed, the language user is said to produce sentences grammatically ill-formed/incorrect. Pragmaticists, on the other hand, talk of Principles and Maxims. They propose that the principles and the maxims of conversation are guidelines. They guide and control the human verbal interactions. These maxims originate from the very rational and orderly nature of conversation. These maxims introduce the communicative values like truthfulness, brevity, politeness, clarity, tact and relevance that operate in society. Therefore Leech (1983: 10) claims "There is no reason to exclude them from our enquiry."

In the previous section, it has been observed that maxims conflict/clash with each other. In such situations the communicators observe one maxim and break the other. Sometimes two or more maxims are sacrificed in the same interaction. Principles, too, conflict with each other. One principle overrides the other depending upon the goal of the ongoing conversation. Taylor and Deborah (1987: 93) succinctly remark "It is not always possible, given certain illocutionary goals, to be both cooperative and polite."

Leech (1983: 82) argues: "The CP has the function of regulating what we say so that it contributes to some assumed illocutionary or discoursal goal(s). It could argue however that the PP has a higher regulative role than this: to maintain the social equilibrium and the friendly relation which enable us to assume that our interlocutors are being cooperative in the first place."

The communicators prioritise the observance of principle. If a situation does demand, they sacrifice one principle to uphold the other. Taking the clue from Brown and Levinson's concept of politeness as 'face-saving' Jacob Mey (2001: 75) opines "People try to build their interlocutors' positive faces" while trying to avoid posing threats to their "negative faces." This is especially important in linguistic interaction since every engagement in conversation opens up the possibility of "losing face".

In a fictional discourse there is character-to-character-level interaction. Characters exploit their verbal interaction to the achievement of their goals. It is generally observed that one of the motives for deviating from the Maxims of Cooperative Principle is to care for the face of the other. In the novels under study one observes situations in which characters break the Quantity maxim for being polite to their co-locutors. Let's see why and how they do so.

The following is an interaction between Vilas and Dr. Vineeta from *Temporary Answers*:

> He said, "When I go out with a woman, I pay."
>
> "You allow for no exceptions?"
>
> "None."

> "Haven't you heard of women's lib?"
>
> "I have heard of it."
>
> "But you don't believe in it."
>
> "I didn't say that."
>
> "You imply it. You wouldn't insist on paying for everything yourself if you were with a man. He did not reply." (31)

Vilas, a childhood friend of Dr. Vineeta, has offered her an opportunity to be a partner in his clinic. One evening he drives her out in his car to a movie. When he wants to pay for the movie, Vineeta offers to pay for it. She even refers to the Women's Liberation. She enquires if he would insist on paying for everything if he is with a man. Vilas prefers to be tongue-tied. He and She have a "relationship in the making." He withholds to reply because he intends not to divulge his view about paying if he is with a man. He, perhaps, thinks that it will hurt Vineeta and will be detrimental to their relationship and partnership in the clinic. By being tongue-tied Vilas opts out of the Quantity maxim. The motive seems to be not to perish but propel his relationship with her. By offering to pay himself, he is being polite to her via being tactful. By remaining tongue-tied he is being polite by making her feel good and comfortable, He explicitly tells her later—"You must know I care for you. A great deal" (33).

> He said, "I am thinking of going away for a couple of weeks as soon as the college closes for the Diwali vacation."
>
> "Where?"
>
> "I haven't decided yet."
>
> "Well, may be I can get away for at least part of the time and join you."
>
> He shook his head unsmilingly. His eyes held an appeal. (158-59)

It seems that Vineeta and Abhijit would talk about getting married. But suddenly Abhijit seems to be sick because he hasn't been able to write anything after his play *Phulpakhrache Pankha*. He has been going through his sterile period. He needs the holiday to restore his faith and balance. He tells Vineeta that he is thinking of going away for a couple of weeks. She asks him if she would join him for some part of the outing. His non-verbal response—shaking head unsmilingly and his eyes holding an appeal—is his opting out of the Quantity maxim. He has been advised by a doctor, a friend of his father, to go out alone. Hence, he believes in going alone and living in the idyllic surroundings for his mental and spiritual renewal. He doesn't want Vineeta to accompany him. If he tells her his rejection flatly, that would hurt her and would sound to be impolite on his part. He breaks the Quantity maxim to make her feel comfortable by not replying to her offer. In fact, later she learns a valuable lesson from this: "even people who love each other feel the need from time to time to get away from each other." This helps her build up her defenses and gather strength in her remaining life. In brief a Professor and a celebrity playwright, Abhijit sacrifices the Cooperative Principle to avoid being blunt to Vineeta.

One observes a different case in *Heat and Dust* in the following talk:

> "What's happening in Khatm?" He didn't answer but shut his eyes again. She said, "I hear there are some sort of riots?" she insisted: "What's it all about?"
>
> "Tell me. No. You must."
>
> After a pause he said fretfully, "How should I know? After all I live in the palace and nothing like happens there, does it?"
>
> "Nothing like what?"
>
> "How should I know" he repeated. "I stayed in my room all day yesterday and this morning. What else can you do in this hideous terrible heat? Have you looked outside? Have you seen what it's like? Once these dust storms start, they go on forever. No wonder anyone goes mad." (71)

Olivia's compatriots Mrs. Crawford and Mrs. Minnies come to her bungalow in the Civil Lines to reassure her that there would be no riots on the Husband's Wedding Day at the shrine of Baba Firdaus. They also suggest that the Nawab could control such riots (communal riots) if he so desires. After they leave, Olivia wonders what part the Nawab has in the riots and how he can control them. When the Nawab's guest and friend Harry visits her, she enquires what is happening in the Khatm and what the riots are all about. She knows that Harry has been the Nawab's friend for many years now. Hence she asks him about the riots. Her intention is to know the Nawab's role in these happenings. The replies given by Harry to her do not answer her queries. He withholds the information he possesses and thus flouts the maxim of giving adequate required information. He implicates that: "He is ignorant not only about the happenings in the Khatm but also about the riots that take place at the shrine of Baba Firdaus." Harry knows the temper of the Nawab. Divulging about the Nawab's involvement in the riots would not only invite the Nawab's fury but also be a dispraise to him. What is striking here is that Harry flouts the maxim of Quantity to be polite to the third party, not the interlocutor. In Politeness parlance he breaks the maxim to save the Nawab's 'positive face'—desire to be admired/praised.

Here is another instance in the same novel in which the concern for politeness overrides the maxim in question:

> "Take the Nawab: I can't deny that he does fascinate me—as I am sure," he told Olivia. "He does you."
>
> "Oh gosh darling" Douglas laughed, "does he?"
>
> "Well" said Olivia, laughing back. "He is a fascinating man... and terribly handsome."
>
> "Really?" Douglas asked, as if he had never seen him in that light.
>
> "Oh, absolutely," said the Major. "He is—a prince.
>
> No other word for him. The trouble is that his state is unfortunately not quite princely enough to satisfy either his ambition or indeed his need for money." (149)

At the dinner in the bungalow of Douglas, Olivia, Major Minnies and Douglas veer to the topic of the Nawab. Major Minnies and Olivia have high praise for the forceful character and the fine qualities of the Nawab. Douglas has rather an antagonistic attitude towards the Nawab. For him the Nawab is the worst type of ruler in India. He can't believe what Major Minnies and his wife Olivia are talking about the Nawab. When he enquires whether the Nawab does fascinate Olivia, she is over-informative. When he asks the Major if the Nawab is really handsome, Major Minnies also flouts the maxim by being over-informative. Whereas Douglas is acerbic and acrid towards the Nawab Major Minnies and Olivia shower their compliments on the Nawab. Major Minnies also expresses his sympathetic and commiserating attitude to the Nawab. Where only 'yes' is sufficient to Douglas' questions, the Major and Olivia provide more information. They contravene the Quantity maxim and compliment and admire the Nawab—the fourth party in absentia.

In Anita Desai's *Cry, the Peacock* we have Maya—the protagonist and Gautama, her husband—at Poles apart—one believing in attachment and love, the other believing in detachment and money-matters. It is interesting to see how they process language to negotiate their relationship. Let's take a look at the following interaction:

> "Who?" Gautama asked, turning it over puzzled. "Arjuna?" he frowned. "But who is that?" and deep lines ran from end to end of his wide forehead on which no bead of perspiration ever stood. "Who is Arjuna?"
>
> I smiled, "My brother. My long lost brother who ran away from home at the age of twenty two and was never heard of again. He has written to me now, to tell me he is working in a canning factory in New York, and fighting the Negro cause. My brother was always that rebel...unlike me." (143)

One day Gautama comes back from the Court in the evening. He notices a long white envelope on the table. This is a letter from Arjuna, Maya's only brother now living in New York. This is the first time he has written to her after many years. Gautama asks her curiously who Arjuna is. What she provides is more than required by Gautama. She unshrouds her long lost brother to Gautama. She does not want her husband to be kept in ignorance. She pours the key bits of information about

Arjuna to Gautama. The implicature she intends to generate is that: Her brother Arjuna is a rebel revolting against the order and juxtaposed against her who holds order close to her bosom. She provides the unsolicited information about Arjuna perhaps because it is he who has referred to the horoscope in his letter—it is the horoscope that has been haunting her as it prophesies that either she or her husband would die within the four years of their marriage. She proceeds to tell about Arjuna because he has addressed her "Dear Maya, Dear sister, dear small stupid silly sweet sister." For her these words have a river-strength in them, no dam can ever halt it. The expression of love provides her a solace for which she hungers at the moment. By giving unrequired information perhaps she wants to minimize the physical cost to Gautama who may proceed to ask her further questions about Arjuna.

Pom, one of the friends of Maya, also sacrifices the maxim in the following conversation:

> "And Birla Mandir—I never thought you would go there to pray. Did she tell you too?"
>
> "Yes, she says I must if I want a son. I suppose she knows," Pom mused, crumpling the petals in her hand, "she has four sons." Then she smiled. "Why? Does it seem funny to you that I should listen to my mother-in-law?" (63)

Once Maya recalls a drive on which her friend Pom had taken her in her car. She was taken to Birla Mandir. On the way Maya asked her whether her mother-in-law advised Pom to pray for begetting a son. Pom told Maya that her mother-in-law had four sons and that she was following her mother-in-law's directive. By flouting the maxim of giving required information Pom implicates that: "She is so superstitious as her mother-in-law. One has to pray to Vishnu in the Birla Mandir so that one can beget a son not a daughter. She, like her mother-in-law, is a typical Hindu wife." Pom deviates from the maxim because in the ongoing conversation she is being kind/condescend to Maya as Maya is not in the same condition she is in (Pom is carrying). Pom plays matronly to Maya suggesting that one should visit temple if one wishes to have a baby, particularly a son. She shows her concern for Maya by being sympathetic at a deeper level.

In Shobha De's *Socialite Evenings* it is the women characters who dominate the action from the beginning to the end. In this novel we have a number of dominant female characters like Anjali, Karuna, Ritu and Si. They talk openly of husband-wife relationship, of sex, of orgasms and marital infidelity. As Swain (2000: 131) remarks "Shobha De's is the picture of women not only as protagonists but also motivating factors in society, initiating and regulating their own lives as well as the lives of others in the voluptuously fascinating world of Bombayites." In this glittering world of socialites one may think that people should have very little concern for preserving the face of others. One does come across encounters in which the concern for being polite to other overrides. Here is one such encounter:

> "Who are you?" I asked suspiciously.
>
> "So good to hear your voice and know that you are in New York."
>
> My God, I thought, thousands of miles from Bombay and it was Him. The ad-film-maker who had driven off so abruptly after being so nice and who had prompted Anjali to sharper her fangs on me. The urbane voice poured smoothly into my ear.
>
> "I ran into Anjali the day I was leaving India—she told me you'd be in New York. I called her up later in the night to ask whether she knew your contact here. And listen, babe, that should be explanation enough. Can I buy you lunch today?" (51)

Karuna is on her trip to New York. She is staying with her Sindhi friend. One night she suddenly receives a call and enquires who the caller is. It is the ad-film-maker who had met at her friend's party. Instead of answering her question he abstains from telling her his name/identity and thus flouts the maxim of Quantity. What he provides her implicates that "Telling her his name does not hold important for him. He is on the hunt for her through her mentor, Anjali." The last question implicates that "he wants to be intimate to her." It is an offer he is making her. Thus, he is maximizing his cost and maximizing benefit to Karuna—he is being tactful and generous. Moreover he doesn't impose the lunch on her. Giving her an option to say 'yes/no' he is being polite via Lakoffian maxims of avoiding imposition and giving option. The ad-film-maker sacrifices to be cooperative in order to show his concern of politeness to Karuna.

There is another interesting exchange between Karuna and Ranbir Roy:

> "Is that good or bad?"
>
> "Good and bad."
>
> "That doesn't answer my question."
>
> "Does it make any difference?"
>
> "May be."
>
> "I'd better run. Didn't know you were such a predatory Female." (303)

Karuna enters into a new relationship and that is with Ranbir Roy, an Indian reporter from America. Though a married man having two kids Americanized, Ranbir intends to have intimate relation with her. He has an eye on her. He sees no chance to make it to the slot of editor as he cannot lick the system. Having no resource to start something of his own he fears his wife would divorce him. When Karuna asks if it is good or bad if his wife divorces him, he does not answer the question in the course of this conversation. He even goes to the extent of calling her 'a predatory female.' Analysed on the touchstone of CP and PP he suspends the Quantity maxim to be friendly to her—this is through bantering. As Leech (1983: 144) proposes "Banter is an offensive way of being friendly." Ranbir's use of the noun phrase 'a predatory female' for her seems offensive. But at deeper level he aims to be intimate and friendly to her. He wants to involve her with him—may be it is through making a documentary on the status of Urban Indian Woman. Briefly, he breaks the maxim of being cooperative to show his concern for Karuna seeming obviously offensive and impolite to her. Elsewhere he compliments her for her ability of creativity when he tells her "I think you've got the stuff in you" (300).

In Shashi Deshpande's *The Binding Vine*, the concern to preserve the other's face dominates in some situations. The following is an illustration:

> I squeeze myself out of the place and am waiting for the lift when Priti comes running to me.
>
> "Urmi, you're going. What is it?"
>
> "Sorry, Priti. I should have told you. I have to go. A friend of mine—her sister's dead."
>
> "Oh, no I'm sorry."
>
> The lift stops.
>
> "I'm sorry, too. I'm going away like this."
>
> "Don't be silly. This is not important. Would you like me to drop you home?"
>
> "No, I'll get a taxi."
>
> "Keep in touch then." (187)

Casual though it appears, this is a beautiful example of how people encode their relationship through verbal interaction. The narrator-protagonist Urmila attends the party organized to celebrate the success of Priti's film on "sati". As the party is in progress, a call from her mother, Inni, has a soul-shattering news for Urmi that Sulu, a rape-victim, Kalpana's aunt, has died and Kalpana's mother, Shakutai, wants to see Urmi. Priti approaching Urmi asks why she is leaving abruptly. Urmi withholds to answer Priti's question as required—avoiding to relate who her friend is and who has died. Her move to withhold the information she possesses is directed to make Priti feel easy. This is the moment of happiness in Priti's life and as such no time for telling her about Shakutai, Shakutai's sister Sulu and Shakutai's daughter Kalpana. Priti's offer to drop her home shows her counter-concern for Urmi. The final utterance 'keep in touch then' from Priti reveals the motive to further the relationship between the two.

The illustrative interactions analysed in this section show that the maxim of Quantity has a back seat when it comes to promote comity rather than conflict in social relations—the function of Politeness Principle. As Black (2006: 25) remarks "Considerations of politeness may inhibit the speaker. This is one of the most crucial aspects of Grice's theory for the interpretation of literary texts."

2.5. Conclusion

In this chapter it has been discussed that there are norms or underground rules that govern, guide and control human verbal communication. The focus here has been on one such underground rule—the maxim of Quantity. As already discussed this maxim demands that the communicators give the required amount of information—neither more nor less. What is striking about this maxim is that characters in fiction time and again deviate from this norm. There are five kinds of non-observing the maxim viz. flouting, violating, infringing, suspending and opting out of the maxim. The motivations for dealing with the maxim in these ways are individual, social, moral and so on. The most significant of these non-observances is flouting the maxim. This is a flagrant breach of the maxim that leads the addressee to calculate an implied meaning called 'implicature' in Gricean parlance.

A close observation of character-to-character level interaction in the five selected novels leads to illuminating revelation that the characters in these novels deal with this maxim in all the five ways mentioned. They flout the maxim when they intend to convey implicature. They do this in two ways: by being more informative and by being less informative than their conversational partner demands.

Sex is an important factor in all societies. This is also a dominant element in human verbal interaction. Sociolinguists observe that language use is determined by the sex of the communicator. Studies in this discipline reveal as Coates (1986: 3) observes "Women and men talk differently" so that there is men's language and women's language. As far as the Quantity maxim is concerned, it is sacrificed in the following types of interaction:

(1) Male-to-Female interaction (e.g. Abhijit-Vineeta, *Temporary Answers,* p. 4)
(2) Female-to-Male interaction (e.g. Olivia-Harry, *Heat and Dust,* p. 71)
(3) Female-to-Female interaction (e.g. Karuna-Anjali, *Socialite Evenings,* p. 74)

It emerges that sex of the characters does not inhibit the non-observance of this maxim.

Another significant observation is that when the characters in these novels face the clash of Quantity maxim with other maxims of cooperation, they sacrifice this maxim to uphold the other maxim/s. In some situations the maxim of Quantity and the other maxim is also contravened. Whether it is a flout or any other type of deviation, the flow of conversation is in no way hindered. Although suspension and opting out of the maxim do not generate any implicature, they can be looked at positively. Withholding the information one possesses has two functions. As Besnier (1989: 333-34) states that it has "A self-serving function as well as a group-serving function." In the former it delays the introduction of particularly scandalous or sensitive or otherwise central piece of information while in the latter case it provides the conversationalists the opportunity to partake in the conversation. One observes that this strategy is adopted by the characters in the novels under investigation.

Linguistic communication is a juggling act. A juggler has to balance himself well, throw a ball up and also catch one that is falling. Communicator while engaged in communication also weighs the principles that operate in communication, though unconsciously. One is reminded of the dance of daffodils in Wordsworth's famous poem *Daffodils* and the dance of the waves in the lake beside these flowers. The dance of the daffodils outdoes the dance of the waves. The principles of conversation also compete with one another. As far as the Quantity maxim is concerned, it is overridden by the principle of being linguistically polite. Grice's Cooperative Principle is the principle of rational and efficient conveying of information. But Brown and Levinson (1978: 100) point out "Politeness is then a major source of deviation from such rational efficiency and is communicated precisely by that deviation."

It is true that the desire to avoid face-threatening forces one to sacrifice the Cooperative Principle or one of its maxims. It could be argued that this is only a partial truth. The analysis of interactions in the selected novels in which the Quantity maxim is contravened could support the argument. In a nutshell not all non-observances of this maxim show the concern for being polite to the other.

In this chapter an attempt has been made to discuss the operation of the Quantity maxim in the five selected novels. Next to this maxim is the maxim of Quality. The next chapter discusses this maxim and the relation between this maxim and the desire to be linguistically polite to others.

3

Quality Maxim in the Five Novels

3.0. Preliminaries

Human beings are social and rational agents. They care about their communicative goals and about maintaining their social relationships. The acts like greetings, complimenting, blessing and congratulating their fellow-beings only help them oil the wheels of their social relationships. They are rational because they care about achieving their goals. The most crucial and significant means they use for this is language. They employ a variety of linguistic devices to consolidate their relationships and achieve their goals. Some such devices are irony, metaphor, hyperbole, symbols and litotes. These assist them to convey their meanings-implied meanings. One observes that they convey more than what their words say. Their words achieve their desired effects only in the appropriate contexts. Hence Katz (1972: 443) remarks "In many cases a sentence means one thing while its utterance (in context) means another." About the power of words/language Leech and Short (1986: 279) pithily comment "Words are like stiletto more discreetly effective weapon than the bludgeon."

Words are dry when used out of context and acquire meanings when used in context. The linguistic devices mentioned above contribute to convey the desired semantic load. They are very crucial and critical to relationships. Taken literally the utterances which are metaphorical, ironic and hyperbolic are false. In pragmatic terminology these are deviations from Gricean maxim of Quality: "Do not say anything which is false." The section that follows discusses how this maxim operates in fictional conversation.

3.1. Quality Maxim and Conversation in Fiction

A novel differs from a play in significant respects. A play has various means to create a world: stage direction, dialogue, gesture and actions of characters. A novel has only language/words to create a world. Language is a double-edged weapon. As Leech (1983: 9) suggests "Language can be used to deceive or misinform." Taken from the point of view of telling the lies most of the words and utterances we use in linguistic conversation have a dual personality. They literally mean one thing and have a different/opposite meaning to convey. People are often heard telling lies. One thing we need not forget is that telling lies is not random and involuntary/indiscriminate. For liars it has some purpose to serve. Lying is either "self-concerned" or "other-centered." As pointed out earlier lies are critical to relationship. Even if a friend is fat, we flatter him/her by saying—"you are so thin as Ethiopian marathoner." If she is ugly, at times we say "no problem, you'll beat Cleopatra for a crown in a beauty contest." We violate the Quality maxim for the sake of nurturing our relationships. Cautioning us about this duality of words/utterances Ryan (2004: 11) says "The world of words is deceptive suggesting unity where there is actually dissonance." This is because words or utterances are semantically loaded. The speaker uses a word or produces an utterance which may have more than one meaning. The hearer has to get at the meaning intended. The recognition of this reflexive-intention leads to successful communication.

Literary or fictional discourse is marked by this use of language. There are ironical, false and metaphorical remarks by characters. They are more effective in literary discourse than in ordinary everyday conversation because they form part of a text as a whole and thus make a greater contribution to the textual meaning. They reveal the characters and the motives of characters. As lying is an integral part of conversation, Black (2006: 24) generalizes "We all lie from time to time for good or bad reasons." Put in other words we deviate from the

Quality maxim on many occasions. This applies to novelistic conversation too.

One comes across characters in stories and novels breaking the maxim of Quality. One reads them telling the lies. A few examples would help see how and why the characters take recourse to deviate from this maxim. The first example is from a famous story *An Astrologer's Day* by R.K. Narayan included in an anthology edited by Shakti Batra and P.S. Sidhu. Here is the conversation between a wayward astrologer and a client:

> "When shall I get him?" he asked clenching his fist.
>
> "In the next world" answered the astrologer. "He died four months ago in a far off town.
>
> You will never see any more of him." (115)

One day a man approaches a wayward astrologer. The man is searching for his killer. Thinking that the astrologer might tell him exactly when he will find out the killer he asked the astrologer about it. The client had in fact been the astrologer's friend in his youth. The astrologer had beaten the friend badly. Thinking that he was dead he had pushed the friend into the well nearby. To save himself he had run away from the village and had become a fake astrologer. The friend was saved by a passerby who had peeped into the well. Now the astrologer recognizes that the client is the man/friend he had tried to kill. He tells the client that his killer had died four months before in a remote town. In the context of the story this is a sheer lie he tells the client. He violates the maxim of Quality. His violation generates a misleading implicature that "the killer is no more in this world. It is futile to search for him." It is amusing to gather that the astrologer was an inveterate liar.

In another story *A Career* by R.K. Narayan in the collection of stories "Under the Banyan Tree and Other Stories" one learns how the narrator is duped by a young fellow, Ramu. The conversation proceeds between the two as under:

> Ramu said "My father, father, cholera, never thought he would get it...." I consoled him. I had never seen him so broken. I said feebly, "He'll be all right, don't worry...." I had hardly the heart to ask him about the shop. He

himself said, "I have handed the keys to mother, and all the account and cash also."

"All right. All right. I will look to all that, don't worry" I said.

The guard blew his whistle. Ramu jumped into a third-class compartment. The train jerked forward. He put his head out of the window and said, "I will be back tomorrow by the night train if my father gets better.... Whatever happens, I won't be away for more than fifteen days. Kittu has asked me to bring him", his voice and face receded, "a wooden elephant on wheels. Please tell him that I will surely bring it. My namaskarams to mother." Tears rolled down his cheeks. Even long after the train had left the platform, he was still looking out of the window gesticulating to indicate "I will surely be back soon" (46).

The narrator has a shop—The National Provision Stores—in Lawley Extension in Malgudi. One day a young fellow, Ramu, presents himself at the shop. He begs for a little food and shelter. The narrator directs him to his house. Ramu wins the confidence of the narrator's wife by helping her cook, clean and scrub the pots. With his attractive ways he becomes popular in the locality. The narrator leaves his shop to his trust and takes on the business of milk and butter supplied to the merchants in Madras. In five years his business of milk prospers by leaps and bounds. One morning he gets down at Malgudi station and finds Ramu leaving for Trichinopoly. He tells the narrator that his father is dying of cholera and he must go at once. He will be back very soon and also bring a toy—a wooden elephant on wheels—for the narrator's son Kittu.

The narrator reopens the shop after a week. To his surprise he notices that the shop is empty. The entries in the credit book are in a mess. The amount of ₹3500 is due to the wholesale supplier, Sadik Sait. An old man in the Extension tells the narrator the spicy story of Ramu—his affair with a tall and a pretty girl and his buying four suits, eighteen silk shirts, velvet slippers, a wrist watch, two rings, a brooch, silk sarees and blouse pieces worth over a thousand rupees. From a relative in Madras the narrator learns that Ramu's father is hale and hearty. Ramu never returns to the narrator. Ramu's tears and gestures at the time of departure are crocodile tears. He tells the narrator the deadly lies—the narrator is left a bankrupt. Leaving the shop entirely in the hands of Ramu proves to be the narrator's hamartia. An experienced man in his career as a shop man the narrator is pitifully duped by a young and a crafty fellow, Ramu. In the Gricean framework, Ramu breaks the maxim of Quality and this mars the relationship between the narrator and Ramu. It turns out later that Ramu loses his eye-sight and is forced to be a wandering beggar. But that is another part of the story.

We come across people who try to camouflage their anti-social and bad habits. Transgressing the maxim of truthfulness is their second nature. If telling lies serves their purpose, then do it they will. If one breaks this maxim, one may not be hanged and legally punished. But on no account could it be denied that being untruthful may lead to sever one's relationship with others. Small and negligible act it may seem, telling lies affects the whole course of one's life. In this context one is reminded of Walter Morel, a coal-miner in Lawrence's novel *Sons and Lovers* constantly telling lies to his wife, Gertrude. The following is one evidence when he is being untruthful to Gertrude:

> She said to him coldly:
>
> "Did you take sixpence out of my purse last night?"
>
> "Me?" he said, looking up in an offended way, "No, I didna. I niver clapped my eyes on your purse".
>
> But she could detect the lie.
>
> "Why, you know you did" she said quietly.
>
> "I tell you, I didna," he shouted. "Yer at me again, are yer?" I've had enough on it. (55-56)

One day Walter had a strong desire to drink. But he had no money with him. As Mrs. Gertrude Morel was in the garden the previous night, Walter had taken the chance to steal sixpence from her purse which was in the top drawer of the dresser.

The next day she wanted to pay the greengrocer but found that the sixpence was missing. When he came home back, she asked him if he had taken the money. Walter denied twice having taken it and thus told her a lie. In fact, the context of the novel tells us that he has stolen the money from her purse. He tells the lie twice in this heated talk by saying—"I didna." A Petty theft this might seem, this serves as an eye-opener for Mrs. Morel. Even before marrying her he had lied to her that he was a tea totaller, the house he lived in belonged to him and the furniture in the house had been fully paid for. He was untruthful before marriage and he continues this practice of telling the lies. This temperament of his makes her extremely unhappy. His lies turn out to be detrimental to their relationship as husband and wife. A crucial part of his nature, this leads her to fix her love on her children, particularly Paul Morel. Thus the violation of the maxim of truthfulness affects the whole course of their life.

We have a very funny and amusing instance of a character deviating from this maxim in Henry Fielding's novel *Joseph Andrews*. The violation occurs in the following conversation:

> "I am afraid," said Lady Booby, "he is a wild young fellow."
>
> "That he is," said Slipslop, "and a wicked one too. To my knowledge, he games, drinks, swears and fights eternally: beside he is horribly indicted to wenching."
>
> "Ay", said the lady, "I never heard that of him."
>
> "O, Madam," answered the other, "he is so lewd a rascal that if your ladyship keeps him any longer, you will not have one virgin in your house except myself. And yet I can't conceive what the wenches see in him, to be so foolishly fond as they are, in my eyes he is as ugly a scarecrow as I never upheld."
>
> "Nay," said the lady, "the boy is well enough."
>
> "La Madam," cries Slipslop "I think him the ragmaticallest fellow in the Family."
>
> "Sure Slipslop," says she, "you are mistaken: but which of the women do you most suspect?"

> "Madam," says Slipslop, "there is Betty, the chambermaid, I am almost convicted, is with child by him." (16)

This is a conversation between Lady Booby, a widowed wife of Sir Thomas Booby, a landed aristocrat and Mrs. Slipslop, Lady Booby's servant-maid. An anaphoric reference is warranted to see how Mrs. Slipslop heaps lies about Joseph Andrews, Booby's footman. On the seventh day after the death of her husband Lady Booby admits Joseph to her bedroom. As he sits down, she begins to talk to him in an amorous tone and puts her hand on his. She addresses him and insinuates to seduce him. When he tells her that he does not understand her, she gets infuriated and sends him away. She decides to dismiss him but before so doing she invites her waiting-woman Mrs. Slipslop to seek her opinion about Joseph.

When Joseph is on the way, he happens to meet Mrs. Slipslop. Funnily enough Mrs. Slipslop has also cast her eyes on Joseph. She invites him to her room for a glass of wine and begins to seduce him. She prepares to lay her violent amorous hands on Joseph like a hungry tigress that has traversed the woods in a fruitless search, sees a lamb within her reach and leaps on her prey. Joseph is the brother of Pamela who is the embodiment of the virtue of chastity. Like his sister he wants to preserve his chastity and hence thwarts the evil designs of Mrs. Slipslop too. Mrs. Slipslop also gets raged at him.

When Mrs. Slipslop appears before Lady Booby, she tells Lady Booby that Joseph is a lewd rascal. He has taken to gambling, drinking, swearing and also wenching. The proof of his lasciviousness is that Betty the chambermaid is pregnant by him. The fact is that Betty has been intimate with a hostler. Betty herself has extraordinary liking for Joseph. She is so swayed by her passion that she embraces Joseph with eagerness. He resists her advances and pushes her into the hall. All these contextual threads are evidence enough that all that Mrs. Slipslop tells Lady Booby are black lies. We as readers know that it is a tug of war between Joseph and Lady Booby and Mrs. Slipslop: One trying to puncture the evil design of the two ladies and the other is trying to seduce Joseph. In the context of this novelistic discourse Mrs. Slipslop violates the maxim of speaking truth. Her information about Joseph shared with Lady Booby misleadingly implicates that Joseph is liable to be dismissed.

The deviation from this maxim in this situation acquires a great significance if considered from the point of view of the theme of the novel—the moral degeneration and vanity of the so-called sophisticated and rich-class people of the beginning of the eighteenth century. Underlying the transgression of the maxim of speaking truth is the realistic exposure of vanity, hypocrisy and pretentions of Booby and Mrs. Slipslop. The exposure of these vices becomes scathing and pungent and we as readers know that Lady Booby and Mrs. Slipslop are more wicked than good.

In the four illustrations above one observes that violating the maxim of Quality is self-concerned. The Astrologer's lie to the client, Ramu's lies to the narrator, Walter Morel's lies told to Gertrude and Mrs. Slipslop's lies to Lady Booby are taken recourse to, to serve their subjective purpose/goal. The phenomenon of lying has another side to it: people are seen telling lies for saving others. Let's take an example of this type from Chaman Nahal's novel *Azadi*. The following is the conversation:

> Sipping the drink he said momentarily: "Look. I might as well be frank with you. I like this woman".
>
> "You better watch yourself—that woman is my sister." (225)

In this conversation between Rahmat-Ullah Khan and Arun it is Arun who makes a false assertion. The woman in question is Sunanda. Rahmat-Ullah Khan has an eye on her. He tells Arun frankly that he likes Sunanda. Arun tells him that Sunanda is his sister. As readers we know that Sunanda is not Arun's sister. On the other hand, there is intimate relationship between the two. Arun recognizes that Rahmat-Ullah Khan wants Sunanda to quench his sexual desire. In order to save her from the clutches of the womanizer Arun violates the Quality maxim to save Sunanda. His intention is benevolent, not malevolent.

Briefly put, the characters in fiction like real people are forced to make false assertions. The purposes behind doing this are individual, social, moral, financial and so on. It could be seen that lying is an integral part of verbal and non-verbal interaction. In the next section, we discuss how the characters in the five selected novels deal with this maxim.

3.2. Quality Maxim in the Five Novels

The verbal exchanges analysed in the foregoing section reveal that characters in fiction contravene the Gricean maxim of truthfulness. The deviation from this maxim is contingent/situation-dependent. In fact in Nimbkar's *Temporary Answers* the two characters—Abhijit and Vineeta show their concern about "lying" as a part of human relationship. For Abhijit a lie is not necessarily destructive to a relationship. For Vineeta however unimportant a lie may seem, it still undermines a relationship. One observes that taking recourse to a lie depends on the goal of the conversers. They tell a lie to protect the interest of the other, to avoid hurting other's feeling, to avoid to reveal the truth learned in confidence or to protect themselves from danger/defame or to get something done for their benefit.

Like the maxim of Quantity the characters in fictional conversation deal with the maxim of Quality in five different ways—flouting, violating, infringing, suspending and opting out of the maxim. In the case of flouting of the Quality maxim the intention is to generate the implicature. The intention is not to deceive the other. In the case of violation the intention is to mislead the other/to generate the false implicature. As Grice (1975: 49) puts "If a speaker violates a maxim, s/he will be liable to mislead." As far as the Quality maxim is concerned, the borderline between the flout and violation is very thin. J. Thomas (1995: 74) observes "There is no principled reason to expect that an implicature will be true-speakers can imply a lie as easily as they can say one."

This section is concerned with why and how the characters in the novels under study deviate from the maxim of Quality. Let's begin with Jai Nimbkar's *Temporary Answers*. One observes that the characters in this novel break this maxim time and again. The following are such instances in which this is done:

> I said, "Don't you realize that your attitude implies contempt for women?"
>
> "On the contrary, it implies respect." (31)

After becoming a partner in a Clinic run by Vilas, Vineeta often accompanies him in his car. He even takes her out for lunch, a movie and a play. She enjoys being with him as a pleasant and an undemanding companion. One day during a drive Vilas emphasizes that when he goes out with a woman, he pays. On asked if he allows no exception or he has heard of women's liberation, Vilas replies that he allows no exception and that he has heard of women's liberation. From what he says Vineeta gathers that this implies his attitude of contempt for women. When he replies that it implies respect for women, Vineeta understands that he is being ironical. This is because she does not see any logical basis for his assertion. For her he blatantly fails to be true. In the circumstances it leads her to calculate that he is a man who would treat a wife like a fragile thing who requires his protection. He would smother and baffle her if she rebels against being a household pet. Thus, the word "respect" he uses means "contempt for women" for Vineeta. Though she is dependent as a widow on her parents, she is a modern woman in the making-craving for independence and equality with men. She interprets his assertion as being untruthful/ironical.

Vineeta's friend Kishori tells a lie in the following talk with Vineeta:

> I said, "How long will you be away?"
>
> "Let me see. If we leave Saturday evening, we should be back by Wednesday morning.
>
> Gangubai will come with the children, so you won't have to do anything except to just keep an eye on them."
>
> "All right, Kishori, I will look after them." (73)

One day Kishori comes to Vineeta's office and tells her that her husband Madhu has his Conference in Hyderabad and that he wants Kishori to be with him. She requests Vineeta to look after her children—Hemant and Smriti. On being asked how long will Kishori be away, she tells that they will come back by Wednesday morning. In so telling Kishori misleads Vineeta. Her misimplicature is that "they will be away only for few days." The same night Abhijit meets Vineeta. He tells Vineeta that Madhu and Kishori will not be back until Saturday. He himself was present when Kishori made the plan for going to Hyderabad and staying there till Saturday. It turns out that Kishori has lied to Vineeta. Put it in Gricean terms Kishori violates the maxim of Quality.

The following is another instance when Kishori does the same thing:

> Kishori said, "We met this really lovely couple and they were going to do some sight-seeing. They said why don't we join them, then we could hire a taxi and share expenses and do it quite cheaply. So we decided to go along. I mean what is the point of going so far if you don't do a bit of sightseeing."
>
> I said, "But Kishori, you could have let me know."
>
> "Well, we thought of telephoning, but it would have meant wasting hours waiting for a call to get through. And telegrams are mostly useless. They are so slow that you would probably not have got a telegram before we arrived anyway." (76)

The context of this conversation between Vineeta and Kishori reveals that Madhu and Kishori return from Hyderabad to Pune on Saturday morning. The couple turns up on Saturday afternoon to collect their children from Vineeta. No sooner do they come to Vineeta than Kishori begins to relate her apologies for her delayed comeback. In this novelistic context the excuses she tells are lame. Now and then we as readers learn that Kishori is a "user", selfish and happy-go-lucky type of woman. She is a sort who would not worry about her children. Her own need is her guiding principle. All other considerations are minor for her. We as human beings are capable of being selfish. But we generally have certain controls and inhibitions that keep most of us away from being completely selfish. This rule does not seem to apply to Kishori.

Thus, the way Kishori deviates from the maxim of truthfulness speaks volumes about what sort of woman she is. When Vineeta realizes Kishori's apparent sensitivity and her real nature, she pays back Kishori in the same coin. One evening Kishori telephones Vineeta and tells her that she has urgent business. Bhanoo Pandit, the musical director, is attending a party and Kishori has also been invited for the same. She wants Vineeta to keep an eye on her children for a few hours. She is so sickened by Kishori's lying that very distinctly she says to Kishori, "I can't have the children today, Kishori. I am going out. I have a dinner appointment" (77). The request from Kishori is summarily declined by Vineeta. Kishori's lying leads to counter-lying from Vineeta and this mars the relationship between the two.

The narrator-protagonist Vineeta is forced to lie in the talk with Kishori:

> "You don't know then if his troubles are over," Kishori said. "Trouble"
>
> I knew as soon as I said it that I shouldn't have. It told Kishori s what she wanted to know. She pounced.
>
> "You don't know about his differences with Mulgaonkar?" she said.
>
> Mulgaonkar was directing the play.
>
> I said, "Oh, that, He did say something about it." (126)

Kishori invites Vineeta to a party on her tenth wedding anniversary. When Vineeta attends the party, Madhu, Kishori's husband, enquires Vineeta if she is very busy in thinking about Abhijit. Kishori asks whether Vineeta knows that Abhijit has differences with Mulgaonkar. Mulgaonkar was the director who was presenting Abhijit's play *Delleeshwar*. He has given the role of Aurangazeb to an actor named Narayan Samant. Samant is fond of grand manner and speaks as if from a political platform. The writer, Abhijit, does not visualize the role of Aurangazeb speaking in a grand and a political manner.

This has caused differences between the director of the play's performance and the writer, Abhijit. When Kishori asks Vineeta if she knows about the differences between the two, she takes recourse to lying. Vineeta, thus, violates the maxim of truthfulness to mislead that Abhijit and she are intimate these days and that Abhijit has told Vineeta about his differences with the director Mulgaonkar.

The fact about Vineeta is that she has not seen Abhijit for quite a few days. She feels so vulnerable when she realizes that Kishori knows about Abhijit and she knows nothing. It stings her that Abhijit has not bothered to tell her about the play, the director and the differences with the differences with the director. To produce the impression that Abhijit does share his troubles with Vineeta she is forced to being untruthful. Thus, circumstances make Vineeta to be untruthful. Fortunately, this happens only among Madhu, Kishori and Vineeta as no guests have arrived for the party yet.

Vineeta's mother-in-law, the mother of her dead husband Nagendra violates this maxim in the following talk:

> I said, "You can tell people that I am no longer your responsibility, then whatever I do won't spoil your name?"
>
> I wanted an open fight, a chance to say the things I had bottled up for years. But she would not give me the satisfaction.
>
> She only said, "You may want to dissociate yourself from us. But you married our son and even though he is dead, we still consider you our responsibility." (136)

This conversation takes place between Vineeta and her mother-in-law when Vineeta lives alone after Nagendra's death. The mother-in-law asked Vineeta to come and live with her or go and live with Vineeta's mother. She also referred to Nagendra's friend, Navin Mehta. People used to talk that Mehta sat patiently through Vineeta's weeping hours. He dealt with thousand matters capably after Nagendra's death. He stood by Vineeta in her bad times. Her mother-in-law felt that some day or the other Mehta would want the price of his devotion and help to Vineeta. It would reflect badly on their family's name. She tries to persuade Vineeta not to live alone. She puts that even though her son Nagendra is dead, Vineeta, her daughter-in-law, is still her responsibility. For Vineeta her mother-in-law's showing her care for her is a sheer lie. Vineeta knows very well that her mother-in-law never really cared for her. There was, in fact, antipathy between Vineeta and her mother-in-law. Her assertion that "we still consider you our responsibility" proves for Vineeta to be false. The false assertion she make reveals her hypocrisy and her desire to establish her right to interfere in Vineeta's life. One also learns that Vineeta's mother-in-law is a woman who is clever at wording her speech. She tries to appear to be a caring mother-in-law but is a hypocrite. For Vineeta her mother-in-law seems to be a snooper in her personal life.

In Jhabvala's *Heat and Dust*, one comes across a few such conversations in which the characters take recourse to telling lies. Let's see how and why these characters deviate from the maxim of speaking the truth. Olivia flouts the maxim in the following conversation with her compatriot, Harry:

> Harry said, "Have you noticed something? That you are never taken to meet the Begum and her ladies?"
>
> "I *have* met them, thank you." She gave a forced laugh. "It was hard going." (102)

Harry is not in good health. Hence, he does not come to fetch Olivia in a car and take her to the Nawab's palace. It is Olivia who visits him in his suite of rooms. When one day she visits Harry, he tells Olivia that despite her frequent visits to the Nawab, the Nawab has been discourteous to her by not taking and introducing Olivia to his mother and her ladies. Olivia replies that she has met the mother (Begum) and her ladies. The truth is that Olivia has never been taken to the Begum. In her reply to Harry Olivia falsely asserts that she has met the Begum. She further tells a lie that her meeting with the Begum was hard going. By flouting the maxim thus she intends to implicate that the Nawab has been courteous enough to take and introduce her to his mother and to ladies in the palace. In the ongoing context her intention seems to reply Harry positively and dismiss that topic quickly. Her purpose in visiting the Nawab's palace is to enjoy the company of Harry and in particular that of the Nawab. She knows that she can't be friendly with the Begum and her ladies because they don't speak Olivia's language—English. She is not interested in meeting the Begum. Her flout of the maxim is thus intentional.

The Nawab of Khatm flouts the maxim in the following conversation with Olivia:

> "Who were those men?"
>
> He didn't answer at once and when he did, it was with another question: "Who do you think they were?" He gave her once of his shrewd looks. Then laughed: "I suppose you think they are bad men. You must have heard many stories I think, isn't it, and you believe they are true".
>
> Again she felt she didn't have to defend herself or answer him.
>
> "But if they are bad men," he went on, "I think they can't be so very bad men because look what they have come here for." He pointed to the mound in the shrine on which some fresh garlands had just been laid and sticks of incense were still smouldering. "You see, they didn't come for any bad purpose but to pay their devotions." (133-34)

One day the Nawab takes Olivia to the famous shrine of Baba Firdaus. When they arrive in the grove near the shrine, Olivia sees some men emerging from the shrine. They are rough and armed. Studying their faces Olivia feels that they are like mediaeval bandits. Curiously she asks the Nawab who those men are. The Nawab's reply to her question is all a falsity. His reply is geared to implicate to Olivia that they are the holy men who have come to pay their devotions on the Husband's Wedding Day. The truth is that they are the dacoits. They cause communal riots and rob the pilgrims at the command of the Nawab. It is he who protects them and receives a rake-off from them for doing so. This is a secret that he does not want to share with Olivia. He intends to implicate that what he is stating is true and thus supplements his statements with non-verbal action-pointing to the mound in the shrine on which some fresh garlands had just been laid. His implicature is that it is those very men who have laid the garlands in the shrine to pray and tell their wishes to Baba Firdaus. In brief, the Nawab's reply is a flout exploited by him to remove Olivia's suspicion about the dacoits and his nexus with them.

The characters in this novel also deal with the Quality maxim in other ways violating and suspending. Harry violates the maxim in his following conversation with Olivia:

> "The Nawab also says he is bored being here, so today everyone is packing."
>
> "He's bored?"
>
> "So he says. But there is something else too." He frowned and went on packing very meticulously.
>
> "What?"
>
> "Oh I don't know Olivia." (142)

One day Olivia visits the Nawab's palace and finds that everyone is running and packing. When she enters Harry's room, she finds that he is packing too. He explains that the Nawab is bored being in palace. One of the ladies of Begum, his mother, has also been advised a change of air. They are, therefore, going to Mussoorie. When Olivia asks Harry whether the Nawab is bored in the palace and if something is the matter with him, Harry flatly replies that he does not know what exactly the trouble is with the Nawab. His flat refusal is to convey to Olivia that he knows nothing of the Nawab's trouble. Harry, thus, misleads Olivia by being a liar. The truth is that Harry knows that the Nawab has at the present at least two troubles: financial and domestic. The Khatm of the Nawab is in bankruptcy. This has been going on for years now. The domestic problem is about the Nawab's wife, Sandy. She is from Cabobpur. The Cabobpurians are trying to bring a case against the Nawab about her dowry. For them the Nawab is a little prince and they compare him with a gross swine.

Harry's deviation from the maxim of truthfulness is an attempt to camouflage these facts about the Nawab. Living with the Nawab for many years Harry knows very well that the Nawab is terribly sensitive when he is talked to about

Sandy and her family. He fumes with anger and makes the other person feel a fool and stupid. Harry wants to hide these things form Olivia and therefore a lie comes handy to him.

Harry deals with the maxim in another way also—suspending the maxim. He does this while attempting to avoid telling Olivia about the dacoits in the following conversation:

> She asked, "What is all this about dacoits, Harry?—Tell me."
>
> She said when he didn't.
>
> He sighed and after a while he said, "Honestly I don't know Olivia. A lot of things go on and I'd as just soon not know about them." (103)

Once introduced to the Nawab's palace Olivia becomes a frequenter to this place in absence of her husband, Douglas Rivers. She particularly enjoys the company of her compatriot, Harry. Harry has been a guest of the Nawab for many years. When one day Olivia happens to visit Harry's room, she realizes that Harry is not in good mood and health. She herself is uncomfortable because she has heard about the disturbances caused at Baba Firdaus' shrine by the rioters. Stories also go about the dacoits. She is eager to know what the matter is about the dacoits and enquires Harry about the same. Harry replies that a lot of things happen in and around the palace and he would not know anything about them.

Harry seems not to divulge many of the stories about the Nawab. Harry knows not only about the character of the Nawab but also about the old Nawab—the Nawab's father. The Nawab has a gang of dacoits that crosses the territory around the palace and strays into the province under Mr. Crawford's jurisdiction. The dacoits raid the villages and get away with cash and jewellery. They also handle the villages—be they men or women—in a rough way. The Nawab protects them and receives commission from them for doing so. Knowing a lot of such things Harry tells Olivia that he does not know about the dacoits. He withholds the facts that he possesses and thus suspends the maxim of Quality. His intention is not only to save the Nawab from disgrace but also himself from inviting the Nawab's fury.

Anita Desai's *Cry, the Peacock* tells us about the mismatched marriage of Maya and Gautama. What strikes us about Maya is that her cry is the cry of an agonized woman and falls flat on her husband's ears. This is because of as Choudhary B. (1995: 59) observes "Her inability to reciprocate." It is this flaw of hers that makes her undergo a series of harrowing mental experiences. Maya and Gautama have been very skillfully juxtaposed by the novelist. The cold war consistently goes on between the two. The verbal encounters between them reveal the hot currents of torn relationship between wife and husband. Maya is aware of this and hence ruminates that her marriage with Gautama is a fiasco and was "broken repeatedly and repeatedly the pieces were picked up and put together again" (40). There is an insurmountable impasse between them. Gautama is very near to, yet very far from Maya. This is due to the gap of communication at the emotional level between the two. The conversations between them insinuate that they are the Poles apart. In this section our concern is with how Maya and Gautama deal with the Gricean maxim of conversation—that of truthfulness. A close observation of the character-to-character-level conversations in the novel reveals that characters deviate from this maxim on a number of occasions.

Gautama flouts the maxim in *Cry, the Peacock* in his following conversation with Maya:

> "Whoever spoke of love?" he said, drawing his fine eye-brows together so that his face drew into a mass of complex lines. He looked very much the mediator beneath the *bo* tree, seated upon a soft tiger skin, too fastidious to touch the common earth, with those long, clean-cut hands of his, too fastidious to admit such matters as love, with its accompanying horror of copulation of physical demands and even, overbearingly, spiritual demands, of possession and rights won and established.
>
> But no, tonight, I would not admire him for this superior plane he always managed to elevate himself onto when I tried to involve him in my matters, my wants and cares, which to him were childish, tiresome and even distasteful.

> Tonight I would hold him down beside me. "I spoke of it." I said loudly and the small white stars of the Queen of the night bush released such overpowering fumes of fragrance, paradisiacal and unearthly that I felt a little giddy, feverish even. "And you will think me a tiresome child for it, for showing what you once called my third-rate poetess's mind."
>
> "I never." (122-23)

This conversation between Maya and Gautama centers around love and poetry. It strikes that there is a wide gulf between Maya and Gautama. This is because they have different taste and different opinions on several matters. For him love has no importance in life. For her love is a powerful force. She has a taste for Urdu poetry. She has learnt from her father that Urdu poetry is evocative. She has a desire to join the party being held outside her room. His friends have been invited and they appreciate the Urdu couplets. She joins the party—a circle of leisurely gentlemen. Her husband Gautama says that poetry is enjoyable because it is unrelated to our life, unclouded by the vulgarity of ill-educated men and over-bearing women. Maya feels the male chauvinism and leaves the party. When later she asks if he thought of her as a tiresome child due to her third-rate poetess' mind, Gautama replies immediately that he never called her a child. As readers we know that he was in a stringent and ironic temper in the party. He does express his contempt for her love for poetry. In saying that he never thought of Maya as a child he is being blatantly untruthful. The novelistic context helps us see that he does believe that "Maya is a child pampered by her doting father. She is a spoilt child who cannot bear one adverse word." Time and again Maya gets the impression from Gautama's behavior that between them "there is no bond, no love—hardly any love" (108). His falsehood stings her and hence she asserts "you did and you believe it now" (113).

In the following conversation too Gautama is being ironical and flouts the maxim of truthfulness:

> "But you see, I can. I have so much to look at, to touch and feel and be happy about. I like to walk about here

> and touch things leaves, sticks, earth, everything. I play with my cat. And if I am lonely, I can visit my friends. The world is full-full Gautama. Do you know what, that means?' I am not bored with it that I should need to hunt another one."
>
> He glanced at me—which was new.
>
> "You are quite right," he said, stamping his cigarette underfoot so that we were completely in the dark and aware of the moon that had risen above the roof, like a shallow vessel, a golden boat in the sky, brilliantly polished and richly vivid.
>
> "You are right. You are, in a fashion, less egoist that I. While I must always have a piece of paper in my hand or a book or people around me, so that I may write of myself, search for myself in them, talk to them of myself. You are the one, who can bear to be absolutely alone, losing yourself in your garden and your pets, strange" he mused, turning away from me and beginning upon a nervous chain of cigarettes, half or quarter smoked, that seemed to be necessary fuel for his ticking brain. "Strange, because then you should be capable of her greater detachment than I, hence of greater peace of mind and stability." (118-19)

This is a conversation between Maya and Gautama on a serene topic—life and its meaning. She points out to him that she is passing her life in activities like playing with a cat, walking in the garden and touching the leaves, sticks and visiting her friends. She is not bored with life at all. Gautama admits that her present state of life is better than the life of his. He further argues that she should be completely unattached with life—with the evils of fame, name and money. She should live life like a lily upon water and the tortoise with its limbs withdrawn from the external world. This would help her attain greater peace of mind and stability. Living like a lily and a tortoise would make her capable of greater detachment than him. In this exhortation to Maya he is being ironical. He knows well that she is attached to the world—garden, pets, poetry and friends. She can never attain detachment—absolute freedom.

It is only people like Christ and Buddha who attain absolute freedom. They are capable of attaining detachment because their joy is within and their light is within and not without as Maya tries to find in the external world. By being ironical he, thus, flouts the maxim to implicate that "she is in a better state than he is."

Maya, the heroine of the novel, breaks the maxim in the following hot exchange with Gautama:

> "Why is your head so hot?" he asked suspiciously. "And damp. Do you have a temperature?"
>
> "No," I said, "No, Gautama, no temperature" and began to move away from him, towards the house.
>
> "Are you sure?" he called after me.
>
> "Sure", I whispered, "Sure." (124-25)

Maya and Gautama differ from each other in more respects than one. For her love is a force that never withers. It is immortal and abiding. He holds that love is cancer. Love loses its intensity and depth with the passage of time. She is a woman of faith in Gods and Goddesses. He is a man of logic. For him Gods are things made of plaster or mud. Our children are real and Gods are not. Maya is unable to stand his logical argument and decides to go inside the house. While he shakes himself free from her grasp, he catches hold of her wrist. He enquires why her head is so hot and whether she has a temperature. She replies that she has no temperature. What is striking is that she intensifies her negation through "No", "No", "No temperature" "Sure" and "Sure". These words are used to mislead that "she is all right".

Maya, thus, violates the maxim of truthfulness. The fact is that Maya has a temperature. Her skin is burning with prickly heat. In the circumstances it is understandable that she would not speak to him the truth and allow him to be intimate with her. He is firm in his views about love and logic. His views about love stand in contrast with hers. He explicitly states that it is quite impossible for him to talk to a woman like Maya who has entirely different views about love and life. She wants security from him but he leaves her to drown in a treacherous sea. Distressed by this behavior of his she desires to turn away from him and a lie comes handy for her to do so.

Quite a few times the characters in this novel are seen dealing with the maxim in other ways—suspending and infringing the maxim. Mrs. Lal, the hostess of a party, does this in the following conversation with a prim lady:

> "Have you no *ayah*?" asked the orange spotted lady, sipping orangeade. A purple flush suffused Mrs. Lal's face and neck. She stammered a little, glancing at her husband, "She does not stay here at night." She said. (70)

Once Gautama takes Maya to a party hosted by Mr. And Mrs. Lal. As the party starts with an orangeade, the little son of Mrs. Lal comes trailing in to his mother. He anchors at the edge of his mother's sari. One of the guests, a Prim lady in an orange spotted sari, catches sight of the child. She asks Mrs. Lal whether she has no *ayah* to look after her little son. Mrs. Lal's face and neck flush. She glances at Mr. Lal. She tells the Prim lady that they have an *ayah* but she does not stay at night. This is a sheer lie she tells in the presence of the guests. She deliberately takes recourse to telling a lie. Admitting that they have no *ayah* would bring a kind of disgrace for her and her husband. This is the party of men and women who try to show off their wealth and degrade others. The Prim lady's question seems to be an attempt to degrade Mrs. Lal. Mrs. Lal glances at her husband and tells a lie to save her husband from degradation—not having an *ayah* for keeping an eye on children. Mrs. Lal could be said to have suspended the maxim of being truthful. The stammer she produces and the glance she takes at her husband before answering the Prim lady's question indicate that she is taking the time and mustering the courage to tell a lie. Underlying her lie is her snobbery. Nevertheless it serves her purpose.

In the following exchange between Maya and Gautama, Maya infringes the maxim by telling a lie:

> "But one thing does disturb me. You never explained it. What was that horoscope that he wrote about? About which there was such a to-do in your household. Why?"

> And softly, softly the drums crept across the desert, stole through the dust. Softly—soft, soft with care, now, Maya with care.
>
> "Gautama", I stammered, stretching out my hands to him, without expecting him to touch them, not even desiring that touch.
>
> "Believe me Gautama, I—I don't remember." (150-51)

Maya's brother, Arjuna, has written her a letter. In this letter he refers to the horoscope that an astrologer has given her. Gautama asks Maya what that horoscope is about. The reply she gives is an attempt to hide the fact from him. She does not want Gautama to know that an astrologer has predicted death of one of them (Maya or Gautama) within four years of their marriage. The reference to the horoscope intimidates her. She knows that Gautama is an unsentimental utilitarian. If he knows the prediction by the astrologer, he might put her in peril of life. It would endanger her. He loves life too—its problems and their solutions. It is she who would be led to death and not he.

In fact, the horoscope is the solid fact of her life remembered and known. It is not a figment of nightmare of hallucination. The thought of the horoscope and the prediction gives her fierce headache—frightening in its intensity. Letting Gautama know the horoscope and the prediction would precipitate het tragedy. In this mental state—fear and headache—she tells him that she does not know the horoscope. Speaking the truth would invite the dangers for her like sudden fires out of the cracked earth. She says to herself later "It must be kept a secret" (153). The fact about Maya is that she has neurotic fear of death. She would not confide it to Gautama. Hence Meerabai (1996: 85) puts "Her inability to come out of fear of her libido hinders her from coming to terms with Gautama."

Socialite Evenings by Shobha De deals with the new ideology of love, sex, marriage and family. Traditionally loyalty has been the basis of marriage and family in India. As Prabhu P.H. (1958: 236) notes "Mutual fidelity till death of the highest law of husband and wife to follow." In the stories of the central female figures in the novel—Anjali, Karuna and Ritu—it seems that this very basis has fallen on the rocks in the lives of these socialites in the Muppyland. Among these socialites adultery is a clog that lubricates the man-woman relationship. A seasoned flirt Ritu, Karuna's friend, educates her about the rules of adultery: "no calls on Sundays, no calls at home, letters to be destroyed immediately after reading...no presents" (171). Very brazenly Ritu takes pride in this and tells Karuna "Don't forget I have a doctorate in the subject" (172). Put it briefly, the novel presents the panorama of the tenets in the lifestyle of the socialites: betrayal, adultery, sexual orgies and gossips.

The phenomenon of lying is very crucial in this world of the socialites—the actors, actresses, producers, directors, admen and film journalists. A close observation of the verbal exchanges among the characters in this novel reveals that they employ lying as strategy to further their relationship and propel themselves in their career. Lying is an integral part of their life style. Let's see how a lie comes handy easily and naturally to the heroine in *Socialite Evenings* in the following brief talk with her father:

> I was sneaking away when I heard him call out. "Where are you going?" he asked. "Oh, I've forgotten my science workbook. I have to get some extra notes for the test tomorrow." (21)

Very early in her school life Karuna befriends her classmate Charlie. In her very school life Charlie gets deflowered in a car by an Anglo-Indian boy. Thrilled as she is by this experience, Charlie wants to share it with Karuna. Standing down Karuna's balcony she calls her by whistling. No sooner does she whistle than Karuna begins to sneak away from her room to meet Charlie. Her father inquires where she is going. Karuna tells him that she is going out to collect her science workbook and some notes for the test. Thus, she flouts the maxim of truthfulness to implicate that "she is going out to meet her girl friend for the academic purpose."

The fact is that she cannot avoid seeing Charlie. She has developed some strange fascination for this girl. This is the girl who was the first girl in their school to wear stretch pants. This is the girl with whom Karuna has seen the first adult movie "Splendour in the Grass" and with whom she has smoked the ciggies. Karuna is obsessed with this fantastic friend of hers. To see this friend Karuna very readily tells her vigilant father a lie. The lie she tells her father has deeper implications. Born in a middle-class traditional family Karuna felt suffocated. From her very school days she clandestinely aspired for the Brave New World. A socialite in the making, her lie is a strategy she cleverly employs. Very expertly Pushp Lata (2000: 68) comments, "She can easily checkmate and outplay all her male counterparts with a strategy which looks beyond the male comprehension as it is too subtle and manipulative a trick." The novelist makes Karuna's father one of the male counterparts that Karuna seems to be very cleverly outplaying.

The protagonist, Karuna, flouts the maxim by being ironical in the following conversation with her mother, Anjali:

> "And she does not mind being talked to like that?"
>
> "Well, five thousands bucks is five thousand bucks. Plus, he recommends her to his producer buddies and she gets the odd role."
>
> "Oh, great! She sounds real classy." I said. (103)

It is Anjali who drags the middle-class orthodox family girl Karuna into the flashy world of directors, producers, actors and the businessmen. One afternoon Anjali calls on Karuna to see a nympho starlet Nisha at Anjali's house. When Karuna reaches Anjali's house, Nisha is there in her white sari and an enormous red bindi on her forehead. Anjali tells Karuna that Nisha's husband likes her in her white sari and big tikka on her forehead. Pleased by her appearance her husband tells Nisha that he imagines that he is screwing a devi and not a "pros". When Karuna asks whether Nisha does not object to his language, Anjali continues that her husband recommends Nisha to his producers. Nisha gets money and also an odd role in the movies. The reply by Karuna is that Nisha seems to be a very great and classic student. Karuna is in fact making a calculatedly ironical comment. Anjali takes it as a compliment and goes on to relate that Nisha has educated in a convent school and speaks English with a good accent. For Karuna Nisha is a "whore" and has a diseased body. She is utterly vulgar and has a vile, obscene and an over-used fellatio mouth. Steeped in the world of infidelity and adultery Anjali takes Karuna's remark at face-value, fails to get at her irony and proceeds to add on to the pluses of Nisha.

Yet on another occasion Karuna passes ironical remark about Anjali's husband, Kumar:

> "Let's see the loo," I suggested. Anjali opened the door and we stepped into miles of marble and granite. Everything was gleamering and perfect. A sunken bathtub, Jacuzzi, a stuffed chair in one corner and fair-sized library."
>
> "What does this man do? Spend half his life in the bathroom? It's so well equipped." (138)

Anjali's trampy friend Si and Karuna are invited by Anjali to her house after her marriage with Kumar Bhandari. After serving them the lunch Anjali leads them upstairs. She takes them around Kumar's bedroom and bar. Karuna suggests that they should now see their loo. Anjali opens the door and they enter into the bathroom. It is perfect—a bathtub, a chair in one corner and a library were inside the bathroom. Seeing this Karuna remarks that it is so well-equipped. She also enquires whether Anjali's husband spends half of his life in this bathroom. Once again Anjali fails to get at the irony. What Karuna intends to implicate is that Anjali's husband Kumar has actually nothing to do as a husband. He is a homo and buggers with his picked-up orphan boy Murty and his boy-friends. Anjali is his third wife—the other two being at Madras and Juhu respectively. Despite having three wives he has a penchant for boys. The irony of the adjective "well-equipped" is that it is well-equipped for Kumar's worse work-outs with boys. The bathroom also has a mini-fridge and a bar cleverly hidden in easy reach of the tub. Thus, the ironical remark by Karuna helps unravel the dirty traits in Kumar's personality.

On a few occasions the characters deal with the maxim in the other way—they violate it. Charlie's distant uncle does this in the following conversation with Karuna:

> "Mr. Chopra would like some photographs of you. I looked quietly at Charlie who winked and mouthed "say, yes!" I was totally confused. I suppose the client thought I would be flattered, but uppermost in my mind was father's reactions. "I haven't asked my parents' permission," I stuttered, "they'll get angry."
>
> "Don't worry we will not print these pictures without your permission. These are just trial shots for our files. Your parents will never find out." Uncleji said. (23)

Charlie is Karuna's college-friend. One day Charlie goes to her distant uncle who runs an advertising Agency. He has asked her to model for a synthetic yarn manufacturer. Karuna is persuaded to accompany her. After going there, the Uncleji first takes Charlie's photographs. Then the Uncleji leers at Karuna. He tells her that a client Mr. Chopra wants to take some photographs of hers. She tenders the excuse that she has not been permitted for modeling. The Uncleji tells her that her photographs are only the trial shots and will not be printed without her permission. Charlie also insists that Karuna should let him take her photographs. In the state of "to be or not to be" her photographs are taken. After a few days it turns out that her photographs are published in a newspaper and are seen by Karuna's father. They are published without her permission and without any payment. He, thus, misleads Karuna and she feels cheated. The discovery of her photograph in a newspaper by her father earns her a tight slap. But it only intensifies her rebelliousness against her father. The ads keep appearing in the newspapers. It means money of her own and quick thrill of excitement. It is an ego-satisfying experience for her. No doubt Charlie's Uncleji cheats Karuna but from there starts her career of modeling via Charlie. Had the Uncleji not taken her photographs and cheated her, we can rest sure that Karuna's life would have taken a different turn.

On one occasion Ritu's husband tries pitiably to save himself from disgrace and thus suspends the maxim in the following conversation with Ritu:

> The minute he walked in, I pounced on him. "So what are these flowers you are sending these days? They sure as hell aren't coming for me." He looked down for a minute and recovered fast enough to say "You mean those? I'd sent them for Gloria and Peter's wedding ceremony. I'd also put your name on the card." (128-29)

Ritu's husband has an affair with a tartlet. Ritu comes to know about this affair through someone. Ritu first has an encounter with the woman and asks her to leave her (Ritu's) husband alone. The woman very plainly tells Ritu that it is not she who is chasing him but he who is chasing her. He calls her now and then and sends her flowers. When Ritu's husband walks back home, she asks him about the flowers he is sending these days. Her husband replies that he had sent the flowers for the wedding ceremony of his acquaintance—Gloria and Peter. This is in fact a sheer lie he tells Ritu. The truth is that he has spent some days with the tartlet in Bangalore. He tells Ritu a lie to save himself from disgrace. The discovery of his affair with the tartlet lands him in trouble. A lie comes handy to him to save himself. He resorts to lying as a defense mechanism.

Ours is a patriarchal society. It is the husband who shouts, criticizes and abuses his wife. It is the wife who listens, tolerates and suffers. Shobha De makes her women characters different. They are not "yes-persons." They muster courage and are bold enough to articulate their protest against their husband/s. It is the male who is marginalized. This encounter between Ritu and her husband illustrates this phenomenon. Ritu's husband is left in a pitiable condition and a lie he takes recourse to cannot save him from being taken to the task. Ritu grabs a huge vase and flings it at him.

Ritu and Karuna are untruthful in the following verbal exchange with Mataji:

> She sat in front of us staring unabashedly.
>
> "What your husband is doing? Business? Or naukri? She asked Ritu.

"Naukri", she said.

I thought Mataji looked disappointed. "Nice. Very nice. And your husband? He is also having job?" That was for me.

"Having job", I lied.

"Good, good, good. Officer-no?"

"Yes—both officers", we chorused. (158)

As Anjali presents Babaji to Karuna and Ritu in a highlighted manner, Karuna and Ritu are intent on seeing Babaji. He invites them to see him at the Taj Mahal Hotel. Karuna and Ritu present themselves at the Taj Mahal Hotel. As Babaji is being given an almond oil massage in his suite, Mataji intercepts them and asks them to wait outside. As they sit down, Mataji queries Karuna and Ritu about what their husbands are. When giving the option—business or naukri, they reply that their husbands are doing naukri. They are officers. We as readers know that Karuna's and Ritu's husband are not in service. Karuna and Ritu are being untruthful to Mataji. Perhaps they want Mataji to misthink that they are the middle-class wives. The lie they tell Mataji is motivated. Their intention is to put off Mataji. They are not interested in Mataji at all. All they want is to see Babaji and know how fake a rajyogi, a Sanyasi he is. They hear that there are romantic ghazals being played in his suite instead of *bhajans*. Karuna and Ritu want the introductory remarks to be finished so that Mataji will stop talking and they will be led inside for Babaji's *darshan*. They use the strategy of lying to sideline Mataji. They are wise wives from the socialite class. They know with whom to talk and whom to put off. The strategy they adopt in this conversation with Mataji is a part and parcel of their lifestyle.

After having discussed how the characters in the four novels *Temporary Answers*, *Heat and Dust*, *Cry, The Peacock* and *Socialite Evenings* deal with the maxim of truthfulness, let's discuss how this maxim operates in Shashi Deshpande's *The Binding Vine*. Even though the focus of the novelist is on the protagonist, Urmila, we have the stories of two other suffering women-Mira-Urmila's mother-in-law and Shakuntala—the mother of Kalpana—a rape-victim. Add to this the tragedy of

Sulu-Shakuntala's sister. These women suffer and share their sufferings with others of their sex. Belonging to middle-class and patriarchal society they are called for protecting themselves from travails and tortures. Lying comes as a protective measure for them. As and when the situation demands, they take recourse to the phenomenon of lying. They do not hesitate to deviate from the Gricean maxim of speaking the truth.

Analysed from the pragmatic angle, the conversations between the characters in the novel reveal that they deal with the maxim of Quality in all ways—flouting, violating, suspending, opting out and infringing. The protagonist, Urmila (Urmi for short) tells her friend Lalita a blatant lie and thus flouts the maxim in *The Binding Vine* as follows:

> Finally she stops for breath and looks at me. I realize she is waiting for me to offer her my history in exchange. I hesitate and I—should have known this would be her first question—she asks me, "How many kids do you have?"
>
> "Only one. A son." (106)

On a Saturday evening Urmila, her son Kartik, Vanaa—her sister-in-law, her children—Pallavi and Mandira—are on the beach spending their leisure time. The children are busy playing the game of building a castle of sand. Vanaa enquires Urmi about her involvement in the case of Kalpana in hospital. Just then a woman passes by them and looks at them curiously. Urmi takes time to recognize that it is her friend, Lalita. Lalita tells Urmi that her sister died last year and her sister's baby is with her. Lalita is curious to know about Urmi and how many kids she has. Urmi replies that she has only one child and it is son. She avoids referring to her infant daughter, Anu who has suddenly died. Urmi, thus, blatantly tells a lie and flouts the maxim: "Don't tell anything which you believe to be false." This is a deliberate move on her part and is meant to implicate that "the only kid she has is a son and not a daughter." The lie she tells is not unpurposeful. The avoidance of reference to Anu is her attempt to drive her away from her memory. Considered in the Indian social context the fact of having a girl means having a lot of problems. Hence most of the Indian mothers would rather prefer to have son. Urmi knows of her mother-in-law Mira wanting her to have a son and not a daughter "I feel the quickening in my womb, he moves" (149). Urmi also knows the agonies of Shakuntala—a mother whose daughter Kalpana is a rape-victim. This novelistic context implies that Urmi's untruthfulness is deliberate. Only the woman as mother knows what it means to have a daughter. Hence Shakuntala cries out: "Why does God give us daughter?" (150)

Urmi lies to Shakuntala too in her reply with Shakuntala:

> She is silent, except when she gives directions to the driver. Once she asks me, "How many children do you have?"
>
> "Only one. A son." (60)

When Urmi visits her sister-in-law Vanaa in a hospital where Vanaa works, Urmi sees Vanaa and the doctor bending over a sobbing woman and offering her a glass of water. The woman is Shakuntala. The doctor, Bhaskar Jain, realizes on examination that Shakuntala's daughter Kalpana has been brutally raped. Kalpana has been hospitalized. Vanaa asks Shakuntala to go home with Urmi. Shakuntala and Urmi get in the taxi. Giving directions to the taxi driver Shakuntala asks Urmi how many children she has. Urmi's reply that she has only one and that is a son is a sheer lie. Shakuntala's intention is to know whether Urmi also has a daughter so that she can share with Urmi the feelings of having a daughter. Urmi witnesses the agonies of a mother whose daughter has been ruined by being raped. It is a traumatic experience for the mother. Shakuntala is sobbing, her nose is blowing and a bit of fluff is clinging to her nostril. More traumatic than this is the blot she has to suffer as the mother of a raped daughter. Urmi's lie is "alter-centred"—"other-centred." She avoids referring to her infant daughter, Anu and her sudden death. By this she wants to avoid adding salt to Shakuntala's psychological injury. Urmi opts out of speaking the truth in order to avoid intensifying the other's agonies and to soothe Shakuntala's mental travails.

Urmila's concern for the other woman—the less unfortunate one-Shakuntala—can be seen on another occasion when she deviates from speaking the truth:

> "My daughter—my daughter—." Shakuntala's cry eddies around me.
>
> "What is the matter?" Inni asks
>
> "Nothing." (63)

Reaching Shakuntala to her home, Urmi comes back her home. She has her bath. She makes chapattis and she sits for meal with her son Kartik and her mother Inni. She cannot forget Shakutai and her plight. Shakutai's cry "My daughter—my daughter" rings in her ears. As she mutters the words, her mother Inni enquires what the matter is. Urmi replies that there is nothing. As readers we know that there is a lot she knows about Shakutai and her daughter Kalpana. She deviates from speaking the truth to her mother. Once again the deviation from speaking the truth is motivated. Telling her mother about Shakutai and her daughter Kalpana would mean bringing a bad name and disgrace for Shakutai in a male-dominated Indian society. Truth will come as a double-edged devastating weapon: a disgrace for the rape-victim's mother whose husband has already left her and ruining the marriage prospects of not only Kalpana but also her younger sister Sandhya.

The protagonist Urmila is a new Indian woman in the making. The truth she withholds to speak underlines her female bonding and her penchant for helping another woman and saving her from disgrace and defame. Later in the novel Urmila positively comes forward despite Vanaa's and Inni's reluctance over her involvement in Kalpana's case. It is Urmila who brings the case in the limelight and the culprit, Prabhakar, the husband of Sulu, Shakutai's sister, is exposed. Taken in the whole novelistic context Urmi's lying to her mother speaks volumes about her and hence acquires an uncommon significance.

As against the protagonist, Priti turns out to be a pseudo-feminist. Priti violates the maxim in her conversation with Urmi:

> "Would you use your own mother's life?" I asked Priti.
>
> And she said, "Yes. One has got to be objective: One has to distance one self." (40)

Priti, a friend of Urmila, comes to console Urmila after the sudden death of her infant daughter, Anu. A reference to Mira, her mother-in-law flashes an idea in Priti to make a movie on Mira's life. She requests Urmila to give her the story of Mira and write a script for the movie. Mira is her mother-in-law, the mother of her husband Kishori. She does not like the idea of using Mira's story for the movie and refuses to write the script for the movie. When Priti tries to convince Urmila that Mira will be used only as a symbol, Urmila tells her that Mira has written on her books "strictly private and confidential." Urmila asks Priti if she would use her own mother's life-story for the movie on womanhood. Priti replies positively and says that her mother's life will be dealt with objectively. As the novel proceeds, it turns out that Priti never makes the movie on her mother's life. She misleads Urmila that her mother's life will be objectively presented in the movie. The truth is that Priti's mother has become a maniac depressive and an alcoholic. Priti has left her mother in America and blocked her own mother out of her life. It transpires that Priti's attempt at making a heroine of herself and linking a personal life to a national drama only presents her as a pseudo-feminist. The lie she tells makes herself an object of satire on her pseudo-feminism.

We come across an instance of the maxim suspended by Shakuntala for social reason as follows:

> "Malcolm, this is Shakutai, her daughter is a patient here.... Tell him about it yourself, Shakutai."
>
> "What is wrong with your daughter?" Malcolm asks in polite disinterest. He'll listen only because I've asked him to.
>
> Shakutai falters, looks at me, finally says, "It was an accident."
>
> Sensing something, Malcolm waits for her to go on. "Car accident?" He prompts her when she doesn't.
>
> "You tell him, Urmila", Shakutai pleads with me. (69)

Urmila visits the hospital where Kalpana has been admitted for four months now. As Urmila is with Shakutai, Malcolm calls Urmila by her name. He is her friend. He and Urmila have studied together in a college. Now he is working as a journalist for a newspaper. Seeing him it strikes Urmila that the way Kalpana has been treated in the hospital can be reported in the newspaper. She introduces him to Shakutai and entreats her to tell him about Kalpana so that it can be printed in the newspaper. Shakutai tells him falteringly that Kalpana has been hospitalized due to her car accident. When he further prompts her to go on, Shakutai withholds speaking the truth and pleads Urmila to tell him about it.

Shakutai's deviation from being, truthful is not without purpose. A typical Indian mother in a patriarchal society she knows well that speaking the truth to him about Kalpana and getting it published in the newspaper will ruin her family's name. It will bring her disgrace and ruin the prospects of not only the marriage of Kalpana but also that of her younger daughter Sandhya. If her daughters will not be married off, they will be socially vulnerable. Shakutai wants to hide the truth but her attempt at doing so only underlines her agony, fear and helplessness. She suspends the maxim of truthfulness for this social reason and reacts in the way that most Indian mothers of unmarried daughters would do. She tries to suppress the truth but it only expresses the trauma of a woman in the land governed by the Manu's laws.

As it has already been stated that a maxim is infringed when a speaker has imperfect command over language or because of cognitive state like excitement, nervousness some abnormal psychological condition. In the novel under study an instance of infringing the maxim of Quality occurs at the outset of the novel when Urmila is grieving over a sudden death of her infant daughter, Anu. There is nothing left for her she feels. She has hallucinations about Anu sitting by her and breathing by her side. In this state she recalls how she and the children said false things in her childhood in her childhood when they played round a disused well in Ranidurg. This is how they broke the maxim:

> The point was to say the most horror-rousing things:
>
> "I can see long soft wriggly worms...."
>
> "I can see green frothing bubbling scum—something is coming out of it—I can see one eye." (21)

The children-Amrut, Urmi's brother, Vana, her friend and Urmila herself played round the well. They peeped in its depth. They decided to describe the horrors they could see in the well. All that they said were the false things. Truly speaking there was nothing in the well. There was only darkness and smell. In the state of hallucination now Urmila realizes that it was the smell of hopelessness. She experiences this hopelessness now after the death of her daughter, Anu. Urmila and the children infringed the maxim in the state of excitement and ignorance of the world around them. Their intention was not to generate any implicature as such.

In this section it has been discussed how the maxim of truthfulness is exploited by the characters in character-to-character level interactions. The analysis of the phenomenon of lying helps shed light on how the characters in the novels under investigation negotiate their relationships, propel in their career and show their concerns for others and the society. As the nature of the maxims suggests, they compete/conflict and complement with each other in conversation. The following section deals with the play between Quality maxim and other maxims of Cooperative Principle.

3.3. Quality Maxim and the Other Maxims of Cooperative Principle

Clarity, brevity, truthfulness, tact and politeness are communicative values. These values are reflected through the communication of human beings. They suggest how human beings as members of a social group give preference to one value rather than another. The Gricean theory of communication helps us as a framework to analyze these values through analysis of the activity of conversation. The Gricean maxims of conversational cooperation are typically characteristic. Unlike the grammatical rules they can co-occur, compete and complement one another. Leech (1983) gives a beautiful example of how the maxims clash with each other and the language user upholds one maxim at the expense of the other. Here is the conversation between A and B:

A: When is Aunt Rosie's birthday?

B: It's sometime in April.

In this conversation the reply given by B is not what is expected by A. He does not give the right amount of information needed by A and thus violates the Quality maxim. From the reply given by B, A derives an additional piece of meaning/implicature: B does not know the exact date of Aunt Rosie's birthday. A arrives at this implicature through the following stages:

(1) B has violated the Quantity maxim by not giving the right amount of information.

(2) B has done this to observe the Cooperative principle at some deeper level.

(3) B does not know Rosie's birthday except that it is in April. He does not want to risk telling a lie. That is—he wants to uphold the Quality maxim.

A significant point that arises from this conversation is that B has given preference to the Quality maxim over the Quantity maxim. The situation and the background knowledge force one to violate one maxim and follow the others. In some cases the converser is called for to reverse the process. This section is concerned with the conflict between Quality maxim and the other maxim/s of the Cooperative Principle.

In the previous section it has been observed that the characters in the novels under study sacrifice the maxim of truthfulness in their conversations with other characters. The situation and the goal of the converser specify the kind of the non-observance of the maxim like—flout, violation, suspension, opting out and infringement. In the following conversations analyzed, it is observed that the characters break the maxim in order to uphold the other maxim of conversational cooperation. Let's take an example to see how the clash between the Quality maxim and that of Manner is faced by the protagonist in *Temporary Answers* in the following conversation:

> She telephoned me one evening at the office and said in the breathless way she had "Vineeta, I know I have no right to ask you to do this, but could you possibly have

> the children just for a few hours? Something urgent has come up. There is this party I have got the invitation for. Bhanoo Pandit is going to be there, you know, the music director. There's some chance that he might consider me for playback singing for his next picture. Wouldn't that be exciting? The only problem is that Madhu is out of Pune and Gangubai, damn her, took off yesterday because some cousin died and is not back yet. She was supposed to be back by now."
>
> When it sounded as if she was going to stop for breath, I said, "I am sorry, I can't."
>
> "What was that? Speak up, will you please? I am in this coffee house and there's an awful racket going on, I can't hear you."
>
> I said loudly and distinctly, "I said I can't have the children today, Kishori. I am going out. I have a dinner appointment." (77)

As it is obvious, Vineeta's friend, Kishori, requests Vineeta to look after her children for a few hours because she wants to attend a party. Her husband Madhu is out of Pune and the housemaid Gangubai is not back yet. The request by Kishori is squarely rejected by Vineeta: "I am sorry, I can't. I can't have the children today. I have a dinner appointment."

The fact is that Vineeta has no such planned appointment for dinner. Thus, she tells Kishori a lie. And why not? Vineeta has realized that Kishori is an inveterate liar and is a user. She has already used Vineeta once when she went to Hyderabad with Madhu. She had said that they would be back by Wednesday morning. They returned to collect their children on Saturday afternoon. Add to this Abhijit's explanation that she is innocent and Kishori is completely selfish. Kishori's guiding principle is her own need. She does not bother even if she hurts other/s. This selfishness of Kishori has stung Vineeta and angered her. She would, therefore, not hesitate to be direct and straightforward to reject Kishori's plea. Put it in the Gricean terms, Vineeta violates the Quality maxim to uphold that of Manner in a delicate relationship like that of friendship one is struck by

Vineeta's directness and bluntness to reject her friend's plea. Of course, she has more than one reason for doing so.

In Vineeta's previous conversation with Kishori, we have a strange situation in which Kishori violates not only the maxim of truthfulness but also of Quantity and Relation. This is how the conversation proceeds:

> I said, "How long will you be away?"
>
> "Let me see. If we leave Saturday evening, we should be back by Wednesday morning. Gangubai will come with the children, so you won't have to do anything except just keep an eye on them." (73)

Kishori's husband, Madhu, has his Conference in Hyderabad. He wants Kishori to accompany him. As the maid Gangubai is not trustworthy, Kishori asks Vineeta to look after her children for a few days. She tells Vineeta that they would come back by Wednesday. The truth is that Madhu and Kishori have planned their trip and they have made the bookings for the return on Sunday. By telling that they will be back by Wednesday Kishori violates the Quality maxim. Vineeta's question "how long will you be away" is also not requiredly answered by Kishori. The reference to Gangubai also seems to be irrelevant to Vineeta's question. The sacrifice of these maxims by Kishori speaks volumes about her. She is an inveterate liar, selfish or self-centred, a user and a persuasive sort of woman. Vineeta readily accepts to look after the children. We also realize how gullible Vineeta is.

In Jhabvala's *Heat and Dust* the clash between Quality maxim and other maxims seems to be operating in a few of the conversations. Take, for example, a look at the following conversation between Olivia and her compatriot Harry:

> Harry said, "Have you noticed something? That you're never taken to meet the Begum and her ladies?"
>
> "I *have* met them, thank you." She gave a forced laugh: "It was hard going." (102)

As Harry was not in good health, he would not come to the Civil Lines to fetch Olivia and take her to the palace of the

Nawab. Olivia herself would visit Harry and the palace. Harry has observed that the Nawab has been rather discourteous to Olivia. Despite her frequent visits to the palace, the Nawab has not introduced her to the Begum (his mother) and her ladies. On this visit Harry asks Olivia whether she has been taken to the Nawab's mother. Olivia replies positively and violates the maxim of truthfulness. The truth is that the Nawab is not interested in introducing Olivia to his mother nor is Olivia interested in meeting the Begum. She adds a clause to her lie "It was hard going." It means she wants to emphasise and clarify to Harry that she has had a meeting with the Begum and that the meeting was hard going. She does not want to leave any kind of vagueness in the mind of Harry about her introduction to the Begum. Perhaps Olivia takes it that not being introduced to the Begum despite her frequent visits to the palace and her intimacy with the Nawab would be making herself an object of ridicule. She, therefore, replies to Harry's question positively and in a straightforward, clear and direct way. The context of situation—her intimacy with the Nawab—forces her to be a liar and to speak in a clear and in an unambiguous manner. If a lie is going to help her save her from ridicule, then tell it she will. She does it in this conversation with Harry in a brief and clear way. She prefers to be clear rather than speak the truth. The readers know the truth—The Nawab never spoke to her about his mother. (152)

Harry violates the Quality maxim in the following conversation with Olivia:

> "The Nawab also says he is bored being here, so today everyone is packing."
>
> "He's bored?"
>
> "So he says. But there is something else too." He frowned and went on packing very meticulously.
>
> "What?"
>
> "Oh, I don't know Olivia." (142)

As Olivia got pregnant, she wanted to tell it to the Nawab first. As she arrives in the palace, she finds everyone is packing. On being asked why they are packing, Harry tells Olivia that they are going to Mussoorie as advised by the Begum. The Nawab is also bored being here at the Khatm. When Olivia enquires why the Nawab is bored, Harry replies that he does not know what the matter is with the Nawab. The truth is that Harry knows well that the Nawab is in both the troubles: financial and domestic. His Khatm has been bankrupt and his wife Sandy and the Cabobpurians are bringing a case of dowry against the Nawab. By withholding this truth he violates not only the maxim of truthfulness but also that of Quantity. Harry knows that answering Olivia's question as required by Quantity maxim and by telling the truth about the Nawab, would be inviting the Nawab's fury The Nawab's is terribly sensitive. In any case speaking the truths to her about the Nawab would do good neither to the Nawab nor to Harry himself. He straightforwardly denies telling her about the Nawab's troubles and thus sacrifices both the maxims in the present conversation.

In *Cry, the Peacock* too there is a clash between Quality and other maxims of cooperation in a few conversational situations. Characters prioritise the observance of a maxim and sacrifice one at the cost of the other. This happens in the conversation between Maya and Mrs. Lal, the hostess of a party. This is how it happens:

> "Have you hurt yourself?" I asked her at last, for she seemed unable to recover what poise she might once have had.
>
> "No," she said, with surprising decisiveness and the line of her lips plunged downwards in a queer, hard grimace of unutterable bitterness. "That was the accidental part of it." She said. (72)

Once Gautama takes Maya to a party hosted by Mr. and Mrs. Lal. As the guests gather in the dining room, Mrs. Lal begins serving the dinner. One of the guest ladies asks Mrs. Lal whether she has no air-conditioner. This gives Mrs. Lal a nervous jerk. She swings into her pot-bellied husband and knocks aside his plate piled with rice and pickles. Mrs. Lal then hits her forehead against his chin. Maya asks her if she has hurt herself. Mrs. Lal replies that she has not been hurt.

The truth is that she has hurt not only her head but also her eyes. She rubs the eyes furiously till they are weeping and red. Mrs. Lal, thus, lies to Maya. She further adds that she has accidently hit against her husband's plate. Mrs. Lal's intention is to explicate and clarify to Maya that there is nothing serious with her. Her addition that—"that was the accidental part of it' is a deliberate attempt to clarify and explicate her reaction to her hitting. Briefly put she is being untruthful but attempts to be clear—to observe the Manner maxim.

In the following conversation between Maya and Gautama, Maya violates the maxim of Quality but is relevant, clear and brief:

> "Why is your head so hot?" he asked suspiciously, "And damp. Do you have a temperature?"
>
> "No," I said, "No, Gautama, no temperature," and began to move away from him towards the house.
>
> "Are you sure?" he called after me.
>
> "Sure," I whispered, "Sure." (124-25)

This conversation between Maya and Gautama follows the expression of differences in their attitude to love. For her love is a force in life. For him love's tragedy is that it cannot survive death, death cuts love short. His logical argument with her exasperates her. It makes her skin burn with heat. Her tongue is dry and thick with thirst. On being asked by him whether she has a temperature, she replies negatively. She, thus, tells him a lie. Her reply to his question is not just a verbal reply. Behind this is her intention to sever herself from him. She answers him as required—neither more nor less, also in a relevant way. She observes the maxims of Quantity and Relation but violates that of Quality. She does not hesitate to tell him a lie because in the present circumstances she does not wish to further her talk with him. She requiredly and repeatedly asserts "sure" "sure". Taking recourse to telling a lie by Maya only suggests that the chasm between her and Gautama is further widened.

The illustrative examples of conversation from *Temporary Answers, Heat and Dust*, and *Cry, the Peacock* reveal that the maxim of Quality (of speaking the truth) clashes with the other maxims of verbal cooperation. The circumstances in which the characters find themselves force them to tell the lies but be relevant and clear and brief. One notices this interplay of the maxim of speaking the truth and the other maxims of cooperation in the other novels under study: *Socialite Evenings* and *The Binding Vine*. In *Socialite Evenings*, it is very interesting to see how the characters pitted in the Muppyland exploit the phenomenon of lying and other maxims of cooperation. The protagonist Karuna violates the Quality maxim in her following talk with her father:

> I was sneaking away when I heard him call out "Where are you going?" he asked.
>
> "Oh, I've forgotten my science workbook. I have to get some extra notes for the test tomorrow." (21)

Karuna's father was on his bed. He was surrounded by a pile of his office files. Karuna's friend Charlie gave two shrill whistles and signaled to Karuna to come down. This was the system she had adopted to communicate with Karuna when her parents were at home. No sooner did Charlie give the whistles than Karuna started to sneak away to meet Charlie down stairs. Her father enquired where she was going, Karuna replied that she was going to get science workbook and some notes for the test the next day, as readers we know that she was sneaking away to meet Charlie and not to get the workbook nor the notes. She tells her father a lie because her father and mother thought that Charlie was a bad influence on their daughter and they would not want this girl in their house.

In telling her father the pretext of getting notes and workbook Karuna, thus, sacrifices the maxim of truthfulness. She would not hesitate to tell her father a lie because Charlie is the girl through whose prism Karuna sees the world in her school life and initially in college. A close observation of this conversation also reveals that Karuna has violated the maxim of Quantity and Manner. Her father's question 'where are you going?' has not been answered as required by her father. Karuna is being indirect too thus, violating the Manner maxim. This conversation between Karuna and her father is highly suggestive. It suggests the violation of not only the conversational norms but also the norms for the middle-class daughter-obedience to parents. The sacrifice of the maxims suggests Karuna's protest and rebelliousness against the so-called patriarchy in the Indian society. The later part of the novel shows how the norms of patriarchy in Indian society are shattered by the socialites like Karuna, Charlie, Anjali, Ritu, Nisha and even the male counterparts like Abe, Shirish, Kumar Bhandari and Ranbir Roy.

Ritu and Karuna deal with the above-mentioned maxims in a different manner in their encounter with Mataji:

> She sat in front of us staring unabashedly.
>
> "What your husband is doing? Business? Or Naukri?" She asked Ritu.
>
> "Naukri" she said.
>
> "I thought Mataji looked disappointed. "Nice. Very nice. And your husband?" He is also having job?" That was for me.
>
> "Having job," I lied. (158)

Ritu and Karuna visit Anjali's house on the occasion of Janmashtami party. There they see an extra-ordinary good-looking man, clad in a Sadhu's saffron robes. He is Babaji—an enlightened being, a Sufi saint, the final avatar of Krishna. Ritu and Karuna are sure that he is one of the fake Hindu Sanyasis. Ritu, in particular, is fascinated by Babaji. He asks Ritu to visit him in the suite of the Taj Mahal Hotel the next day. Ritu is aware of his vile intention. Anyway she is eager to know how he handles her. The next day Ritu and Karuna visit the Taj Mahal. Mataji, a woman disciple of Babaji comes out of the suite and throws her glance at Ritu and Karuna. Babaji is being given an almond oil massage inside. Mataji asks Ritu and Karuna to wait for a while. As they sit waiting, Mataji stares at them. She enquires Ritu if her husband is a businessman or in naukri. Ritu replies that he is in naukri. Mataji then asks Karuna what her husband is doing. Karuna answers that he is having a job. Both Ritu and Karuna thus tell Mataji a lie. One thing that strikes us is that their replies are brief, clear and relevant. They tell Mataji neither more nor less than required by Mataji. Mataji's intention seems to get to know the background that Ritu and Karuna come from and she begins enquiring them about their husbands. The way Ritu and Karuna answer her questions is their calculated move to put off Mataji. They are interested in Babaji not Mataji. With this purpose they very readily answer Mataji that that their husbands are doing naukri. They are shrewd enough to answer in brief and as required. In Gricean terminology, they face the clash between speaking the truth and answering in clear and relevant manner. They sacrifice the maxim of speaking the truth at the cost of being relevant, clear and brief and follow the norm of giving required amount of information. If compared, these two instances of conversation in this novel reveal that in the former Karuna sacrifices the maxim of Quality whereas in the latter the maxims of Quantity, Relation and Manner are observed in preference to that of Quality.

In *The Binding Vine* too the conflict between the maxim of speaking the truth and that of being relevant and clear could be seen in a number of situations. Let's begin with the following conversation:

> "Would you use your own mother's life?" I asked Priti.
>
> And she said, "Yes. One has got to be objective: One has to distance oneself." (40)

Priti is a friend of Urmila. She comes to condole Urmila over the death of Urmila's baby-daughter, Anu. In the course of their conversation, Urmila refers to mother-in-law, Mira's life-story revealed through her poems and diary. Priti is excited by the story and wants to make a movie on Mira's life. She asks Urmila to write the script of the story for her. Urmila refuses to do so. She asks Priti if she would use her own mother's story for the movie. Priti replies that she would use her own mother's story for the movie. As it turns out later this never happens. Priti, thus, sacrifices the maxim of speaking the truth. She further adds that—"one has to be objective. One has to distance oneself." By adding this she provides more information that required by Urmila's question. Moreover, she does not state plainly that she would use her own mother's story in an objective manner. Analysed from the Gricean point of view Priti breaks the maxim of speaking the truth, giving required information and being direct and clear. She seems to do so with the intention of persuading Urmila do the thing for her—write the script of Urmila's mother-in-law's story for the movie. An America-returned girl Priti wants to give an air of a progressive girl—a feminist. As readers we learn in the later part of the novel that her action is far removed from the reality. For us she remains a pseudo-feminist.

Urmila deviates from speaking the truth to her mother by way of suspending the maxim in her conversation as follows:

> "My daughter...my daughter...." Shakutai's cry eddies around me.
>
> "What's the matter?" Inni asks.
>
> "Nothing." (63)

After reaching Shakutai to her home, Urmila comes her home back. She has a bath and makes the chapaties. She, her son Kautik and her mother Inni sit for the meal. As they are having the meal, Shakutai's words—"My daughter...my daughter" ring in her ears. Her mother Inni asks curiously what the matter is. Urmila briefly replies 'nothing' and deviates from speaking the truth. The truth is that she knows a lot about Shakutai and her daughter, Kalpana—a rape-victim. We expect that Urmila should share her feelings with her mother. But Urmila prefers to suspend from speaking the truth. Urmila has in fact linked what has happened to Kalpana with what has happened with her mother-in-law, Mira also a victim of marital rape.

By saying "nothing" Urmila, thus, intends to save Shakutai from disgrace and defame. A woman in a man-dominated society Urmila knows well what it means to be the mother of a raped mother and what it means to be the mother of a daughter raped before marriage. If she tells Inni what has happened to Kalpana, it would bring disgrace for mother and daughter (Shakutai and Kalpana). It would also ruin the prospects of not only Kalpana's marriage but also that of Kalpana's younger sister, Sandhya. Very compassionately Urmila withholds from speaking the truth. In using the single negative word 'nothing', she also withholds the information she possesses. Thus, she prefers to suspend the maxims: Quantity and Quality. She thinks if it is going to help her Shakutai, then do it she will. She, thus, uses lying as a strategy to defend the others.

Shakutai also takes recourse to lying in her conversation with Malcolm:

> "Malcolm, this is Shakutai, her daughter is a patient here. ...Tell him about it yourself Shakutai."
>
> "What is wrong with your daughter?" Malcolm asks in polite disinterest. He'll listen only because I have asked him to.
>
> Shakutai falters. Looks at me, finally says, "It was an accident," Sensing something Malcolm waits for her to go on. "Car accident?" he prompts her when she does not.
>
> "You tell him, Urmila," Shakutai pleads with me. (169)

Malcolm is Urmila's friend. He and Urmila were college-mates. Now he is a reporter for a newspaper. Urmila and Shakutai happen to meet him at the hospital. Urmila wants what has happened to Kalpana to bring into limelight—getting it published in the newspaper. Her intention is to get the incident published and get justice for Shakutai and her daughter. She introduces Shakutai to Malcolm and asks her to tell him what has happened to Kalpana. When enquired by Malcolm, we see how both Shakutai and Urmila avoid speaking the truth. By withholding the truth Shakutai suspends the maxim of Quality. Hers is an attempt to save herself and her daughter from social disgrace. Urmila's request to Shakutai to relate the happening to Malcolm is a deliberate attempt to test whether Shakutai is prepared to get it published and known publicly. They possess the information but refuse to relay it. They, thus, suspend the maxim of giving required information. This is a very sensitive situation in which they are caught "to speak the truth or not to speak it." Shakutai's domestic status (her husband has left her for another woman) and her place in the society force both Shakutai and Urmila to deviate from speaking the truth and answering Malcolm's question requiredly to avoid the social dangers Shakutai and her daughter will be victims of. They take recourse to lying. Shakutai's reply that 'it was an accident' (meaning-Kalpana has met with an accident and has, therefore, been hospitalized) is geared to varnish the lie she is telling. It is quite understandable why these two women avoid speaking the truth and relaying the information they possess.

In this section, we have discussed how the maxims of verbal cooperation clash with one another. The maxim of Quality in particular clashes with those of Quantity, Relation and Manner. The characters face the clash between telling the lie and being informative, relevant and clear. The social and individual factors force them contravene the maxim of speaking the truth at the expense of the others. When a character tells a lie, it signals his/her intention to convey something. We as readers know the contextual clues in the novels and this helps us to get at the intended meaning of the characters. Telling a lie is either 'self-concerned' or 'other-centered'. It is taken recourse to either to save oneself or to save the others. The section that follows discusses how the characters in the novels under study tell the lies for saving others—for being polite to others.

3.4. Quality Maxim and the Politeness Concern in the Five Novels

There are many occasions when people are heard telling lies. The reasons for doing so are contingent and unpredictable. The situation in which a lie is told suggests why a person has done so. The lies people tell can be grouped into two categories: malevolent and benevolent. If a person tells a lie for deceiving the other, it could be called a malevolent lie. On the other hand, if a lie is told to save or to protect the other or to help him/her, it is a benevolent lie. Let's take an example of a situation in which a lie may be benevolent or malevolent. A friend of mine asks me for lending him/her a thousand rupees. I do posses the amount of money he/she needs. Despite this I tell him/her that I have no money and am unable to help him/her. The lie I tell is malevolent. If, on the other hand, I lend him/her the money, I am being benevolent to him/her at the expense of my pocket. In the pragmatic terminology—I am being impolite in the former case but being polite in the latter. In lending him/her the money, I am preserving my positive face—desire to be liked/admired by others and I am being polite to him/her via being generous and via the Lakoffian maxim of making the other feel good and comfortable.

The fictional characters are like real-life people. They lie and exaggerate. They are ironical. Their conversations are mimetic of real-life interactions. This section is concerned with how the characters in the selected novels use the phenomenon of lying for saving themselves and for saving and helping others. The characters in these novels hail from the middle and socialite class of the Indian society. In a few situations one observes that these characters deviate from speaking the truth for others. Their deviation from maxim of Quality is 'alter-centred.'

This is what Shobha in *Temporary Answers* does in the following situation:

> "Can you think of anyone else who might have been with her, any one with whom she is particularly friendly?"
>
> She hesitated before she said, "No, I don't think so." (55)

Madhuri is Vineeta's younger sister. She is in her adolescence. Her hair-style, clothes and staying out late lead to constant conflict between her and her mother. One night she goes to a movie. She is expected to be back at nine thirty but does not return till eleven. Vineeta's mother sends Vineeta to Mrs. Kibe, whose daughter Shobha is supposed to be with Madhuri. This conversation takes place when Vineeta visits Shobha. She asks Shobha if there is anyone with whom Madhuri is friendly and who might be with Madhuri. Shobha hesitantly tells that she does not think that Madhuri is friendly with any boy. In saying so Shobha deviates from speaking the truth. The truth is that Shobha knows that Madhuri goes around with a boy named Ram Sawant. Ram is in-charge of the Bicycle Stand at the college in which Madhuri is studying. Shobha has seen Madhuri talking to Ram in the college that morning. Despite this she flatly refuses to tell Vineeta about Madhuri's friendliness with Ram. Shobha hesitates to speak the truth because her mother Mrs. Kibe is present. They want to avoid gossiping about Madhuri's running away with Ram Sawant.

Mrs. Kibe and Shobha are sociable enough to withhold the truth they know. Shobha in particular thinks that the daughter of a professor has run away with a cycle-stand assistant is a social disgrace for Madhuri's parents whose elder daughter Vineeta is already a widow living with her parents. Speaking the truth at this time would make Madhuri's parents hide their faces from the people. They would be the object of social ridicule and abuse. It would threaten their positive face-desire to be liked by others. These social considerations force Shobha suspend the maxim of speaking the truth. Two days later Vilas brings Madhuri home and the cat comes out of the bag. It turns out that Madhuri was with Ram Sawant. Put it briefly, Shobha tells a lie to show her concern not only for Madhuri but also for Vineeta and her parents, people from a respectable family.

Madan Bhingare, a boy from a poor family, also violates the maxim for the social reason in his conversation with the Police-Sub-Inspector:

> He asked Madan, "Did you take the milk powder?"
>
> "No."
>
> "What did you do with it? Who did you sell it to?"
>
> "I didn't take it."
>
> The slap sounded like something suddenly exploding. I gasped with the suddenness of it. Madan's eyes watered and the finger-marks on his chick swelled into welts. There was anger in his eyes.
>
> He said, "I didn't take it." (88)

Madan Bhingare is a twelve-year-old-boy employed by Vineeta at the Charity Clinic. A woman Parvati Bhise working at the Clinic reports that some milk powder is missing. Vineeta takes Madan into confidence and tries to elicit the truth from him. But he keeps on saying that he didn't take it. Vineeta threatens him saying that she would take him to the police station. When Madan refuses to admit his theft, he is finally taken to the police station. The Police-Sub-Inspector enquires Madan if he has stolen the milk powder from the clinic. Madan repeatedly answers that 'he didn't take it.' By this he tries to mislead that he has not taken the powder and could be said to have violated the maxim of speaking the truth.

With the help of the context of the novel it could be put that Madan is an inveterate liar. Once he stole money from the counter of Ramusheth—a shopkeeper. On being asked he said nothing and thus refused to speak the truth. On this occasion too he is being untruthful. It transpires later that Madan has stolen six five-kilogram tins of milk powder and sold them to a man named Chandanmal. The lie he tells serves his double purpose: it is meant to save himself for his anti-social act and also his family from social disgrace. His father works in a dyeing factory. There are five children in the family. The eldest son has pulmonary tuberculosis. The daughter has infantile paralysis. The father spends a great deal of his money on drinking. Madan is the only child in the family who is bright and grown-up in his speech and manners. Circumstances force him behave in the way that he does. He commits stealth and on being caught he refuses to admit it. The reason is more than obvious—he wants to save himself, particularly his poor family from being incriminated.

Vineeta's mother-in-law also breaks the maxim to show her concern and care for her widowed daughter-in-law. This is how she does it:

> I said, "You can tell people that I am no longer your responsibility, then whatever I do won't spoil your name."
>
> I wanted an open fight, a chance to say the things I had bottled up for years. But she would not give me the satisfaction. She only said, "You may want to dissociate yourself from us. But you married our son and even though he is dead, we still consider you our responsibility." (136)

After the death of Vineeta's husband (Nagendra), Vineeta's mother-in-law suggested that she should live with her or ask Vineeta's mother come and stay with her (Vineeta) at Bombay. Vineeta refused to do so. The mother-in-law then referred to Nagendra's friend Navin Mehta who stood by Vineeta after

Nagendra's death. The mother-in-law intended to insinuate at Vineeta's intimacy with Mehta and the resultant disgrace it might bring to her mother-in-law's family. Vineeta asked the mother-in-law to tell the people that Vineeta is no longer the responsibility of Nagendra's family. The mother-in-law replied that even though Nagendra is dead, they still consider Vineeta their responsibility. In saying this, the mother-in-law breaks the maxim of speaking the truth. Vineeta has experienced that there was antipathy between her and her mother-in-law. All that the mother-in-law says now is a lie and thus reflects her hypocrisy. She is being untruthful to express her care and concern for Vineeta—a daughter-in-law widowed at thirty. She is being polite now because she is letting Vineeta free to dissociate herself from the family of her dead husband. She contravenes the maxim of Quality for being polite to Vineeta via being sympathetic and by not imposing her will on Vineeta.

In Jhabvala's *Heat and Dust* characters could be divided into two broad categories: Western (British) and Indians. To the former belong Douglas Rivers, Olivia, Dr. Saunders, Major Minnies, Harry and the young narrator. The Nawab, the Begum (his mother), Inder Lal, Ritu, Inder's mother and Maji belong to the latter category. The conversations between the British and the Indian reveal their attitudes towards one another. Jhabvala has very skillfully dealt with these characters having intimate relationships: The Nawab-Olivia, the narrator-Inder Lal, and Harry and the Nawab. One of the central concerns in the novel is cross-cultural conflict. Though the English and the Indian try to assert their supremacy over the others, one finds that they do try to protect their counterpart on a few occasions.

Harry is a guest of the Nawab. He has come to India with the Nawab. He has been given the best guest suite by the Nawab in his palace. The suite has marble rooms and has been charmingly furnished with fine pieces of European furniture. Though an English counterpart to the Indian Prince/the Nawab, Harry's interactions with Olivia project him as an image-saver for the Nawab. Even if a lie is needed to be told, he does it. There are two glaring instances of Harry's conversation with Olivia in which he deviates from speaking the truth. The first is this:

> She asked, "What's all this about dacoits, Harry? Tell me,"
>
> She said when he didn't.
>
> He sighed and after a while he said, "Honestly I don't know, Olivia. A lot of things go on and I'd just as soon not know about them." (103)

Olivia has seen in her very first summer stay in India that there was rioting in Khatm on Husband's Wedding Day. Baba Firdaus' shrine had been taken over by Hindu worshippers. This excited the wrath of the Muslim inhabitants in the State of Khatm. They created disturbances on simple issues on the day of the fair, not necessarily at the shrine but in the bazaar. The rioters were supported and protected by the Nawab. As the Husband's Wedding Day fair was drawing near that year, Olivia felt restless. Now she is eager to know about the riots. Hence she visits Harry in his suite. As Harry has been living with the Nawab for many years now, Olivia thinks Harry might tell her about the riots. When she asks Harry about the riots, he replies that he does not know anything about the riots. His reply is a move to protect the Nawab from being exposed in having nexus with the rioters. Harry knows very well that the Nawab is very much excited if anything goes against him. By telling Olivia about the riots and the rioters Harry does not wish to invite the wrath of the Nawab. Harry also knows very well that there is an intimate relationship between Olivia and the Nawab. Creating even a suspicion in her mind about the Nawab's involvement in the riots would tarnish the Nawab's image. To save the Nawab from incurring a bad name Harry uses a lie as a protective measure. Thus, he could be said to have suspended the maxim of speaking the truth to preserve the Nawab's positive face.

Harry is seen employing this move again in his exchange with Olivia on another occasion:

> "The Nawab also says he's bored here, so today everyone is packing."
>
> "He's bored?"

"So he says. But there is something else too." He frowned and went on packing very meticulously.

"What?"

"I don't know." (142)

Olivia is Douglas Rivers' wife. Rivers is busy in his work as the Assistant Collector of the State of Satipur. The environment in which Olivia is wrapped suffocates her. The limited friend circle with her compatriots in the Civil Lines and the negligence of her emotions by Douglas Rivers force her to be irresistibly drawn to the handsome Indian Prince the Nawab. She finds emotional security in the Nawab and thus develops intimacy with him. She becomes the fallen Eve of the English society and becomes pregnant from the Nawab. Initially she puts this fact off from her husband and decides to tell it to the Nawab first. When she arrives in the palace, she finds that everyone including Harry is packing. On being asked Harry tells Olivia that they are all going to Mussoorie at the advice of the Begum. Olivia tries to dig out the reason for their going to Mussoorie. Harry relates that the Nawab is bored being in the palace. As Olivia eagerly inquires why the Nawab is bored, Harry replies that he does not know.

Harry in fact knows that the Nawab is in two troubles at the moment: domestic and financial. The Nawab's wife Sandy is at Cabobpur (Simla) and her family is threatening to bring a case of dowry against the Nawab. Financially the Khatm is bankrupt. Harry is reluctant to divulge these truths to Olivia. He knows that the Nawab is terribly sensitive and will be outraged if he is exposed. Harry does not want to lead Olivia to the dark sides of the Nawab's life and hence he suspends the Gricean maxim of speaking the truth to save the Nawab's 'face'.

In this connection one observes that the Nawab himself takes recourse to telling a malevolent lie in his encounter with Olivia to save himself from defame and disgrace. This is how the encounter between the two proceeds:

> "Who were those men?"
>
> He didn't answer at once and when he did, it was with another question: Who do you think they were? He gave her one of his shrewd looks, then laughed? "I suppose you think they are bad men. You must have heard many stories I think, isn't it and you believe they are true." Again she felt she did not have to defend herself or answer him.
>
> "But if they are bad men," he went on, "I think they can't be so very bad because look what they have come here for." He pointed to the mound in the shrine on which some fresh garlands had just been laid and sticks of incense were still smouldering. "You see, they didn't come for any bad purpose but to pay their devotions." (133-34)

Once the Nawab drives Olivia to the shrine of Baba Firdaus. He leads her up the rocky path to Baba Firdaus' grove—the grove near the shrine of Baba Firdaus. As they enter the grove, Olivia sees some rough men emerging from the shrine. Olivia is shocked when they fall at the feet of the Nawab. The Nawab talks to them easily and in a familiar way. The Nawab dismisses them and calls her into the shrine. Eagerly she asks who those men are. The Nawab's reply to her question is a move to camouflage the truth from her. They are a gang of dacoits from whom he receives the commission for protecting them. They loot the people in the villages nearby at his instance. If he speaks the truth to her, the sky will collapse. The lie he tells Olivia is intended to save himself from being exposed. He points to the mound in the shrine on which the fresh garlands have just been laid. The non-verbal strategy he employs serves as an accessory to his false verbal reply. To save his 'positive face' a lie is very skillfully worded by the Nawab. Compared these three conversations, one could say that the lies told by Harry in the former two are "alter-centred" while the one in the latter by the Nawab is "self-centred/self-concerned."

In *Cry, the Peacock* the two central characters—Maya and Gautama—have been juxtaposed. The character of Maya has also been revealed through comparison with the other minor figures—Leila, Pom, Nila and Mrs. Lal. The novel deals with human relationships—man-woman relationship in particular. The novelist has used language very deftly to show how these characters negotiate their relationships. In a few situations, it could be observed that the characters contravene the maxim of speaking the truth to show their concern for other/s. In other words, the maxim of Quality is sacrificed for the sake of being polite/for saving other's face.

Mrs. Lal sacrifices the maxim in question in the following conversation with Maya:

> "Have you hurt yourself?" I asked her at last, for she seemed unable to recover what poise she might once have had.
>
> "No," she said, with surprising decisiveness and the line of her lips plunged downwards in a queer, her grimace of unutterable bitterness. "That was the accidental part of it," she said. (72)

Once Gautama takes Maya to a party hosted by Mr. and Mrs. Lal with the intention that going out would make Maya feel relaxed. While serving the food to the guests Mrs. Lal swings into her pot-bellied husband. She knocks aside his plate piled with rice and pickles. Finally, she hits her forehead against his chin. Maya asks her if she has hurt herself. Pat comes the reply "No" from Mrs. Lal. In fact, Mrs. Lal's head or perhaps her eye has been obviously hurt. Mrs. Lal her eye furiously till it gets red. Mrs. Lal deliberately tells a lie to Maya. Maya, Gautama, a prim lady and Harbans Singh, her husband are Mrs. Lal's guests. In Indian culture a guest is like God—*Atithee Devo Bhav*. People see to it that there is no harm and inconvenience caused to the guest/s. Care is taken to see to it that the guest's stay is comfortable and he is served good food/feast.

Mrs. Lal has obviously been hurt. She is unable to recover her poise/pose. Still she tells Maya that she has not been hurt. She suspends the maxim of speaking the truth. As a hostess she knows that if she shows that she has been hurt, it would make her guests uncomfortable. Suspending the maxim of speaking the truth is her expected strategy to minimize the physical cost and discomfort to her guests, in particular Maya. Her purpose is to be tactful and to make her guests feel comfortable. For these considerations Mrs. Lal does not hesitate to break the maxim of truthfulness.

On the same occasion Mrs. Lal sacrifices the maxim to save herself and her husband from disgrace. This is what happens between the Prim lady and Mrs. Lal:

> "Have you no *ayah*?" asked the orange-spotted lady, sipping orangeade.
>
> A purple flush suffused Mrs. Lal's face and neck. She stammered a little, glancing at her husband. "She does not stay here at night." She said. (70)

Mrs. Lal's small son trails into the dinning-room. He anchors himself to the sari of his mother. He whimpers softly and comes crab-wise to his mother. The orange-spotted Prim lady asks Mrs. Lal whether she has no *ayah* to look after her small child. Mrs. Lal glances at her husband and tells the lady that the *ayah* does not stay at night. The men and the women in the party try to show off their wealth. They attempt to air their social grace in their discourse with others. The Prim lady's intention is to degrade and ridicule Mrs. Lal. Mrs. Lal recognizes the intention and thus to save herself and her husband from disgrace in the presence of the guests she tells the lady that they do have an *ayah* and she does not stay at night. The truth is that Mr. and Mrs. Lal have no *ayah*. The appearance of their inner house itself is very disgusting. The mosquito nets are patched. The electric fan above their heads is not working properly. It revolves noisily. The vegetables for the party are colourless. The rice is cold and lumpy. Having an *ayah* and an air-conditioner are signs of being wealthy. To say that they have no *ayah* would be degrading for them (herself and her husband). To save herself and her husband from social disgrace in the presence of the guests Mrs. Lal suspends the maxim of truthfulness.

A lie comes handy as protective measure for Maya when the following talk between her and Gautama centers around the horoscope mentioned by Maya's brother, Arjuna in his letter:

> "But one thing does disturb me. You never explained it. What was that horoscope he wrote about? About which there was such a to-do in your household? Why?"

> And softly, softly the drums swept across the desert, stole through the dust. Softly...soft, soft, with care now, Maya with care.
>
> "Gautama" I stammered, stretching out my hands to him, without expecting him to touch them, not even desiring that touch. "Believe me, Gautama, I, do not remember." (150-51)

Maya's only brother, Arjuna has been disowned by her father. Arjuna has left his cozy home and been working in a canning factory in America. After many years he has addressed a letter to his dear, small stupid, silly sweet sister Maya. In it he has referred to the horoscope. According to the astrologer's horoscope one of them (Maya or Gautama) would die within four years of their marriage. Maya shows the letter to Gautama. Gautama is eager to know about the horoscope mentioned in Arjuna's letter. When he questions Maya about it, she hides the truth from him. She tells him that she does not remember the horoscope.

The novelistic context tells us that the horoscope is a solid fact of Maya's life. She knows that Gautama is unsentimental and utilitarian. She fears that if Gautama comes to know about the prophecy in the horoscope, he might put her to death. He might put her life in peril. She determines that Gautama should never know about the horoscope, not even guess about it. This consideration leads her to suspend the maxim of truthfulness. She, thus, tells a lie to save herself from impending danger. It could be said that Maya sacrifices the maxim for saving herself. Her deviation from the maxim is self-centred.

But this is only a partial truth. Observed at a deeper level the conversation also reveals Maya's concern for Gautama. She ponders, "Did he not love life too? It's problems? Their solutions, the method of solution" (151). As readers we know that Gautama is against the emotion of love. He argues that love loses its intensity in course of time. We also know that Maya constantly craves for love of her husband. On this occasion she seems to be thinking as much of her husband as of herself. Her consideration for Gautama leads her to suspend the maxim of truthfulness about the horoscope. Hence Prem Sagar (2000: 55) holds "It will be a folly off the mark if it is presumed that Maya had no love for her husband."

In *Socialite Evenings* and *The Binding Vine* too one observes that characters deviate from the maxim of speaking the truth for the sake of being polite to other/s. The world of *Socialite Evenings* is a world of difference. It is the world of socialites: actors, actresses, models and cinema producers and directors. This is the world in which the people's personal gains matter most. Hence one rarely comes across the deviation of the maxim which is 'alter-centred.' But one does come across an instance in which consideration for other leads one to tell a lie. This happens in the following interaction between Ritu and Karuna about her husband:

> "Sounds sleazy. Did your husband find out about this encounter?"
>
> "You bet he did. The minute he walked in I pounced on him. "So what are these flowers you are sending these days? They sure as hell aren't coming for me." He looked thrown for a minute and recovered fast enough to say, "You mean these? I'd sent them for Gloria and Peter's wedding anniversary. I'd also put your name on the card." (128-29)

Someone tells Ritu that her husband has an affair with a tartlet, a secretary somewhere. Ritu goes to the tartlet's office and asks her to leave her husband alone. When her husband gets home back, she inquires him about the affair. He tells her that he had sent the flowers to Gloria and Peter—his acquaintances—for their wedding anniversary. Ritu narrates this encounter to Karuna. It is clear that Ritu's husband does have an affair with the tartlet. When asked by Ritu about it, he is being untruthful. He is wise enough to understand Ritu's fury and thus to save himself from disgrace he does not hesitate to suspend the maxim of truthfulness. Reflecting about the lie from Ritu's husband one could say that the recourse he takes to telling lies is doubly motivated. He is already exposed but does not want the tartlet to be exposed and thus taken to task by Ritu. At a deeper level the maxim is suspended by him to save his 'positive face' and also that of the woman of immoral character. It could be stated further that Ritu's husband prefers to be a liar in order to save the tartlet. His deviation from the maxim is 'other-centred'.

In *Binding Vine* too the consideration of politeness overrides that of being linguistically cooperative. The two principal characters—Urmila and Shakutai—serve as protective cover for Kalpana—Shakutai's eldest daughter. Kalpana has been raped and she has been hanging between life and death in a hospital. Whenever the topic surfaces in the course of their interactions, Urmila and Shakutai suspend the maxim to camouflage the truth about rape. The following two instances reveal this strategy of Urmila and Shakutai respectively:

> "My daughter—my daughter" Shakutai's cry eddies around me.
>
> "What's the matter?" Inni asks.
>
> "Nothing." (30)
>
> "Malcolm, this is Shakutai, her daughter is patient here—tell him about it yourself, Shakutai."
>
> "What is wrong with your daughter?" Malcolm asks in a polite disinterest. He'll listen only because I've asked him to.
>
> "Shakutai falters, looks at me, finally says, "It was an accident." (169)

In the former case Urmila suspends from speaking the truth about Kalpana to her (Urmila's) mother Inni. In the latter it is the mother Shakutai who does this to save her daughter, Kalpana, from social disgrace. In the male-dominated Indian society the preservation of her character is the most important thing for a woman or a girl. The virtue of a woman or a girl is very often figuratively described as "a pot of glass"—a very delicate thing to preserve. People give utmost importance to preservation of character. Most of them have the conviction that "If wealth is lost, nothing is lost. If health is lost, something is lost. But if character is lost, everything is lost." This is truer about the character of a girl or of a woman whether married or unmarried. Even a suspicion about her character in the mind of people around her is necessarily damaging to her personality.

The truth is that Kalpana has been brutally raped by Prabhakar, the husband of Sulu, Shakutai's sister. Urmila, Shakutai, Dr. Bhaskar Jain, Vanaa—Urmila's sister-in-law—all know the truth. But it is a question of Kalpana's future, Sandhya's future (Kalpana's younger sister) and also that of Shakutai whose husband has already deserted her. To save Kalpana's and Shakutai's 'positive and negative faces' Urmila, Shakutai herself, Vanaa and Dr. Bhaskar Jain try to deviate from speaking truth. In the two instances above Urmila and Shakutai suspend the Quality maxim for socio-cultural and individual reasons. Put it pragmatically the Cooperative Principle is sacrificed by them to uphold that of Politeness.

3.5. Conclusion

In this chapter we have discussed how the Gricean maxim of Quality operates in the character-to-character-level conversations in the novels under study. A general observation is that characters in these novels deviate from being truthful on many occasions. The departures from this maxim fall into different categories: flouting, violating, opting out and suspending the maxim. Very rarely does one observe that the maxim is infringed by the characters. The non-observances of the maxim are highly motivated. They are both 'self-centred' and 'other-concerned.'

India is a multi-religious country. The scriptures teach us that telling a lie is a sin—*zooth bolana paap hai.* Despite the teaching of the scriptures characters pitted in the Indian socio-cultural background do not hesitate to break the maxim of truthfulness. Circumstances force them do so. They break the maxim by telling lies and being ironical. If a lie serves their communicative purpose/goal, the maxim in question is flouted or violated. The cases of opting out and suspending the maxim are particularly 'alter-centred'. The characters in these novels opt out of and suspend the maxim to save other/s from social disgrace and for maintaining their relationship with their fellow-beings. In a nutshell, lying, being ironical and exaggerating are the instances of deviating from this maxim. They are very important phenomena in terms of conveying conversational implicatures and being linguistically polite to others. Another important phenomenon in conversation is being relevant-making relevant contribution to the ongoing conversation. The next chapter discusses how the 'Relation maxim' is dealt with by the characters in the five selected novels.

4

Relation Maxim in the Five Novels

4.0. Preliminaries

By its very nature conversation is a multi-featured activity. It is a cooperative activity between speaker and listener. It is organized and this organisation is complex. The conversational organization has various devices that hold utterances in conversation together. Mention could be made of devices of conversation like topic and reference (anaphoric and cataphoric reference i.e. back-pointing and forward-pointing reference). Conversation is a cohesive activity—it has cohesion. There are ties that hold utterances together. The factors of cohesion are repetition, pronouns, ellipsis, substitution, tense-blend, etc. The apparently unconnected utterances in conversation have implied or underlying connection with each other/one another. For a conversation to be successful it has to have cohesion as well as observance of an unwritten agreement called cooperation. This is very important as Crystal (1997: 117) observes "The concepts and relationships expressed should be relevant to each other, thus enabling us to make plausible inferences about the underlying meaning."

In Gricean pragmatics there is a maxim of Relation to be followed by conversational partners. This helps the partners to interpret meaning as it is intended in conversation. The next section discusses and illustrates the Relation maxim with regard to the topic of conversation.

4.1. Relation Maxim and Conversation in Fiction

In its simplest form the maxim of Relation states: 'Be relevant' as you engage in conversation. This maxim demands that a conversational partner should make contribution which is related to/relevant to his/her co-locutor's utterances. This can be done by sticking to the topic of ongoing conversation. This maxim of Relation/Relevance is defined in a broader sense too. Leech (1983: 94) says "An utterance is relevant to a speech situation if U can be interpreted as contributing to the conversational goal/s of speaker or hearer." Making a contribution relevant to a speech situation implies holding on to the topic of the ongoing conversation. For Stenstrom (1994: 150) "The topic is what the speakers talk about". The speakers talking about something depends on a variety of factors: their relationship (formal/informal), their shared experience/ knowledge, their assumption and their cultural background(s). If a speaker and a listener have formal relationship, they use a pre-topic sequence-Greeting-Greeting and this follows the introduction of a topic. If they have an informal relationship and know each other well, they begin the conversation directly with a topic.

Talking about something is not as simple as it appears. It involves strategies called topical strategies. Broadly speaking the topical strategies are: introducing a topic, changing or shifting a topic, terminating a topic and resuming a topic. This implies that talking involves a lot of rituals. Introducing a topic is bringing a topic (new) in conversation. Changing or shifting a topic involves moving from the current topic to another topic. Terminating a topic is closing the topic or the entire conversation. Resuming a topic is a strategy of bringing back the old topic into conversation. As far as the Relation maxim is concerned, one observes that the maxim is followed by introducing a topic, developing it or elaborating it and resuming the old topic into the conversation. To follow this maxim is as Wardhough (1986: 292) comments "To link utterances together thematically." In other words it means making a contribution which is in consonance with that of the co-locutor. One has to provide a bit of information which has a contextual effect in a given context. For Sperber and Wilson (1986) an item of information or a contribution is relevant if it has a contextual effect in a given situation. An item of information or a contribution has contextual effect if it allows a derivation of a contextual implication. If a conversational partner apparently sticks to the topic of ongoing conversation, it helps the listener establish easily the relevance of the contribution. This is what happens in the following conversation from Anita Desai's novel, *The Village by the Sea*:

"All she said was "Lila, have the girls gone to school?"

"Yes."

"And Hari to the fields?"

"Yes, Hari to the fields "

"Then you must sweep and go to the market and cook, Lila"

"Yes, Ma," said Lila." (11)

This is a small talk between a village girl Lila and her mother in the village, Thul, on the western coast of India. Lila's mother has been ill for a long time. Lila's brother Hari brings the milk from a cowherd in the village. Lila makes tea and brings a tumbler of tea for her ill mother. Seeing Lila the mother asks her whether the girls—Bela and Kamal—have gone to school. Lila replies with 'yes.' When asked about Hari, she replies that he has gone to the fields. The mother asks Lila, to do the household chores and pat replies Lila "Yes, Ma." In the Gricean terminology all the replies from Lila are exactly relevant. Lila answers what her mother enquires. The mother's questions and Lila's answers fit explicitly into one another. One could also say that Lila observes not only the maxim of Relation but also those of Quantity, Quality and Manner. The flow of conversation runs smoothly. This helps Lila's mother interpret Lila's replies easily and carry on the conversation.

But one observes that not all utterances in conversation explicitly fit into each other. The conversational partner provides information/bits of information which is/are not connected to that of the speaker. In this case one is said to have deviated from this maxim in question. The goal behind doing so motivates the converser in being irrelevant. One thing very important in this respect is that if an utterance is irrelevant or disjointed, the interpretation process will grind to a halt and so may the very act of conversation. Of interest is to investigate why and how a co-locutor deviates from being relevant and what implication it has in the ongoing conversation. A couple of examples would help us to see how characters in fiction attempt to establish the relevance of apparently irrelevant responses.

Thorat (2000) cites a beautiful example of how fictional characters are irrelevant and there irrelevance generates implicature for the co-locutor. This is the encounter between Rahmat-Ullah Khan and Arun from Chaman Nahal's *Azadi:*

> "All right, we'll let that pass. But I was saying if you promise to bring her here one evening, I'll personally take you and your parents to the Jammu border in my jeep. You people will reach safely in less than half an hour."
>
> "I'm afraid I must leave, he said curtly and walked out of the room." (228)

The novelistic context tells one that Rahmat-Ullah Khan is a womanizer. He has evil designs about a woman Sunanda. In fact, he tells Arun freely that he likes this woman. In this conversation, he attempts to bribe Arun to procure Sunanda for him. Instead of replying 'yes' or 'no' Arun says 'I'm afraid I must leave.' In so far as Arun says neither 'yes' nor 'no' the maxim of Relation is flouted. His deviation implicates that he does not want to be a mediator between Khan and Sunanda and that he does not want to be an accomplice in Rahmat-Ullah Khan's seductive attempt on Sunanda. Arun's intention is to safeguard Sunanda from the clutches of debaucherous Rahmat-Ullah Khan. Khan understands Arun's implicature and eventually one day rapes Sunanda.

Let us take another example from an interesting story *The Apple* by H.G. Wells in an anthology *Popular Short Stories* edited by Board of Editors. In this story a character who is a stranger (his name has not been given) breaks the Relation maxim by beginning his conversation abruptly with Mr. Hinchcliff. This is how the conversation begins:

> "I must get rid of it," said the man in the corner of the carriage, abruptly breaking the silence. Mr. Hinchcliff looked up hearing imperfectly. He had been lost in the

> rapt contemplation of the college cap tied by string to his portmanteau handles—the outward and visible sign of his newly gained pedagogic position—in the rapt appreciation of the college cap and the pleasant anticipation it excited. Mr. Hinchcliff had just matriculated from London University and was going to be a junior assistant at the Holmwood Grammar School—a very enviable position. He stared across the carriage at his fellow traveller.
>
> "Why not give it away", said this person. "Give it away! Why not?"
>
> He was a tall, dark, sunburnt with a pale face. His arms were folded tightly and his feet were on the seat in front of him. He was pulling at black moustache. He stared hard at his toes.
>
> "Why not?" he said.
>
> Mr. Hinchcliff coughed.
>
> The stranger lifted his eyes—they were curious, dark grey eyes—and stared blankly at Mr. Hinchcliff for the best part of a minute perhaps. His expression grew to interest.
>
> "Yes", he said slowly. "Why not? And end it?"
>
> "I don't quite follow you, I'm afraid," said Mr. Hinchcliff with another cough. (60)

Mr. Hinchcliff has been appointed as an assistant teacher at Holmwood Grammar School. He is standing near a carriage going to Holmwood. His co-traveller, a stranger, begins to speak abruptly—"I must get rid of it". It is interesting to notice that there is no exchange of greeting between the two. There is no introduction. There is no small talk about weather and enquiry about each other's health. The stranger's utterances seem irrelevant to Mr. Hinchcliff. The stranger goes on saying—"I must get rid of it", "why not give it away?" and "why not?" The result is that Hinchcliff is unable to follow the stranger.

The stranger is irrelevant because he has been so much obsessed and restless since he purchased it (the fruit/the apple) from an Armenian man. He can neither throw it out nor eat it. He is afraid that if he eats the apple—the fruit of knowledge—

he would suffer what Adam and Eve suffered after eating the fruit in Eden. He won't be able to tolerate consequences of being a man of knowledge like Adam. Eating the fruit would bring about his Fall. This consideration makes him speak irrelevantly. It is only after a complaint from Hinchcliff that the stranger shows Hinchcliff a small, smooth, golden and yellow fruit. Even though the stranger is being irrelevant, Hinchcliff has a strong assumption of his cooperation. This leads him to complain that he does not follow the stranger. This in turn makes the stranger unravel how he got the fruit from an Armenian man. The stranger suspends the maxim of Relation. This sets the tone of the story.

In this section an attempt has been made to show how 'relevance' is an important aspect of utterance interpretation. The conversational partners are either straightforwardly relevant or deviate from being so. A strong assumption of cooperation and contextual background make the listener interpret what relevance the seemingly irrelevant utterance has in ongoing conversation. In the next section our concern is to investigate why and how the characters in the five novels deviate from this maxim and what semantic significance it has in the conversational and the novelistic contexts.

4.2. Relation Maxim in the Five Novels

The previous section is an attempt to define and illustrate the Gricean maxim of Relation in conversation. It has attempted to show how characters exploit the topical strategies. What is important is not to follow the maxim but to deviate from it. The departure from the maxim has thematic, character-revelation and intentional value. The following section deals exhaustively with the non-observance of Relation maxim in the novels under study.

Let's begin with *Temporary Answers*. At the very outset of the novel the protagonist Vineeta coincidently meets her friend Kishori on the pavement near Fergusson College Road. This is how the talk proceeds between the two:

> "How are you, Kishori?" I asked coolly, not able to express the friendliness I did not feel. The question was unnecessary.

> She looked radiant, happy and busy. If she had been pretty before, she was beautiful now.
>
> "You must come and see us sometime", she said. "And I don't mean it the way people usually do. You know, I say you must come sometime and you say yes and we both hope the sometime never comes."
>
> I felt a laugh bubbling up in my throat and reluctantly let it escape.
>
> "What about tomorrow evening," she said. "We are having some people over. Just an informal dinner."
>
> "Well, I don't really."
>
> She did not let me finish. She had already launched into detailed directions for getting to her flat.
>
> "You must come, I won't accept any excuses," she said. "Madhu would love to meet you." (2)

Seeing Kishori after several years Vineeta enquires how Kishori is. Instead of answering the question, Kishori states—"You must come and see us sometimes." Next, she invites Vineeta to a dinner at her flat the next evening. It is obvious that Kishori flouts the Relation maxim. What she implicates is that 'how she (Kishori) is', is immaterial. It is unnecessary for her to answer Vineeta's question. What is important is to invite Vineeta to a dinner at her flat. Kishori importunates Vineeta by using 'must' twice—'You must come and see us sometimes' and 'You must come. I won't accept any excuses'.

In this context Kishori's irrelevance in her conversational contribution seems to be motivated by her sense of guilt. Kishori has not bothered to come and condole Vineeta after the death of her husband Nagendra. As she happens to meet Vineeta, she intends to air her love for Vineeta. Hence, she would not answer Vineeta's question 'How are you, Kishori?' and she would not even let Vineeta put her excuse. 'Well, I don't really—.' Kishori also irrelevantly brings her husband Madhu in her conversation—Madhu would love to meet you." Kishori intends to hide the fact that she has been untouched by what has happened to Vineeta. It is more than obvious that various considerations make Kishori evade answering Vineeta's query and thus being irrelevant.

Vineeta, the protagonist, is also being irrelevant in her following conversation with Vilas:

> Vilas asked, "Is anything the matter?"
>
> "No."
>
> "You seemed preoccupied."
>
> I surprised myself by saying conversationally, "I met the author once." (32)

Once Abhijit Gokhale's play, *Phulpakhranche Pankha* was on at Balgandharva Theatre. Vineeta bought two tickets. She requested Vilas to accompany her to the theatre and he readily did. When the first Act was over, Vineeta and Vilas came outside. As they talked outside about the people who had come to see the play's performance, Vineeta was raking the audience. Vilas asked her why she was raking the audience and why she looked pre-occupied. Her reply was—"I met the author once". This reply is unrelated to his question. A moment's observation shows one that through her reply she intends to implicate—"she is pre-occupied with the thought of the author whom she met once a couple of months before." Her reference to the author of the play signals that she is raking the audience because she is eager to find out whether Abhijit is among the audience. It suggests how Vineeta has been fascinated by Abhijit she first met at Kishori's party. Abhijit is a tall, thin man with a slight stoop and glasses with a wide black frame, who has cast his spell on Vineeta in the first meeting.

One observes that Vineeta answers Vilas's first question with "No" and the second question by referring to the author of the play. Her fascination for the author Abhijit further underlines that she has started thinking of Abhijit as her prospective life partner. It is understandable why she unsolicitedly refers to Abhijit. After her husband Narendra has died, she is widow at thirties. Moreover, she cannot fit into her parents' household. Her mother and sister, Madhuri have constant bickering between them. They do the same things, they talk about the

and what he called them. By changing the topic abruptly, she deviates from maxim of Relation.

Douglas answers her three questions relevantly: he called them a pack of rogues, they like being told that in Hindustani and she must learn Hindustani to understand his deadly insults administered to the Indians. The question is—why does she change the topic? By not holding to the topic of their ongoing conversation Olivia implicates—"She is interested in knowing about Indians and her husband's attitude towards them." This is a part of her coming to India like other foreigners. Her topic-shift underlies her state of mind—state of excitement to know 'marvellous India'—as it happens with foreigners.

One is reminded of the author's own comments on the cycle through which the Westerners pass in India. Jhabvala (1971: 7) says, "First stage, tremendous enthusiasm—everything Indian marvelous; second stage, everything Indian not so marvelous; third stage, everything Indian abominable." Olivia has been in India several months now. But she has been unable to stand India's 'heat and dust.' Her stay in the Civil Lines Bungalow has been uneasy and suffocating for her in the absence of Douglas. Her departure from the topic of their conversation is a token of the fact that Olivia is in the 'first stage'. She is eager to know about India—her people. She has not adjusted yet to India and her society. A renowned critic of Indian English fiction Shahane (1976: 38) observes "Jhabvala is, of course, very much concerned with the problems of European men and women, trying to get adjusted to Indian society and its mores." In the ongoing conversation Indians and Douglas' attitude towards Indians are significant for Olivia and nor her soft, brown velvet cloth—perhaps a pet topic of conversation for females.

In the following exchange between Olivia and Douglas, it is Douglas who deviates from their ongoing topic:

> She cried, "Must you smoke that dashed *pipe*? In this *heat*?"
>
> He stayed calm, knocking ash into an ashtray carefully so as not to spill any on the table cloth. At last, he said, "You should have gone to Simla."

> "And do what? Take walks with Mrs. Crawford? Go to the same old boring dinner parties—oh, oh," She said, burying her face in despair, "One more of those and I'll lie down and die." (116-17)

One morning Olivia and Douglas took their breakfast and talked about Harry's health. As Douglas finished his breakfast, he now lighted his smoking pipe. Olivia saw him smoking the pipe and asked him if he must smoke the dashed pipe in this heat. Douglas was calm and carefully knocked the ash into the ashtray. Then, he came with a suggestion that Olivia should have gone to Simla (with her compatriots—Mrs. Crawford and Mrs. Minnies). This suggestion of his is not in consonance with her question and renders Douglas as being irrelevant in his reply. The flout of being relevant he commits has two implicatures: one—her concern for his not smoking is immaterial for him and two—he is deeply concerned with Olivia's going to Simla as she cannot stand the heat.

Circumstances help one to infer that Olivia is linking Douglas' smoking to his ability to conceive her—to make her pregnant. There is no doubt that she loves him deeply for his qualities—his solidness, his strength and his imperturbability. But feminine instinct flickers in her. She ponders what use is his solidness for her—he can't get her pregnant. Douglas fails to understand this. Even when she tells him explicitly that she is not getting pregnant and that she would like to consult Dr. Saunders, he just asks her to wait a while so that things will be all right for her. In the course of this exchange about a very delicate, sensitive and crucial topic Douglas reiterates his statement—"I wish you'd have gone to Simla" (118) and again deviates from sticking to the topic. He leaves for his duty. One learns that she looks not in the direction Douglas has left but towards the Palace of the Nawab. Thus, his failure to stick to and discuss a sensitive issue with Olivia has far reaching repercussions on their relationship. One learns later in the novel how detrimental this irrelevance proves—she is drawn towards the Nawab, gets pregnant from him, gets the baby aborted and he (Douglas) divorces her.

Let's see how Olivia herself departs from this Gricean maxim in her conversation with Harry on the same topic later:

> "Are you quite crazy?"
>
> "Douglas is terribly happy too. And making all sorts of plans. There is a christening robe in their family that was worked by some nuns in Goa. His sister has it at the moment—her littlest one was christened in it a couple of years ago at Quetta where they are stationed but Douglas is going to send for it. He says it's awfully pity.
>
> Cascades of white lace—very becoming to the Rivers' babies who are very very fair. Douglas says they all have white-blond hair till they are about twelve." (162)

Olivia goes so close to and becomes so intimate with the Nawab that she conceives—she becomes pregnant from him. She tells about it to the Nawab first and not Douglas. The Nawab is delighted with her pregnancy. Never does he doubt that the child is his. Olivia's feminine longing is going to be fulfilled. But what about Douglas? She comes to Harry's room in the palace to confide him. She has the Nawab on one side and Douglas on the other. She thinks to have an abortion and tells Harry about her thought. Harry is shocked and asks her whether she is crazy. Her question needs just 'yes' or 'no' from her. But Olivia relates to him Douglas' plans of christening his would-be baby. She refers to Douglas' sister, a christening robe and the English have white-blond hair till they grow twelve.

All this that Olivia tells him renders her reply irrelevant. She is blatantly irrelevant. She repeats the name of Douglas 'thrice' in her answer. It implicates—'she is worried about Douglas—his reaction to the baby if it is born with black hair.' She has seen that Indian babies are born with lot of black hair. The colour of her would-be baby's hair haunts her. There is another thing as Paul, P. (1993: 72) records "The physical features of the baby will tarnish her social image."

Olivia is a sentimental, idealistic and romantic woman by nature. She sways in her emotions. The Nawab boosts her ego and these qualities of hers. The irrelevant reply she gives Harry suggests that she is afraid of being exposed to her husband

Douglas Rivers. Her emotionalism has now started dissolving its own accord like sugar in water. It suggests that 'Douglas is in her mind' and that she is mentally disturbed. Her departure from the maxim of Relation speaks volume about her. It is altogether different that Harry comes to vouchsafe her and arranges her abortion by the Begum (the Nawab's mother) and her midwives.

The Indian Prince, the Nawab of Satipur in Pre-Independent India, has been skillfully sketched by Jhabvala. Olivia's falling for the Nawab sets the theme—'East meets West' or 'West meets East'. It is true that Olivia has high praise for the virtues of her husband Douglas Rivers. It is truer that in the Nawab's company she is just a victim of his magnetism. Frustrated with her husband she is drawn to the Nawab. She finds herself in a situation where 'she could not escape even if she wanted to' (137). Even though the Nawab succeeds in having intimacy with her, he seems to keep a lot of dark side of his personality under a carpet. However intimate he is to her, he tries to camouflage his secrets from her. This is what he does in his following conversation with Harry and Olivia:

> "She's been talking about the dacoits," Harry said.
>
> As the Nawab's eyes were at that moment so fully looking into hers she saw expression in them which he might normally have taken care to hide. And for a few seconds longer he searched her face. Then he turned away.
>
> He said in a mild voice: "I hope Olivia, whenever you wish to know something—if something is strange to you—that at such times you will ask not Harry, nor other person, but 'myself only.' He leaned forward:" who has spoken to you? What have they said? No, you must tell me. If you don't tell me, how can I defend myself against the slanders people may bring against me. You must give me this chance." (104)

It is obvious that Harry knows about the Nawab's nexus with a gang of dacoits and rioters. He wants the Nawab to unveil this truth to Olivia. When Harry asks the Nawab to relate her about the dacoits, the Nawab averts to do the same very skillfully. Rather he tries to take Olivia into confidence. He admonishes an innocent Olivia not to ask Harry if she wants to know something about him. He puts himself in the hands of Olivia and pleads her to commiserate him and give him a chance to justify his stand. A volley of questions he pours on her makes her speechless at the moment. There is a whole gamut of things about his nexus with the dacoits. He had associated himself with them. They had been rounded up by the police and all had been sentenced to death for murders, dacoities and loots. The Nawab had visited them in prison. He had also accompanied them to the place of their execution. Telling Olivia about this horrible and nauseating story of his association with the dacoits would certainly have shocked her and made her raise her eyes. The Nawab deploys his 'irrelevance' as a manoeuvre to save himself from shattering his image so far protected by Harry and himself. Thus, the Nawab suspends the maxim of Relation to save himself from self-incrimination.

He repeats this strategy to save himself from shame when Olivia sees this gang of rough and armed men on her visit to the shrine of Baba Firdaus with the Nawab on the occasion of the Husband's Wedding Day. When she asks him about these dacoits, he very deftly averts to tell her about his liaison with them. This is how the exchange between the Nawab and Olivia proceeds:

> "Do you really believe I'd do that," she said with such sincerity, indeed indignation—that he was satisfied with her. He respectfully touched her arm with his fingertips.
>
> "No, I don't believe," he said "And this is why I open my heart to you and tell you everything—don't think please that I want you to say only he is a very good person, a fine and noble soul. Not at all. Of course I would like to be a fine and noble soul—it is necessary for all of us to strive for this—but also I know how far I am from such a goal. Yes, very far indeed." He said and I looked discouraged. (134-35)

When Olivia and the Nawab entered the grove near the shrine, a gang of rough and armed men emerges from the shrine.

Looking at the Nawab they fall at his feet. He asks Olivia to sit under the tree and goes to talk to them familiar manner and easily. She observes how they stand in humility and with adoration before him. Then he dismisses them soon. Olivia asks him who these men are. He falsely tells her that they are holy men and have come to pay their devotion, pray and tell their wishes to Baba Firdaus. He persuades her to admit that she will not tell in Satipur that he is a bad person having nexus with outlaws and dacoits. The fact is that he is disheartened and digresses from the topic of his talk about being a fine and noble soul. He also irrelevantly points out the need for all of us becoming noble souls. Later in the conversation he drifts deftly from himself to his ancestor Amanullah Khan, relates her about Amanullah Khan's gories against the Mahrattas, the Rajputs or the Mughals or the British. All this he does to camouflage his nexus with dacoits.

Harry, a friend of Olivia and a guest of the Nawab also deviates from being relevant. Instead of sticking to the topic of their ongoing conversation—the Begum—he introduces the new topic—the Nawab's desire to go out to Mussoorie. The following is the conversation between Olivia and Harry:

> "Oh?" said Olivia, "Do you see her often?"
>
> Ever since the day Harry had pointed out that not being received in the purdah system was a discourtesy to Olivia, they had not mentioned the Begum. But Olivia was aware that Harry was received there on a footing of intimacy.
>
> "Every day," he said, "We play cards, she likes it." He changed the subject: "And the Nawab also says he is bored being here, so today everyone is packing." (142)

Olivia finds that she is pregnant. She decides to tell about her pregnancy to the Nawab first and not Douglas. She arrives in the palace early morning. She finds that everyone is packing. Harry is packing too. At the insistence of the Begum they were all going to Mussoorie for change of air. Olivia asks Harry whether he sees the Begum often. He replies relevantly that he sees the Begum every day. Instead of elaborating the topic—the

Begum-Harry changes the topic and relates that the Nawab is also accompanying them to Mussoorie.

This digression of the subject by Harry seems to be doubly motivated: One intention is to keep the topic of the Begum under carpet and divert Olivia's attention from the discriminatory treatment meted out to Olivia by the Begum. Another intention is to bring the Nawab in the focus. Harry wants to share his feelings with Olivia about the Nawab's present troubles: domestic and financial. The Khatm is bankrupt and Cabobpurians (the family of the Nawab's wife Sandy—her real name is Zahira) are threatening to bring a case about Sandy's dowry. Harry wants to equip Olivia about the dark and hidden sides of the Nawab's state of affairs. Put it briefly, Harry's digression of ongoing conversational topic implies his concern for Olivia. By referring to how he is received by the Begum with intimacy and how Olivia has not been introduced to the Begum yet, Harry does not want to offend and hurt Olivia. Hence, he opts out of the maxim of Relation.

We have already stated that *Cry, the Peacock* juxtaposes the two characters: Maya and Gautama—the wife and the husband respectively. We learn how their marriage is a fiasco as it is a mismatched one. They are the two beings with basically different attitude towards life and love. Most of the verbal encounters in the novel are between these two characters. Their encounters reveal how they fail to reciprocate with each other. One observes that very rarely do they become concerning and intimate to each other. A girl brought up 'princess-like' by her father. Maya yearns for Gautama's love and company. He, being cold intellect, thwarts her attempts to do so. There are changes in the topic of their conversation. They suggest how their relationship is sick and out of joint. In the following verbal exchanges one observes how the characters in the novel are being irrelevant:

> The first illustration of the conversation between Maya and Gautama shows how Maya blatantly deviates from the Relation maxim.
>
> He said, "Where would you like to go?' Darjeeling?"

> "Father would be there," I confessed and felt something spring up amidst my crushed spirits like fresh grass after rain. (42)

After her marriage with Gautama, Maya learns that not only Gautama but also the whole family of his—his mother, his father and his sister would talk on any topic but love and emotion. This makes her sad. She desires that she and Gautama would go away for the summer. She insists on going away just for a short holiday. Unwillingly he asks if she would like to go Darjeeling. Instead of saying 'yes' or 'no' Maya responds that her father would be there. The glaring implicature it generates is that: 'her father has a programme to go to Darjeeling.' The mention of her father's name is very comforting and equally exciting for her. This is because she retrospects how her father was doting and affectionate as against Gautama. The irrelevant utterance 'father would be there' by Maya is geared to express her hope that Gautama would say 'yes' and they would go away to Darjeeling. But Gautama is without is any excitement and sarcastically says that she can go to Darjeeling with her father. She *can* go but he (Gautama) would not.

Maya's father also ostensibly deviated from sticking to the topic in his talk with Maya when she was at Lucknow—her father's house. This was how the conversation between Maya and her father proceeded then:

> "Why was she wearing a dirty sari?" I ask him, still standing there clutching my toys. "She had not even done her hair," I add with displeasure equal to his for that crumpled garment, that strangling hair, those hot tears had been something shocking, something unsavoury to me, in the context of this flowering garden, the four mandarin trees, one in each corner, the folded white napkin on the starched white tablecloth. "She was a mess."
>
> Suddenly my father laughs. It is not a forced laugh as an older man's at a child, but laughter that comes naturally from a life that has as much room for love and pleasure as for order and discipline. He is delighted that I should have shown a share in his tastes, amused by my observation.

> He forgives me the blobs of broken fruit all over the lawn. "Come, let me see you," he says and waves aside newspaper that has arrived for him. "We shall see how high you can toss this orange." (46)

Saddened by her present life with Gautama, Maya takes shelter into her past. She recollects how she lived happily with her father before marrying Gautama. Her father narrated to her the glorious and bravado of Indian mythology, the lovely English and Irish fairy tales. Once, she and her father sat in the garden for breakfast. The servant announced that the cook would make orange marmalade. Using the small oranges Maya would play battledore and shuttlecock. Just then a woman with loose, strangling hair sobbingly stated that she would leave her husband, Sapru, immediately. Sapru was her father's friend. Her father sent Sapru's wife away in a gray car. Maya asked her father why that woman was wearing a dirty sari and why she had not done her hair. Her father only laughed and asked Maya to play battledore and shuttlecock with orange. He was interested in seeing how high she would toss the orange.

It is more than obvious that Maya's father blatantly produced an irrelevant utterance. His irrelevant utterance implicates that he cares more for his daughter than his friend's wife. It is geared to implicate that he takes pleasure in his daughter playing the game. He is in the situation in which he has to choose between carrying on the conversation about Sapru's wife of exhibiting his love for his daughter. He prefers the latter. His non-verbal action too—his waving aside the newspaper, which had arrived for him—suggests his preference for seeing his daughter playing. It is easy to gather that her father was a doting and affectionate father who would do anything for his motherless daughter. In the context of the novel this deviation from the maxim of Relation juxtaposes Maya's father and her husband Gautama and serves to highlight the contrast between the two.

Harbans Singh—the Prim lady's husband—also blatantly deviates from answering Gautama's question in the following talk:

> "Are they, Harbans?" murmured Gautama pointedly in a tune that would have destroyed to me.
>
> But the man continued unabashed. "Sometimes it helps to have a little guidance.
>
> Especially, women—they are less adventurous than us and they like to know in advance and prepare for it. Now, is that true or isn't it?" (79-80)

At the party hosted by Mr. and Mrs. Lal the guests pick up the topic of palmistry. Harbans Singh, the husband of the Prim lady, takes pride in having made prophecies about Gautama and the prophecies coming true. Gautama is a disbeliever and makes fun of palmistry. For him the patterns of the astral bodies—the earth, the ice and the rock or the lines formed in the hands of monkey or gorillas can have no influence upon the deeds and lives of men. Harbans reacts that Apes and monkeys know only how to eat and mate. But men's lives are more complicated than theirs. Gautama asks Harbans if they really are. The reply from Harbans is not in consonance with Gautama's query. He refers to the need of guidance in our lives—especially women. The irrelevance of his remark implicates his male superiority. His motive seems to get support for his assertion, especially from Maya. He realizes that Gautama won't be on his side and hence intends to test Maya's reaction for his viewpoint expressed in his utterance. Instead of answering Gautama's question in a word 'yes' Harbans attempts to convince Maya how prophecies direct us prepare in advance to face them if they are about misfortunes. His attempts to convince Maya of his viewpoint makes him deviate from answering Gautama's question relevantly. The readers know that Maya is scared of the topic of prophecy made by the astrologer because the term prophecy reminds her of the astrologer's prophecy about her and Gautama. She repeatedly states—"I don't know","I really don't know", "I don't know" in the course of their conversation to skip the topic.

The following exchange between Maya and Gautama is another instance showing the gulf between them as Gautama departs from being relevant:

> "I don't care! These old foggies need a bit of embarrassing—a bit of shaking up. All I wanted was to be outside—with you." I turned to look at him then. "Near you," I added and put out my hand to touch his cool white sleeve. "But you made me to go away," I breathed and drew back my hand without touching it.
>
> He sighed, fumbled, lit himself a cigarette as though he had not heard me at all, were no longer aware of me. The small flame of the match lit the cave of his cupped hand into a ruby grotto, then was flung away into the dark when a startled dog was silent and there was only the insignificant glow of the cigarette left. Then Gautama shifted.
>
> "He who is free from all attachments," he said softly, "and neither rejoices on receiving good nor is vexed on receiving evil, his wisdom is all established." (111)

Once Gautama has a party with his friends in the front lawn. They enjoy Urdu couplets and their music. Maya joins the party of leisurely gentlemen. She feels that the male chauvinism would not permit her share friendliness and is forced to leave the party. After a while Gautama enters her room. He brings with him the odour of cigars and whisky. He sits down on the steps beside Maya. His act of unprecedented indulgence excites in her an emotion of love. She craves for his love. Her desire for his love is rekindled with his indulging act. She tells him that she joined the party not for the old foggies—his friends but she wanted to be near him. But Gautama as we know is a wooden block-devoid of desire and emotion of love. Instead of responding to her love he begins to quote from the Gita and exhorts her. Taking the sustenance from the Gita he advises her not to be attached with the materialistic world.

According to Gautama the one who is free from attachment is wise and his wisdom is established. His preaching from the Gita to Maya, thus, renders his response irrelevant to her proposal of love. Nevertheless his ostensible deviation from the Relation maxim generates a truck load of implicatures for Maya. First, she understands his attempt to elevate himself onto superior plane. Second, his stoicism and third implicature is that Gautama is not a mind reader at all. He utterly fails to understand what she desires for from him in the circumstances.

The following is another instance of exchange between Maya and Gautama which helps us to understand Maya's psychological state:

> "You look hot. Why don't you drink lemon juice instead of tea?"
>
> "No, no, no. Where is the postman? Why won't he come? He *knows*, I am waiting so." I went to the window and raised the bamboo screen. The morning light struck me like a white—hot block of heavy metal. (128)

Maya has hardly slept the previous night. Gautama has brought a cat for Maya so that she loves it and be comfortable. As the cat is hot, Maya pushes the cat away. Gautama asks her to drink lemon juice instead of tea. The initial word 'no' used three times by Maya answers his question but what she queries then seems to have no relevance to his suggestions. Maya deviates from making relevant contribution. Her reference to the postman bringing a letter from her father suggests what is on her mind. Completely distressed by Gautama's indifference and lack of love for her, Maya turns mentally to her past, to her father. She is eager to hear from her father writing her about his plans for going to Darjeeling in the summer. Her reference to her father is a tip of an iceberg. Below it there is a heat of suffocation in her. It is strange that Gautama does not instantly ask her why she is waiting to hear from her father. Her apparent irrelevance suggests that she has some sort of premonition that she would receive a letter from someone/her father. It also implies that Maya and Gautama are a step forward in their separation from each other.

Maya again irrelevantly answers Gautama's question when reference to the horoscope in Arjuna's letter is made. This is how she does it:

> "Who was the letter from then?" he asked, settling back comfortably. He had had a good day in the courts, hence, his excellent mood.

> It embittered me further. "Here," I said and flung onto the table. (142)

Gautama returns from the court in the evening. He notices that a letter has finally come for Maya. As Gautama knows nothing about Arjuna—her brother, he is sure that it is from her father. Maya is utterly disappointed by the letter because if she refers to the horoscope from the astrologer. Gautama asks her who that letter is from. Maya replies that it is 'here' and flings it onto the table. In so doing she blatantly deviates from the maxim of Relation. Her motive is to avoid the reference to the letter—especially the horoscope that Arjuna has mentioned in his letter. We have already discussed elsewhere why Maya desires to camouflage the solid fact about the horoscope. It is only after Gautama's insistence on knowing who Arjuna is that Maya unshrouds her long lost brother to Gautama. Later she goes to the extent of feigning that she does not remember the horoscope at all—"Believe me, Gautama, I—I do not remember" (115).

Let's now examine how this maxim is exploited by characters in Shobha De's *Socialite Evenings*. In the previous chapter we have already pointed out that this is a novel with a new ideology of love, marriage, sex and family. The female characters in this novel are free talkers. They talk unhesitatingly on delicate and sensitive matters like love, sex and adultery. It is obvious that they freely explore the topic of their ongoing conversation—be it sex, love or adultery. One expects that there is no reason for them to avoid the topic or shifting from it abruptly. However, one comes across a few encounters in which they deviate from making relevant contributions or sticking to the topic. Some such encounters in *Socialite Evenings* are as follows:

> "Did you aim for his crotch or his head?"
>
> "I would have missed either—but what happen later was awful. He came at me like a maniac. First he pulled out leather belt from the trouser and then he stood over me with his eyes blazing. *Phatak*—I felt the leather on my arm and I was so stunned. I couldn't even scream. Before

I could open my mouth, it landed on my arm again. I lost my balance—I was sitting on the edge of the carpet. He was still standing at the same spot with his arm raised. Suddenly I felt a sharp kick in my side. And another one. Then I heard him say "shit! There goes my Ballyshoe." Can you believe it? Then he threw his belt away and started to slap me around. One hard hit cracked against my nose. Before I knew it, my favourite Anokhi dupatta was drenched in blood—my nose was like a geyser with blood gushing from it. May be it was the sight of all that blood that made him panic. He stopped and yanked my face up by the hair. "shit! I would better get a doctor. Is there any ice in the fridge?" I was still there under floor with the dupatta struck to my nose. Some of the blood fell on the carpet—the stains are still there. I walked to the kitchen slowly to get some ice. It was so unreal, the whole thing I went to the bathroom to wash my face. I was shocked out of my wits. The whole thing was swollen—twice its size. My eyes were beginning to puff and one side of the face was turning purple where it had got badly bruised. There were thick welts across my arms. But do you know something—I quite enjoyed the whole thing. You must think I am crazy. But really it was thrilling in its own way. Not the pain but the experience. He didn't look like a pipsqueak any more. I thought of Marlon Brando in *"A Streetcar Named Desire"*. Have you seen the film? You must." (129)

Ritu comes to know that her husband (his name has not been given) has an affair with a tartlet—a secretary somewhere. When he comes home, she talks him to task. Unable to control herself she grabs a huge vase and flings it at him. Karuna asks her if she aimed at his crotch or his head. It is more than obvious that Ritu deviates from the topic—how she took her husband to task. Karuna asks how she handled him. Ritu relates her how she got thrashed by him. Her reply is a picturesque and minute narration of how he handled and humbled her. Her reference to Marlon Brando in Tennessee William's play *A*

Streetcar Named Desire is a blatant departure from the Relation maxim in her reply to Karuna's query.

It underlines Ritu's love for getting thrashed. It shows that she loves it because she feels so much better after it. It leads to terrific sex-orgasms. Such beatings bring her and her husband closer. She respects him more as he looks macho in such moments. Ritu's romanticisation of getting thrashed has multiple implicatures and lessons for Karuna to learn: Ritu is chirpy sort of woman. She has no self-respect/dignity as such. Perhaps orgasm is the only thing that matters most for Ritu in her marriage.

Anjali, the protagonist Karuna's mentor, is also being irrelevant in her following encounter with Karuna:

> "Anjali, have you been reading Mirabai?" I asked her.
>
> "I knew you would say that. You have become so predictable. You girls haven't lived my life. You won't be able to understand what spiritual bliss is all about." (139)

After her marriage with Kumar Bhandari Anjali invites Karuna and Si to see her house. After serving them sumptuous meal Anjali leads them upstairs to her *pooja* room. As soon as they enter the room, Anjali bends down on her knees and she touches her forehead to the floor. She is lost in a trance for about a minute. When she raises her head, she tells Karuna and Si "I have found him and I am at peace at last" and points to the deity of Krishna installed in a shrine. Seeing this change in Anjali Karuna asks her if she has been reading a great saint Mirabai. Instead of answering Karuna's question Anjali gets excited and enraged at Karuna and exhorts them what spiritual bliss is about. Her reply is not in consonance with Karuna's question and thus Anjali ostensibly deviates from maxim of Relation.

Her deviation from the Relation maxim generates the implicature that—"Anjali has transformed from orgasm to spiritualism." It comes as a shock for both Karuna and Si that Anjali has developed a strange fascination for bhajans, mantras and prayers. Now to utter the four letter-word 'fuck' makes her impure. She gargles immediately if the word comes out by mistake. In fact, Karuna's intention in asking a question is to make mockery of Anjali. But Anjali is lost in the spiritual or religious ecstasy. For her it is Krishna who is far more significant than Mirabai. She even warns Krishna and Si—"I have Krishna with me constantly and nothing either of you says will affect me now" (139). Thus, her departure from being relevant reveals a new aspect of Anjali's personality for Karuna and Si.

Anjali blatantly breaks the maxim of Relation in her conversation with Karuna as the conversation centers around Anjali's husband—Kumar. It happens thus:

> "That's great. But don't overdo this trip. You know how disappointed you feel when things don't work out the way you've planned them?" But your temple is very beautiful. It smells lovely better than your Nina Ricci and I'm glad you've got this room to escape to when things get rough. We haven't really talked today. How are things between you and Kumar?
>
> "There is a lot to tell you—but I made a mistake. I shouldn't have asked Si to come here. I can feel her bad vibration everywhere. She spreads *paap* wherever she goes. She is so morally corrupt." (141)

In the course of her chatter Si makes some vulgar and cheap remarks about Anjali. Karuna asks Anjali to forgive Si for her misdemeanor. Karuna is intent on knowing about Anjali's life with Kumar and Bhandari. To persuade Anjali to answer her question Karuna first compliments Anjali by telling that her temple is very beautiful and that she has her pooja room to get solace when things get rough. Then Karuna asks her how the things are between her and her husband Kumar Bhandari. Anjali withholds what she wants to tell about Kumar. She takes Si to task instead—"She is morally corrupt." She spreads *paap* everywhere." Her pungent and blunt remark on Si is her strategy to evade answering Karuna's question. There is a lot she has to tell about Kumar. But she avoids doing it and turns on Si instead. In fact, there is no life (conjugal) as such between Anjali and Kumar. He is a homo and has kept a cute boy

Murty. He gives Murty presents from time to time—watches, shirts, shoes plus an extra allowance on his birthday. Anjali does not mind it as she is herself fed up with sex. Anjali does not intend to reveal these dark sides of Kumar's life—style. Thus, she deviates from answering Karuna's question relevantly by way of suspending the maxim.

Towards the end of this conversation Anjali again suspends the maxim as she averts to talk about Murty:

> "Why don't you send Murty? Might as well start the training programme—and what better way than to collect the Memsaab's chappals?"
>
> "You're horrid! But useful. Bye for now." She'd had the last word as usual. (150)

Anjali's life takes a new course after her marriage with Kumar Bhandari. He is delighted to allow her start the business of interior decoration in partnership with Mrs. Kripalani—once a movie star, now the wife of a producer. Anjali is a superstitious woman. She has fixed a good mahurat of Janmashtami celebration for launching the new venture. She has placed an order for new chappals to shoe-shop 'Joy'—to be put on the occasion. She requests Karuna to go there and pick up the chappals for her (Anjali). Karuna sarcastically remarks that it would be better for her to send Murty who might start the training programme (probably of sodomy) than collect the chappals for his Memsaab. Anjali does not even mention the name of Murty in her reply. Rather she remarks that Karuna is horrid but useful. She suspends the maxim of Relation. She is now in a totally different world, the world of spiritual bliss and the world of prayers, Lata Mangeshkar's *bhajans* and chanting the *mantras*. On thing is crystal clear. Anjali is no more interested in Kumar Bhandari and his liaison with Murty. The words 'sex' and 'orgasm' are as if not in her dictionary. Her body is fed up with these and the soul is searching. Further than this Anjali does not intend to carry on the topic—Kumar, his vile acts, Murty and their gizmos. And hence she hurries to say bye to Karuna.

Let's now investigate how the characters in *The Binding Vine* exploit the maxim in question in their conversation with one another. A perusal of this novel from the point of view of the Gricean framework particularly the maxim of Relation suggests that the characters like Shakuntala, Vanaa and Dr. Bhaskar Jain exploit the maxim on a few occasions to negotiate their relationships with others. In the following instance Shakuntala blatantly deviates from the maxim:

> "I move away, lifting the chair we over-turned when we moved the woman. Vanaa and the doctor hide her away from my view, but in a moment I hear her moaning.
>
> 'Will you drink some water?' Sit up, that's right."
>
> She drinks awkwardly, the water running down the sides of her mouth.
>
> "Do you feel better now?"
>
> The woman bursts into sobs, the painful sobs of one not used to cry. I can hear the words, 'my daughter', 'my Kalpana.' (57)

One day Urmila visits the hospital where her sister-in-law Vanaa works. As she enters the room, she sees Vanaa bending over a sobbing woman. A white-coated doctor Bhaskar Jain comes in with a glass of water. He offers the woman the glass of water and asks if she feels better after drinking water. The woman is Shakuntala. She only cries sobbingly 'my daughter', 'my Kalpana'. It is clear that she has not answered the doctor's question relevantly. She is flagrantly irrelevant. This generates the implicature for the doctor that "the woman (Shakuntala) is dying to know what has happened to her daughter Kalpana." He knows the truth—Kalpana has been brutally raped. It is understandable that the doctor calculates this intended implicature of Shakutai. To calm her down he appeals to her—"Don't think of it," (57) (don't think of what has happened to her).

Urmila's sister-in-law Vanaa flouts the maxim in her following conversation with Urmila. We quote below the conversation:

> "What a scene!" Vanaa exclaims. "What will Bhaskar think?"
>
> "That you live a normal family life, what else? How did he turn up?"
>
> "I was waiting for a taxi, you know how it is when you want one badly, there seem to be none. I was getting frantic when I saw him and asked him for a lift—you know Urmi there was a time when I wanted to get married, have children and look after my family. I thought that was happiness." (73)

Vanaa's daughter Pallavi is sick. Pallavi's sister Mandira and Urmila try to test her fever with a thermometer. Just then Vanaa returns from work. Bhaskar Jain also incidentally happens to visit Urmila. They have tea. Bhaskar suggests that Mandira should join him to go out and eat masala dosa. Vanaa hesitates to permit Mandira go with Bhaskar. But Mandira's face lights up. He reassures Vanaa that Mandira would be happy. Mandira joins Bhaskar despite Vanaa's reluctance. When Mandira and Bhaskar are gone, Vanaa asks Urmi what impression Bhaskar will gather about the relationship between Vanaa—the mother and Mandira—the daughter. Urmila replies that the mother and the daughter are living a normal life. Urmi then asks Vanaa how Bhaskar turned up all of a sudden. Vanaa explains how she happened to meet him and asked him for a lift. The latter part of Vanaa's reply refers to her theory of bringing up children and having happiness in life.

The preceding and the following context of the novel tells us why Vanaa refers to her desire to marry, have children and look after them and provides irrelevant bits of information. Mandira's resentment at her mother and her hatred for her (Vanaa) have hurt Vanaa. Even when Mandira went with Bhaskar, she avoided saying anything to her mother. How Bhaskar turned up is not material to Vanaa now but how Mandira has behaved with her is crucial to her. Hidden under her irrelevant reference to her desire to marry and have children is Vanaa's feeling of repentance to have done the same. Vanaa's reference to her theory of marrying and getting children may seem irrelevant. But broadly speaking it hints at one of the concerns of the novelist—the attitude of mothers to daughters and vice versa. The daughters are demanding and the working mothers like Vanaa fail to fulfil their demands. Urmila works out this implicature and is reminded of how she herself was kept away from her mother and sent away to Ranidurg to live with her Aju—her grandmother. At a deeper level Vanaa's deviation hints that she agonises over her children. It is a part of her being a mother taking parenthood seriously.

Dr. Bhaskar Jain tries to establish an intimacy with Urmila. In this attempt he abruptly changes the topic in the following exchange with Urmila:

> He picks up his tea, sniffs, "What is this?"
>
> "Lemon grass. Inni loves it. We grew it in a pot on our balcony."
>
> "It smells good."
>
> There is silence again. Then he puts cup down with determination.
>
> "I wish I'd known you before your Anusha died." (85-86)

Urmila is whiling on the beach and suddenly encounters Bhaskar Jain passing her. He offers her a lift in his car. Unwillingly she gets into it and he drops her at her house. She is intent on getting off him. But he looks at her expectantly and with ingenious curiosity. She asks him to come up and he agrees immediately. She gets him a cup of tea which has a mixture of tea powder and lemon grass. Bhaskar complements her saying—"It smells good." She remains silent. Then he blurts out—"I wish I'd known you before Anusha died." One could observe and state that he intently suspends the topic of their ongoing conversation (tea) and brings in that of her daughter Anu who has died. He is curious to establish rapport and a greater ease with her. The tea smells good but that does not count for him now. What is important for him is to commiserate and sympathise her. He wants to indicate that he shares her feelings of grief, shock and bitterness.

It may seem that he is intruding into an unsolicited area—her daughter—Anu and her death. But the wish he expresses to share her grief leads to establish a greater ease between them. She realizes he is neither awkward nor embarrassed. This paves the way for her to enquire him about what has happened to the girl—Kalpana—still in hospital. His deviation from the topic tea leads their conversation to the topic of her interest—Kalpana. This helps her feel at home and dare to ask him about Kalpana. Dr. Jain suspends the maxim of Relation purposefully.

One is reminded of one more occasion when Bhaskar Jain blatantly shifts the topic and answers irrelevantly. He does this in the following talk:

> "Well," I say at last feebly, with a laugh, but the laugh comes off more awkwardly than I'd intended. "What will your mother say?"
>
> "You never speak of your husband." (161)

Bhaskar is solicitous and determined. He realizes that Urmila does not respond to his insinuation—his zest for her. He directly invites her to his home for lunch. After the lunch he is on the drive to drop her. He tells her that his mother wants him to get married with a sweet, homely, fair and convent-educated girl. But he obliquely asserts that he has fallen in love with a dark, sharp-tongued married woman. Urmila recovers that this description relates to her. She is taken unawares. She asks him what his mother would say of his love for her (Urmila)—a married woman with a six-year-old son. He goes on to accuse her "You never speak of your husband" and thus departs from the topic—his mother's reaction to his proposal. It implicates that "What his mother would say does not bother him. Urmila has to tell him about her husband—whether she loves him." Urmila readily calculates the intended implicature and counter-questions—"Should I?" (161).

We know that Bhaskar has so far suppressed his desire. He cannot hold it up now. He straightforwardly forces her to tell him about her marriage, her husband and her love for her husband. He asserts a moment later—'it is the most important thing to me right now' (161). His blatant deviation from answering her question, thus, projects him in a new role for her—that of a lover.

Shakuntala, the other suffering woman in the novel, goes about chastising Urmila and departs from the Relation maxim. This happens in one exchange as follows:

> "What is wrong with lipstick, Shakutai?"
>
> "You don't understand Urmila, it is not only the lipstick. Here the boys are like—they are like dogs panting after bitches. And if you paint and flaunt yourself, do you think they'll leave you alone? Ever since Kalpana grew up, I have had to live this fear. But Kalpana does not understand. Once she started earning, she thought she could do what she wanted." (146)

Urmila meets Shakutai at her home to take stock of the situation about Kalpana. Shakutai shows her Kalpana's photographs taken with her friend Madhuri. Kalpana had applied lipstick for being photographed. The conventional typical Indian mother Shakutai had exhorted Kalpana to wipe off the lipstick but Kalpana had gone without replying to her mother. Urmila is a modern woman. For her applying lipstick is a sign of one being in her adulthood. She asks Shakutai what is wrong in using lipstick. Shakutai replies figuratively. Lipstick does not mean just applying a cosmetic to beautify oneself. It means a girl is making herself a bitch and inviting the boys—the dogs—to follow her. It means inviting an assault from boys and inviting amorous glances from boys/men. Shakutai goes on to relate how Kalpana was simply unaware of impending danger and she (Shakutai) has been under fear for Kalpana since Kalpana grew up. The later part of Shakutai's reply also implicates how an adult daughter—Kalpana was slipping out of her mother's hands. It underlines Shakutai, the mother's, cry of rage and despair over Kalpana's behavior as she started earning. Urmila's question to Shakutai is a rhetorical question and its connotation is that there is nothing wrong by an adult girl applying lipstick. For Urmila the word 'lipstick' has positive semantic load. Shakutai's reply suggests that for her the word has derogatory meanings.

In this section an attempt has been made to investigate how the characters in these novels deal with the maxim of Relation.

Gricean maxims are characteristically subject to deviation—flouting, violating, suspending, opting out and infringing. This section has focused on why and how the characters deviate from the maxim. The number of instances of departures from the maxim clarify that the characters in the novels do not infringe this maxim due to physical impairment and inadequate linguistic command. It only signals that the deviations from the maxim are highly motivated. The deviations reveal their personality traits and are symptomatic of their broken relationships as well as their attempts to further their relationships. The section that follows attempts to analyse how this maxim conflicts/clashes with other maxims of Cooperative Principle.

4.3. Relation Maxim and the Other Maxims of Cooperative Principle

It has already been discussed that the maxims are the guidelines for conducting conversation. They assist one convey information efficiently and effectively. Analysis of conversation within the framework of these maxims reveals that people can convey more by deviating from the maxim/s than by following them to their letter. The situations in which conversation takes place are infinite. People face problems of choice of linguistic form—register, address term, and pronouns. They choose a linguistic form according to their motivation/goal—conversational goal as well as social goal. Just as they face such problems of linguistic choice, they also face the situation in which it is necessary to withhold the information they possesses, to tell the things for which they have no evidence, to introduce a new topic in the ongoing conversation and to be vague or indirect. In Gricean parlance they are forced to deviate from the maxim of verbal cooperation. They face a situation of what Burt (2002: 993) defines "Maxim confluence-a situation in which two maxims enjoin the same linguistic behavior on the part of the speaker." Put it in simple terms they come across a situation in which they either follow or break a maxim at the cost of the other in the same conversation.

This section attempts to analyse such instances of conversation in which the Relation maxim is contravened either to follow or break other maxim/s—Quantity, Quality and Manner. The focus here is on why the characters in the novels deviate from the Relation maxim and whether the consideration of being informative, truthful and clear has something to do with the deviation.

In *Temporary Answers* one comes across a few verbal exchanges in which the Relation maxim enjoins the other maxims. The protagonist Vineeta faces a situation—whether to be informative, to be truthful or to be clear—in the following conversation:

> Vilas said, "Is anything the matter?"
>
> "No."
>
> "You seemed pre-occupied?"
>
> I surprised myself by saying conversationally, "I met the author once." (32)

Vilas and Vineeta are outside the Balgandharva Theatre after the first Act of Abhijit Gokhale's play is over. They stand near the coffee-house counter. Vineeta is raking the audience. Vilas asks her if there is any matter that she is raking the audience. Vineeta's reply is "No". On being asked why she looked pre-occupied, she replies that she met the author Abhijit once. It is clear that Vineeta is disappointed by the fact that the author has not come to see the fiftieth show of his play. Hoping to find him she is raking the audience. Through her reply "No" to Vilas's first question she is being untruthful. By being so she intends to hide her search for Abhijit. Admitting the truth would invite other question from Vilas about Abhijit—where and how she met Abhijit and she is eager to see him. Her second reply—"I met the author once" appears irrelevant to his question. But it has some relevance to convey—she is pre-occupied with the thoughts of Abhijit.

Vineeta faces the situation in which she has to decide whether to be truthful and relevant. She decides to deviate from being both. She is a widow in her thirties. Hope lies in her to find her prospective partner in Abhijit. But she has already started whiling her time with Vilas—spending evening with him, going out for a movie or a play and going to his house for lunch. She enjoys being with him. There is another prospect that she might fall for Vilas. She has met Abhijit months before and he has not bothered to contact her. Here is Vilas with whom she is being close. She fears that speaking the truth to Vilas about Abhijit might take Vilas away from her. These considerations lead her to be untruthful and irrelevant.

The following are two more exchanges between Vineeta and Abhijit in which the Relation maxim enjoins the other maxim:

> "Don't you like your work?"
>
> "I like the fact that I am doing it. It gives me a little self-respect which is very important to me just now. Without it I couldn't continue living at peace with myself. But it troubles me that I didn't go into this line of work because I have any particular sense of dedication. It was not a matter of a positive choice at all. I got good marks in S.S.C. and took science rather than arts because it was the prevailing idea than the better students took science. Then I went to medical college because I had sufficient marks to get in. So now I am a doctor because I have to earn a living and medicine is the only thing I am trained at. Not a good enough reason." (51-52)
>
> "What are you thinking about?" Abhijit said, he voice suddenly gentle.
>
> I shook my head. Nothing. Nothing that needed to be shared with him. He took me in his arms but it awoke no desire in me because I felt none in him.
>
> I said, "When do you plan to leave?" (161)

In the former exchange we have Vineeta and Abhijit spending evening on the hill behind Fergusson College. She asks him how she goes on with his work of writing. He enquires her whether she likes her present work as an honorary doctor. His 'yes/no' question should have been answered by Vineeta by saying "Yes/No". But she pours in information about her schooling, her college and the present work. It is more than obvious that Vineeta has flouted not only the maxim of being informative but also that of being relevant. Had she been neither more nor less informative, it would not have helped her convey the implicature—"she has had no choice in her education and in her career." Her move is to provide unsolicited and irrelevant bits of information to create proximity with him, confide the truth of her life and possibly arouse his sympathy for her.

In the latter exchange Abhijit asks her what she is thinking about and she enquires him when he plans to leave/get away. He has decided to get away alone for a couple of weeks for self-renewal. She offers to join him but he squarely rejects it. This has stung, bruised and humiliated her. This has made her learn to look inside herself. She had hoped for a future with him and here she is betrayed. She has a bitter lesson to learn that even people who love each other feel the need to get away from each other. The whole gamut of thoughts is simmering within her. On being asked what she is thinking about she just shakes her head pointing 'nothing'. She asks him when he plans to get away. Putting aside her torture and travail she asks him about his planning for outing. It is a ray of hope that Abhijit would propose her one day that seems to force her being untruthful, under informative and deviate from answering his question relevantly. In the next section on 'Relation maxim and politeness concern' we will elaborate a little more why Vineeta sacrifices the three maxims—Quantity, Quality and Relation.

Let's now turn to the "maxim confluence" in *Heat and Dust.* A close perusal of verbal encounters between the characters in this novel excitingly reveals that the characters face the situation in which they have to decide whether to follow the Gricean maxims or deviate from them, which to follow and which to deviate from. The following instances illustrate this interesting interplay of maxims. Here is the first instance:

> She cried, "Must you smoke that dashed *pipe*? In this *heat*?" His stayed calm, knocking ash into an ashtray-carefully, so as not to spill any on the table cloth. At last he said, "You should have gone to Simla." (116)

One morning Douglas took his breakfast and lit his smoking pipe. He started puffing at it slowly. Olivia had loved him for his English solidness, strength and his manliness. Still she grieved over his inability to make her pregnant. She seems to have linked his inability to impregnate her with smoking in this unbearable heat. In fact, this is her rhetorical question which implies that he (Douglas) must not smoke. Instead of answering her question relevantly he suggests that she should have gone to Simla with Mrs. Crawford and Mrs. Minnies. Thus, he is blatantly irrelevant. At a deeper level Olivia's appeal to him not to smoke in this heat leads him to infer that she herself is unable to bear the heat. It would have been better for her, had she gone to Simla to enjoy the cool climate there. His flout from being relevant implicates two things: One—Olivia need not worry about him in this heat (he can stand the summer heat as well as the heat of the pipe) and two—he cares for her. His concern for her leads him to flout the maxim of Quantity and that of Relation—sticking to the topic—his smoking.

The Nawab faces the situation in which he has to decide whether to be requiredly informative or stick to the ongoing topic. This happens in the following talk with Olivia:

> "Do you believe I'd do that", she said with such sincerity—indeed with indignation—that he was satisfied with her. He respectfully touched her arms with his fingertips.
>
> "No, I don't believe," he said, "And this is why I open my heart to and tell you everything—Don't think please that I want you to say only he is a good person, a fine and noble soul. Not at all. Of course I would like to be a fine and noble soul—it is necessary for all of us to strive for this—but I also know how far I am from such a goal. Yes, very far indeed," he said and looked discouraged. (134-35)

The Nawab takes Olivia to the shrine of Baba Firdaus. As they enter the grove, Olivia sees some rough men emerging from the shrine. They see the Nawab and fall at his feet with humility and a look of adoration. He too looks familiar with them. On being asked who those men are, he tells her that they are holy men and have come to pay their devotions to the shrine. He repeatedly implores her not to tell in Satipur that the Nawab is a bad person liaisoning with the dacoits. She asks him if he believes that she would do that. The Nawab replies that he does not and goes on to relate to her that he believes in her and hence tells her everything about him. In fact he desires to be a fine and noble soul. He also points out to her that it is necessary for all of us to try to be noble and fine.

In his rumbling talk the Nawab is over-informative, tells a lie that he tells her everything and irrelevantly stresses the need for all of us to be noble and fine. In fact "No, I don't believe" would have sufficed to answer her question. But his goal at the moment is to save himself from self-incrimination and save his positive face-desire to be liked and admired by Olivia. He attempts to convince her that he is sincere at heart. He pitiably tries to drive away every possible trace of doubt in her mind about his nexus with the outlaws—the dacoits. To divert her attention from the topic—the dacoits—the Nawab suspends all the three maxims—of being informative, being truthful and being relevant.

In *Cry, the Peacock* one comes across a number of occasions in which the norm of being relevant is broken by characters. This is their deliberate and calculated move either to evade the topic of ongoing conversation or to achieve their current conversational goal. The characters face the situation in which they have to decide whether to be informative as required by co-locutor, to be truthful and to be relevant or not. Let's see how they behave linguistically in such exchanges.

The following is a conversation between Gautama and Maya. Maya asks him if they would go away for the summer. She insists that he get away with her just for a short holiday. Without any excitement and with indignation he asks her where she would like to go. The conversation proceeds as follows:

> He said, "Where would you like to go? Darjeeling?"
>
> "Father would be there," I confessed and felt something spring up amidst my crushed spirits, like fresh grass after grain. (42)

Maya genuinely wishes that they should get away for the summer together. Gautama is intent on not doing so. He is rather ready to let her go with her father and manage without her. But when insisted on getting away, he enquires if she would like to go to

Darjeeling. Maya replies him that her father would be there. In fact, "Yes" or "No" would have been an expected reply from Maya. But she refers to her father's being at Darjeeling. She has to decide whether to answer him as required. If she says "Yes", Gautama would perhaps be ready to get away. If she says "No", he would take it as a chance to cancel instantly their getting away. She withholds 'yes'/'no' and produces the utterance—'father would be there' instead. It is geared to articulate her hope that Gautama would be ready to join her father. Hopefulness prompts her to withhold—'yes'/'no' and refer to her father's programme of going to Darjeeling.

Her father also faces the situation of maxim-confluence/ maxim clash in the following conversation:

> "Why was she wearing a dirty sari?" I ask him still standing there, clutching my toys. "She had not even done her hair," I said, with displeasure equal to his, for that crumbled garment, that straggling hair, those hot tears had been something shocking, something unsavouring to me, in the context of this flowering garden, the four mandarin trees, one in each corner, the folded white napkin on the starched white tablecloth. "She was a mess."
>
> Suddenly my father laughs. It is not a forced laugh as an older man's at a child, but laughter that comes naturally from a life that has as much room for love and for pleasure as for order and discipline. He is delighted that I should have shown a share in his fastidious tastes, amused by my observations. He forgets me the blobs of broken fruit all over the lawn. "Come, let me see you play," he says and waves aside the newspaper that has arrived for him. "We shall see how high you can toss this orange." (46)

Maya recalls how she spent her princess-like life with her father in Lucknow. Once she and her father sat in the garden for breakfast. Just then Maya saw a woman in a dirty sari and undone hair. The woman was Sapru's wife—the wife of her father's friend Sapru. The woman announced that she would leave her husband immediately. Maya looked at her and asked her father why the woman had a dirty sari and why she had not done her hair. Maya's father laughed and replied, "Come, let me see you play. We shall see how high you can toss the orange." He faced the dilemma whether to answer the question why Sapru's wife wore a dirty sari and why her hair was undone or to hide the reality from Maya. His reply is not in consonance with Maya's question. Thus, he flagrantly deviates from giving required information and carrying on the topic—Sapru's wife. It obviously implicates that he cares more for his daughter than for his friend's wife. A man living a life of love and pleasure her father intends to take pleasure in his daughter playing shuttlecock and battledore with orange. Further at a deeper level it makes Maya to recover the implicature that "her father was an affectionate and a doting father." He deviates from the maxim to protect his daughter from unpleasant realities of life.

We have already analysed in the previous section another situation of maxim confluence/clash in which Harbans Singh, the Prim lady's husband, flouts both the maxims—Quantity and Relation—while answering Gautama's question at Mrs. Lal's party. He sacrifices these maxims to hint at his male superiority and galvanise Maya's support for his assertion that our lives are more complicated than those of Apes and monkeys.

Shobha De has emerged as a pioneering writer as she is the first Indian woman novelist who tries to shatter the traditional ideology of marriage, family and sex. Hence, she claims as Surendran (1992) observes "To be among the first to explore the world of the urban woman in India." She seems boldly determined to tear down the patriarchal social structure of India. In this effort of hers language becomes a very powerful and deadly weapon to marginalize the male characters in her novels, particularly *Socialite Evenings*. De has as Swain (2000: 135) observes "The technique of manipulating language in order to deconstruct the male ego." The women in De's novel assert themselves boldly and unhesitantly. In this fit of theirs the norm of conversation—being relevant to the ongoing conversation—is blatantly broken by them.

A couple of instances would help clarify this technique of manipulation of language by women characters to assert themselves. The first instance of verbal exchange between Karuna and Anjali is follows:

> "Anjali, have you been reading Mirabai?" I asked her. "I knew you would say that. You won't be able to understand what spiritual bliss is all about." (139)

The setting of this verbal exchange is Anjali's *pooja* room. As Anjali and Karuna enter Anjali's pooja room, Anjali bends down on her knees and touches her forehead to the floor. She is lost in a trance of a minute. When she raises her head, she utters, "I am at peace at last." She points to an exquisite image of Krishna in the shrine of the *pooja* room. Karuna is surprised by this transformation of Anjali and her air of spiritualism. She sarcastically asks Anjali whether she has been reading a well-known religious poetess Mirabai. In her heightened state of trance Anjali replies that Karuna has not lived her (Anjali's spiritual) life and hence won't understand what spiritual bliss is about. In giving this reply she is being ostensibly over-informative and irrelevant. The reply does not even mention the name Mirabai. It conspicuously implicates that Anjali has transformed into a religious-minded devotee and she is on a higher plane that her counterparts—Karuna (and Si). She has now found a wonderful power in religion. Karuna initially fails to recover this implicature. Her relationship with Anjali in the past forces her not to accept the implicature generated. Anjali cracks on Karuna and asserts—'nothing either of you says will affect me now. I have Krishnaji with me constantly' (139). Karuna gets at what Anjali has intended when Karuna says—'All this is marvelous, my dear' (140). Faced with the clash of being informative and sticking to Karuna's question, Anjali sacrifices both to counter-attack Karuna's sarcasm.

The following is another instance in which the maxims of being informative, being relevant and being clear enjoin:

> "That's great. But don't overdo this trip. You know how disappointed you feel when things don't work out the way you've planned them. But your temple is very beautiful. It smells lovely—better than your Nina Ricci and I'm glad you've got this room to escape to when things get rough.

> We haven't really talked today. How are things between you and Kumar?"
>
> "There's a lot to tell you—but I made a mistake. I shouldn't have asked Si to come here. I can feel her bad vibrations everywhere. She spreads *paap* wherever she goes. She is so morally corrupt." (141)

Si and Karuna sarcastically make fun of Anjali's taking to religion as non-sense and rubbish. Karuna is intent on knowing how the nuptial life between Anjali and Kumar is going on. She first praises Anjali's temple and the lovely smell in the *pooja* room. Taking her into confidence Karuna asks her about the things between her and her husband. The presence of Si makes her not to divulge the facts about Kumar. The pungent and cheap remarks from Si excite Anjali and she pours her venom on Si—"she spreads *paap* everywhere. She is morally corrupt." Anjali understands that telling them (Karuna and Si) about her private life with Kumar would be like putting a key of a wardrobe in the hands of a thief. It would make Si more pungent in her remarks about Anjali. Instead of answering Karuna's question as required and relevantly Anjali serves the deadly blows to Si. Put in Gricean terms—Anjali withholds what she knows, is being irrelevant but is clear, succinct and brief in her attack on Si.

In *The Binding Vine* too one observes that the maxim of Relation clashes with that of Quality. Shakuntala faces the clash between being informative and being relevant in the following conversational piece:

> "Will you drink some water? Sit up, that's better."
>
> She drinks awkwardly, the running down the sides of her mouth.
>
> "Do you feel better now?"
>
> The woman bursts into sobs, the painful sobs of one not used to crying. I can hear the words, "My daughter," "My Kalpana." (57)

The one who asks questions is a white-coated doctor Bhaskar Jain. The one who deviates from answering his questions is Shakuntala—the mother of Kalpana. Kalpana has been hospitalized after being brutally raped. Bhaskar Jain offers Shakuntala water and asks whether she feels better after having it. Shakuntala's sobby reply is—"My daughter", "My Kalpana." Shakuntala has either to answer the doctor's question or to express her concern for her daughter. She naturally prefers the latter. Thus, she flouts the maxim of giving information and that of Relation. Taken in the Indian social context it is quite understandable why Shakuntala flouts both the norms of conversation. The flout implicates the mental state and feelings of a typical Indian mother.

This section has attempted to illustrate how the maxim of Relation conflicts with other maxims of Cooperative Principle. One general observation which emerges is that it is sometimes difficult to demarcate the non-observance of Quantity maxim and that of Relation. Characters deviate generally from both these maxims in the same verbal encounter. The next section is concerned with the maxim of Relation and the concern for being polite to other.

4.4. Relation Maxim and the Politeness Concern in the Five Novels

In the second and third chapter we have discussed that the Gricean maxims of Quantity and Quality are sacrificed by characters in the novels for preserving the other's face and being polite to other. Pragmaticists claim that one of the motivations for deviating from the Cooperative Principle is to be considerate and polite to other. This claim applies to some of the departures of the maxim of Relation too in the five selected novels. In this section an attempt has been made to investigate how the characters break the maxim of Relation to show their politeness concern to other/s.

In *Temporary Answers* the characters do not follow the Relation maxim on a number of occasions. Their contributions are not in consonance with the topic of the conversation underway. Nevertheless, their attempt at being irrelevant is deliberate and has some semantic import for the co-locutor to gather. On a couple of occasions the protagonist Vineeta behaves as follows:

> "What are you thinking about?" Abhijit said, his voice suddenly gentle. I shook my head. Nothing. Nothing that needed to be shared with him. He took me in his arms but it awoke no desire in me because I felt none in him. I said, "When do you plan to leave?" (161)

Abhijit has decided to go away for a couple of weeks. This is for his spiritual renewal and for restoring his faith in himself. Vineeta wishes to accompany him at least for a part of his going out. He squarely tells her that he is going away alone. Vineeta feels sick. The sky falls on her. It makes her crest-fallen. A host of thoughts arise in her mind—Couldn't he achieve mental and spiritual space through her? How has she been a fool enough to offer to go with him? Is she a cripple? On being asked by Abhijit what she is thinking about she shakes her head and asks him when he is planning to leave. Her question is explicitly unrelated to his question. She attempts to be considerate to him. She allows him freedom to go away without her. It is for him—his spiritual and mental renewal and peace that she suppresses her bruises. Telling him her thoughts would have hurt him and perhaps deprived him of pleasure and freedom of going away alone. Putting aside what is simmering in her, Vineeta enquires him about his plan to leave. Thus, she opts out of the Relation maxim in reply to his question. Once rejected squarely she does not want to impose herself on him. She deviates from answering his question for his sake.

In the following final exchange too Vineeta shifts the topic of her conversation with Abhijit:

> "What happened to your forehead?" I asked.
>
> "A hailstone hit me," he laughed.
>
> A laugh from him was a lovely sound. I must be able to hear it always.
>
> I said, "Abhijit, do you understand? You must go away. You must leave me deal with my problems in my own way. You must trust me." (173)

Abhijit turns up one night and knocks at her door. As she opens the door, she finds him wearing a raincoat. She begins speaking with him in anger. He reacts—"Don't talk like this, Vineeta, I love you" (172). He comes closer. She finds a red weal on his forehead. She asks him what happened to his forehead. Laughingly he replies "A hailstone hit me." Instead of holding on to this she begins to chastise him saying—"You must go away. You must trust me." It might seem an act of impoliteness on her part not to ask him about his bruise/weal. At a deeper level she lets him to be free. In fact, this is a chance for her to decide to accept his love and marry him. Instead, she offers him the freedom to leave her. She lives in the society which has accepted widow marriage in practice. She gives him the option to accept or not to accept her. Perhaps, she is sure he will give her his hands. Borate (1993: 234) expertly comments "She has not lost hope completely. The answers she has received may have been temporary, but she is certainly looking forward to a panacea." In pragmatic terms Vineeta deviates from sticking to Abhijit's reply and thus opts out of the Relation maxim to be negatively polite to him.

In *Heat and Dust*, the characters give irrelevant responses in a number of their verbal encounters. Some of these deviations from being relevant are 'self-centered' while others are 'alter-centered'. The motivation for being irrelevant is obviously to show concern for the others. This is what the principal characters like Douglas, Harry and Olivia do in the following conversations. Let's begin with how and why Douglas Rivers deviates from the maxim in the following conversation:

> She cried, "Must you smoke that dashed *pipe*? In this *heat*?" He stayed calm, knocking ash into an ashtray—carefully so as not to spill any on the tablecloth. At last he said, "You should have gone to Simla." (116)

Douglas has developed the habit of smoking pipe and that too in the unbearable heat. Olivia is unable to stand the heat. One morning when Douglas starts smoking the pipe, Olivia asks him if he must smoke the pipe in this heat. Instead of replying to her in the affirmative or negative, he suggests her that she should have gone Simla with her compatriots Mrs. Crawford and Mrs. Minnies. This suggestion is not in consonance with her question and thus Douglas flouts the maxim of Relation. It has two glaring implicatures: one—her concern for his smoking is immaterial for him and two—he is deeply concerned with her going to Simla, a pleasant and cool place to stay during the Indian summer. He reiterates this concern for her "I wish, you'd have gone to Simla" (118). In the context of this conversation it is more than obvious that Douglas is being irrelevant. He is so because of his consideration and concern for her. His departure from being relevant is an act of 'self-neglecting' and 'other-caring.'

The Nawab's guest and Olivia's friend Harry too opts out of this maxim. This is to save Olivia from being offended and hurt. This consideration leads him to abruptly change the topic of ongoing talk with Olivia:

> "Oh" said Olivia. "Do you see her often?"
>
> Ever since the day Harry had pointed out that not being received in the purdah quarters was a discourtesy to Olivia, they had not mentioned the Begum. But Olivia was aware that Harry was received there on a footing of intimacy.
>
> "Every day," he said, "we play cards, she likes it." He changed the subject: "And the Nawab also says he is bored being here, so everyone is packing." (142)

When Olivia gets pregnant from the Nawab, she decides to tell about it to the Nawab first and not her husband Douglas. As she arrives in the palace, she notices that everyone is packing. Harry is packing too. She asks Harry why they are packing. He informs her that they are going to Mussoorie at the insistence of the Begum for the change of air. On being asked if he sees the Begum often, Harry replies that he sees the Begum every day. Without elaborating the topic—the Begum—Harry irrelevantly reports that the Nawab is also bored being at the Khatm. In so doing he deviates from the Relation maxim. This is his doubly motivated act. His one intention is to keep the topic of the Begum under carpet and divert Olivia's attention from the discriminatory treatment that the Begum has meted out to him and to Olivia. By elaborating how he is received by the Begum with intimacy and Olivia has not been introduced to the Begum yet, Harry does not intend to hurt Olivia. His other intention is to bring the Nawab in the focus. He intends to insinuate to Olivia about the domestic and financial troubles of the Nawab. Both these motivations make Harry to brush aside the topic of Begum and bring in the Nawab in their talk. The abrupt change in the topic of their talk is, thus, an act of his consideration for her. Already not introduced to the Begum by the Nawab Harry does not wish to add salt to her (Olivia's) injury.

Olivia is ostensibly irrelevant in her reply to Harry's following question:

> "Are you quite crazy?"
>
> "Douglas is terribly happy too. And making all sorts of plans. There is a christening robe in their family that was worked by some nuns in Goa. His sister has it at the moment—her littlest one was christened in it a couple of years ago, at Quetta where they were stationed. But now Douglas is going to send for it. He says it is awfully pretty. Cascades of white lace—very becoming to the Rivers' babies who are very very fair. Douglas says they all have white-blond hair till they are about twelve." (162)

Since the time Olivia has conceived from the Nawab, she has been restless and in mental turmoil. She comes to Harry to confide to him this fact. The fact is that her maternal instinct is going to be fulfilled. But the problem is with the colour of the baby's hair. She knows that the Indian babies are born with lot of black hair. As it would be the Nawab's child, what would be Douglas's reaction if the baby is born with black hair. She is thinking to get the foetus aborted. But this thought irritates Harry. He asks if she is crazy to get the foetus aborted. His question needs 'yes' or 'no' from her. But she relates him about Douglas' plan of christening her would-be baby. She refers to Douglas' sister, the christening robe and the English babies having white-blond hair till they are about twelve. All this information she pours makes her reply blatantly unrelated to Harry's question.

Olivia's blatant deviation from the Relation maxim implicates that "Douglas is in her mind," she is worried about Douglas—"what would be his reaction if the baby is born with black hair". It would also tarnish her image. It seems that her irrelevance is 'self-centered'. But one could say that at a deeper level—she is concerned not only about Douglas—her husband but also about the Nawab. The flout of the Relation maxim she commits, thus, unravels what is going on in her mind.

One observes about the above instances of deviation from the Relation maxim that the act of deviation is motivated by concern of politeness for the other. Being irrelevant is a strategy that the characters like Douglas, Harry and Olivia use to reveal their concern to be considerate to and to save the other's face. By way of general observation one could state that they engage in verbal interaction with their compatriot and through it they try to protect other.

Anita Desai uses the technique of character-juxtaposition in *Cry, the Peacock*. We observe the character-juxtaposition like Maya-Gautama, Maya's father—Gautama and Maya-Pom-Leila. All these character-pairs help one study, the human relationships—father-daughter, husband-wife and friend-friend relationships. One of the basic social functions of language is to consolidate these relationships. Language is a tool of nurturing such relationship. Looked at from pragmatic point of view one observes that characters sacrifice the principle of cooperation its attendant maxim to maintain their relationship. This applies to the maxim of Relation too. One comes across a couple of verbal interactions in which the concern for the other takes the front seat.

Married to cold and frigid Gautama Maya is frequently reminded of her pre-marriage life with her father. She had no mother and her father brought her up 'princess-like.' Her father would not say 'no' to any of her demands. There were servants who would bring the breakfast out into the flower-beds of their garden. Her father loved her intensely. His intense love for his daughter is revealed when he responds irrelevantly to Maya in the following talk:

> "Why was she wearing a dirty sari?" I ask him, still standing there, clutching my toys. "She hadn't even done her hair," I add, displeasure equal to his, for that crumpled garment, that straggling hair, those hot tears had been something unsavoury to me, in the context of this flowering garden, the four mandarin trees, one in each corner, the folded whit napkin on the starched white table-cloth, "She was a mess."
>
> Suddenly my father laughs. It is not a forced laugh as an older man's at a child but laughter that comes naturally from a life that has as much room for love and pleasure as for order and discipline. He is delighted that I should have a share in his fastidious taste, amused by my observations. He forgives me the blobs of broken fruit all over the lawn.
>
> "Come, let me see you play," he says and waves aside the newspaper that has arrived for him. "We shall see how high you can toss this orange." (46)

Maya recollects how her father brought her up 'princess-like', how he told her the fantastic stories of the Arabian Nights and of princes, regal queens, jackals and tigers. Once they sat for breakfast in the garden. The servant began to collect the orange into a bowl. Maya played battledore-and-shuttlecock using the small bright oranges as shuttlecock. Just then a woman—the wife of Sapru—the friend of her father-sank in the chair and sobbed that she would leave her husband Sapru immediately. Her father sent her away in the large grey car. Maya asked her father why she wore a dirty sari and why her hair was undone. Her father blatantly evaded to talk about the woman and irrelevantly asked Maya to play the battledore and shuttlecock. This ostensibly irrelevant response from her father implicates that 'he cares for his daughter'. It reveals his concern and his love for his daughter. In other words it implicates that her father is a doting and an affectionate father for whom nobody is more important at the moment than his daughter. In fact, he is displeased with Sapru's wife. But to please his daughter Sapru's wife is completely thrown out of his response to Maya.

The marriage between Maya and Gautama is a mismatch. They are the Poles apart in many respects. The reference to a prophecy in her brother Arjuna's letter to Maya gives her nightmares or hallucination. This gives her fierce headaches. In this state she hears the sounds of the dancer's drums. The rhythm of the drums pounds in her ears. She is unable to bear the painful sound. She begs to Gautama, "Stop them, tell them, tell them to stop" (151). Then follows this exchange between the two:

> "What to stop?" Gautama queried, looking up from his book with a face as detached as a mask.
>
> "The drums," I complained once, weakly and then, in horror, was silent, for Gautama must not know. There'd be new dangers then, greater dangers. Secret, Secret all my own.
>
> "Why not go away for a holiday?" he said that night. (152)

Maya is unable to bear the sound of the dancer's drums in her state of fierce headache. She begs her husband to stop the drums. As the convalescent calm follows, Maya searches for the dancer but finds that the dancer has gone. Gautama is busy reading his book. He looks up from the book and queries, "What to stop?" Maya replies—"The drums." Instead of going into the details of the dancer's drums—their painful sound-rhythm, Gautama asks her "Why not go away for a holiday?" He understands that Maya is ill. Hence, he does not intend to cling to the topic—the drums—their painful sound/rhythm. Instead he proposes that she should go away for a holiday with her father, wherever her father goes. Maya refers to the 'drums', Gautama refers to 'her father'. An unexpected change in the topic by Gautama underlines his concerns for her—to make her feel comfortable. The consideration he shows for her serves as "an oasis in a desert."

The world of *Socialite Evenings* is the world of difference. It portrays a new and astounding ideology of love, sex, marriage and family. It seems that everybody in this world is concerned with his desire and intentions. It is the world of gossips, extra-marital affairs and scandals. We have analyzed how language becomes a very crucial and critical weapon of making and marring relationships. The people in this Muppyland break the

Gricean norms of verbal cooperation. They employ the strategies of being over-informative and under-informative, lying and of being irrelevant. Our concern here is with their being irrelevant for the sake of others. This happens with Karuna's one time mentor Anjali in her following conversation with Karuna:

> "That's great. But don't overdo this trip. You know how disappointed you feel when things don't work out the way you've planned them? But your temple is very beautiful. It smells lovely better than your Nina Ricci and I'm glad you've got this room to escape to when things get rough. We haven't really talked today. How are things between you and Kumar?" "There's a lot to tell you—but I made a mistake. I shouldn't have asked Si to come here. I can feel her bad vibrations everywhere. She spreads *paap* wherever she goes. She is so morally corrupt." (141)

It is more than obvious that Karuna asks Anjali about her nuptial life with Kumar Bhandari and Anjali tells Karuna about Si. This is because Si has been rather ridiculous of Anjali—her bhajans, mantras and prayers. She is still unable to swallow that Anjali has transformed into being religious and spiritual. Si passes vulgar and cheap remarks about Anjali. Hence when Karuna asks Anjali about her married life with Kumar, she tells Karuna about Si—her bad vibrations, her *paap* and her moral cooperation. More than this Anjali intends to hide the dark sides of Kumar. He is a homo and has kept a cute boy Murty. He has three wives. The first one keeps out of Kumar's way. The other one has left Kumar for the present but has left her photographs, clothes, records, cosmetics and shoes in Kumar's house. Anjali is his third wife. He has been so attentive and generous to Anjali. He doesn't mind on her spending lavishly on furnishing and *mandir*. In the presence of chatty Si Anjali doesn't want to disclose these secrets about Kumar and damage his 'face'—his image. Hence, she suspends the maxim of Relation for the sake of her husband.

Anjali again suspends the maxim of Relation when reference to Murty is made by Karuna in the following exchange:

> "Why don't you send Murty? Might as well start the training programme—and what better way to collect the memsaab's *chappals*?"
>
> "You're horrid! But useful. Bye for now." She'd the last word as usual. (150)

Anjali has placed an order for six *chappals* to the shoe-shop-Joy. She wants Karuna to go and pick up the *chappals* for her. She requests Karuna to do so. Karuna suggests that it would be better for Anjali to send Murty. He might not only collect the *chappals* for his Memsaab but also start the training programme (of sodomy). This remark of Karuna is sarcastic. In her reply Anjali avoids even to mention the name of Murty. Instead of talking about Murty she describes Karuna as horrid but useful and hurries to say bye to Karuna. This strategy of Anjali is motivated by her intention to save Murty. Anjali knows that talking about Murty inevitably leads to talking about Kumar—her husband. She is fed up with fuck-shuck and talking about it. She does not want Murty (and Kumar) to be exposed about their gizmos and buggerings. For that will damage Murty's positive face-desire to be liked. It will bring a kind of disgrace for him. To save his 'face' and him from disgrace Anjali suspends to carry on the topic—Murty.

Shashi Deshpande's *The Binding Vine* deals with a sensitive and delicate issue of rape (in the case of Kalpana) and marital-rape (in the case of Urmila's mother-in-law, Mira). In the Indian socio-cultural context nothing is more damaging to a woman than to be raped and exposed. This happens to Kalpana and Mira. Being raped brings an unbearable agony, disgrace and trauma for a woman. This is why the characters in this novel avoid carrying on the topic-rape-in their verbal exchanges. They avoid the topic or change the topic. Their talk becomes irrelevant. Dr. Bhaskar Jain, Shakuntala and Vanaa are irrelevant in their encounters with their conversational partners. In the following conversation with Urmila, Dr. Bhaskar Jain changes the topic and suspends the Relation maxim:

> He picks up his tea, sniffs. "What's this?" "Lemon grass. Inni loves it. We grow it in a pot in your balcony."

"It smells good."

There is silence again. Then he puts his cup down with determination.

"I wish I'd known you before your Anusha died." (85-86)

Urmila offers Dr. Bhaskar Jain a cup of tea. The tea has a mixture of tea powder and lemon grass. Bhaskar compliments by saying that the tea smells good. Then he suspends the ongoing topic—the tea—and brings in that of Urmila's daughter Anusha who has died. It may seem that he is intruding into an unsolicited area—Anu and her death. But at the moment Bhaskar's intention is to commiserate and sympathise with Urmila. The good smelling tea is not important for him. He also intends to share her feelings of grief, shock and bitterness. These considerations make him suspend the topic of tea and refer to Anu. Dr. Bhaskar Jain, thus, suspends the Relation maxim to be polite to her via being sympathetic to her.

4.5. Conclusion

In this chapter, we have attempted a threadbare and piecemeal analysis of deviations from the Relation maxim by the characters in the five novels. It is observed that these characters deal with this maxim in the ways like flouting, suspending and opting out. They employ the strategy of being irrelevant for fulfilling functions like obtaining some advantages for the self, maintaining their relationship with their interlocutor and asserting their viewpoint. Another significant observation is that their departures from the maxim reveal their state of mind—what is on their mind. When they face the clash between being relevant, being truthful and being brief or clear, situations force them to sacrifice all these maxims.

One of the motivations for them to be irrelevant is to show their concern for the other—to be polite to other/s. Their attempts at being irrelevant could be seen as acts of 'self-neglecting' and 'other-caring'. Put it in other words they give irrelevant responses to protect their interlocutor's face and to save them from social disgrace/defame. Irrelevance, thus, emerges as a significant and remarkable strategy in fictional conversation.

In the present novels characters do this by abruptly changing the topic of their ongoing conversation. Very rarely does one observe them using hedges—"by the way", "what else", "what about", "well", or "let me tell you"—to signal topic change. They interpret their interlocutor's irrelevance as having some relevance in the context of their conversation. They recognize what Taylor and Cameron (1987: 93) call "A continuum of degrees of relevance for instance between the extremes of the completely irrelevant and completely relevant." The Cooperative Principle is a way/norm of conveying information efficiently. One can convey what s/he wants to convey in a clear or in an ambiguous way. This is what the Manner maxim is about. The next chapter takes up how the Manner maxim is exploited by the characters in the novels under study.

5

Manner Maxim in the Five Novels

5.0. Preliminaries

Language performs a variety of functions. It is used for serving an infinite number of purposes. Linguists propose different functions of language. Halliday (1973) distinguishes between the Micro-functions and the Macro-functions of language. In his opinion Micro-functions refer to particular individual uses whereas Macro-functions are related to larger and general purposes of language use. Roman Jakobson suggests such six functions of language as emotive, informative, poetic, metalingual, phatic and directive. One can go on adding terms and labels used for functions of language. The point is that all the linguists agree that the most important and basic of all is the informative/communicative function. We need language to communicate our thoughts, experiences and attitudes to others and we need language to understand what others communicate to us. As far as communication is concerned, there are two main aspects: what to communicate? and how to communicate? The 'how' refers to the manner of communication. In Gricean Pragmatics there is a norm or maxim that guides our conversation and that is the Maxim of Manner. The next section discusses this maxim and how it operates in conversation particularly in fictional conversation.

5.1. Manner Maxim and Conversation in Fiction

The Gricean Maxim of Manner demands that the conversational partners are clear, brief and orderly. They have to avoid ambiguity or vagueness and present their ideas or messages in orderly and logical manner. As it seems it demands heavily from the conversational partners about 'how' they have to say what they have to say. It is easier said than done because it is inevitable for the conversers to use words which have more than one meaning. This phenomenon of polysemy adds to the ambiguity in language use. Ambiguity is an aspect of language about which philosophers and linguists have divergent views. The early twentieth century philosopher Bertrand Russell took ambiguity as a deficiency or defect in language. He is said to have proposed to refine language and create an ideal one. Finch (2003: 23) on the other hand claims that "We need language at times to be imprecise and rather vague." Whatever the divergent views philosophers and linguists hold, one cannot deny that on occasions people are vague, prolix and indirect or circumlocutory.

What is indirectness in the first place? Indirectness is as Weizman (1989: 73) defines "Not just as a lack of transparency, such as with the use of unusual words or ambiguous deictic references, but as lack of transparency specifically and intentionally employed by the speaker to convey a meaning which differed, in some way, from the utterance." This lack of transparency reflects in the use of lexical items with more than one meaning, in constructing lengthy sentences, in using euphemistic expressions, deictic terms and proverbs. In English for example there are many words with more than one meaning that cause the difficulty in the process of interpretation on the part of listener. Mention could be made of some such words like post, ring, spring, minute, charge, present and wind. The catchword 'mouse' in the field of computer may lead to misunderstanding if the listener is not acquainted with the field. But all said and done, ambiguity or vagueness and indirectness are inevitable parts of language. J. Thomas (1995: 119) claims that "Indirectness is a universal phenomenon: as far as we know it occurs in all natural languages." People employ the strategy of being indirect for making their language more interesting, increasing the effect of their message and for being polite to the other/to protect the face of the other.

Grice's proposal of the Cooperative Principle and its attendant maxims is geared towards efficient conveying of information. To accomplish this task it is necessary that the conversational partners follow this maxim: 'be clear, brief and orderly'. Agreeing with Grice, Rai and Rai (2003: 128) state "To be clear is to be efficient, but unfortunately, few people take the trouble to be clear." The question is—how to achieve clarity and follow this maxim? Achieving clarity in conversation involves a lot of rituals. The Gricean Maxim demands that the conversational patterns achieve clarity and brevity as they engage in verbal interaction. One can be clear by using simple and short sentences, using simple and everyday words, giving concrete details with names and figures, using punctuation marks like comma and full-stop and presenting one's ideas in a logical sequence. Being brief implies expressing one's idea or message by avoiding superfluous words and details and preferring single words to windy phrases.

Let us take an illustration of the following exchange between a student and a teacher:

> Student: When should I submit the Project Report, Sir?
>
> Teacher: I would appreciate receiving the report as early as possible as arrangements have to be made to send the marksheet so that it will reach the university within the stipulated time.

A moment's observation would tell one that the teacher is rather windy and vague. S/he can be clear and brief by keeping in mind the above-mentioned factors that help achieve clarity. S/he would better say:

> "Please submit the Project Report by 15th March so that we can send the marksheet to the university by 20th March."

The words and phrases—I would appreciate, receiving and arrangement—can be deleted. S/he can also avoid the vague phrases like 'as early as possible' and 'within the stipulated time' and replace them 'by 15th March' and 'by 20th March' which give definite and concrete details. This in the Gricean terminology would help the teacher converse in effective manner.

It would also save the efforts of interpretation on the part of the student.

Now let us turn to the concern of this section—Manner Maxim and Conversation in Fiction. Some experts in the field of literary appreciation and interpretation argue that the Cooperative Principle cannot be applied to the interpretation of literature particularly fiction. Cook (1994) argues that the questions of being informative, truthful, relevant and clear are unhelpful in the interpretation of literature. This is because fictional discourse has no practical or social function. It is not concerned merely with effective conveying of information. The literary discourse has the crucial functions—change our mental representation of the world and refresh our schemata, our pre-existing knowledge structures, and encyclopaedic knowledge, our knowledge of language and textual structure. One could argue that the Cooperative Principle and its attendant maxims are the tools which help one explain how the literary texts can be processed and how one can arrive at interpretation of literary texts. It follows that like the maxims of Quantity, Quality and Relation the Manner maxim can be used as a tool to guide our reading and interpretation of literary works particularly fiction. What is important is to see how the fictional characters deviate from this maxim. As E. Black (2006: 31) suggests "Any kind of deviation from a maxim may be significant."

A couple of examples would help see how conversation in fiction can be interpreted by looking at the deviation from the Manner maxim. The first example is from Dickens' *Great Expectations*. The following is a conversation among Pip, Mr. Jaggers and Wemmick. It is quoted *in extenso* as follows:

> Mr. Jaggers nodded his head retrospectively two or three times and actually drew a sigh. "Pip," said he, "we won't talk about poor dreams; you know more about such things than I, having much fresher experience of that kind. But no about this other matter. I'll put a case to you. Mind! I admit nothing." He waited for me to declare that I quite understand that he expressly said that he admitted nothing. "Now, Pip," said Mr. Jaggers, "Put this case. Put the

case that a woman, under such circumstance as you have mentioned, held her child concealed and was obliged to communicate to fact to her legal adviser, on his representing to her that he must know, with an eye to the latitude of his defence, how the fact stood about that child. Put the case that at the same time held a trust to find a child for an eccentric rich lady to adopt and bring up".

"I follow you, Sir".

"Put the case that he lived in an atmosphere of evil and that all he saw of children was, their being generated in great numbers for certain destruction. Put the case that he often saw children solemnly tried at a criminal bar, where they were held up to be seen; put the case that he habitually knew of their being imprisoned, whipped, transported, neglected, cast out, qualified in all ways for the hangman, and growing up to be hanged. Put the case that pretty high all the children he saw in his daily business life, he had reason to look upon as so much spawn, to develop into the fish that were to come to his net—to be prosecuted, defended, forsworn, made orphans, bedeviled somehow."

"I follow you sir".

"Put the case, Pip, that there was one pretty little child out of the heap, who could be saved; whom the father believed dead and dared make no stir about; as to whom, over the mother, the legal adviser had this power: I know what you did and how you did it. You came so and so, this was your manner of attack and this was the manner of resistance, you went so and so, you did such and such things to divert suspicion. I have tracked you through it all, and I tell it you all. Part with the child, unless it should be necessary to produce to clear you, and then it shall be produced. Give the child into my hands, and I will do my best to bring you off. If you are saved, your child is saved too; if you are lost your child is still saved. Put the case that this was done and that the woman was cleared."

"I understand you perfectly."

"But that I make no admissions?"

"That you make no admissions." And Wemmick repeated, "No admissions."

"I put the case, Pip, that passion and terror of death had a little shaken the woman's intellects, and that when she was set at liberty, she was scared out of the ways of the world and went to him to be shattered. Put the case that he took her in, and that he kept down the old wild violent nature whenever he saw an inkling of its breaking out, by asserting his power over her in the old way. Do you comprehend the imaginary case?"

"Quite".

"Put the case that the child grew up, and was married for money. That the mother was still living. That the father was still living. That the mother and the father unknown to one another, were dwelling within so many miles, furlongs, yards if you like, of one another. That the secret was still a secret, except that you had got wind of it. Put the last case to yourself very carefully."

"I do". (424-25)

Pip—the hero of the novel—had a dinner at the home of Jaggers—a lawyer in London and a mediator between Pip and Pip's unknown benefactor. After the dinner Pip and Wemmick—Jaggers' clerk walked some distance together. Pip had seen during the dinner that the fingers of Estella—a girl adopted by Miss Havisham and the fingers of Molly—Mr. Jaggers' housekeeper—resembled greatly. He had doubted whether Molly was Estella's mother. During the walk he requested Wemmick to tell him about Molly. Wemmick told that twenty years before Molly had been convicted for murder and her case was conducted by Jaggers. He had acquitted her and since then she had been living with Jaggers as his housekeeper. Her daughter Estella had been adopted by Miss Havisham through Jaggers. Estella's father, Magwitch was also a convict.

Pip wanted to verify these facts from Jaggers. With this 'theme' in his mind he comes to Jaggers. He requests Jaggers to be frank and talk about Estella and her parentage. Jaggers then discloses the facts and whereabouts of Molly, her daughter—Estella and her husband. He does this in an oblique and circumlocutory manner. He even does not mention the names—Molly, Estella and Abel Magwitch. For Molly he uses the phrase—'a woman'. He substitutes the name of Estella with—'child' and 'one pretty little child.' He employs the phrase—'an eccentric rich lady' for Miss Havisham. For Molly and Abel Magwitch he uses the substitutes—'mother' and 'father'. He even does not mention his name itself. He indirectly refers to himself as 'a legal adviser'.

It is obvious that Jaggers flouts the maxim—'be clear, brief and avoid prolixity'. He does this by being oblique, indirect and rather circumlocutory. This deviation from the maxim implicates for Pip that "Jaggers' is a sort of sagacious and shrewd man. He is a secrets-keeper—he keeps people's secrets. He is an inscrutable fellow." Nonetheless, Pip's inferences about Estella's parentage are confirmed by Jaggers' roundabout manner of disclosing the facts related to Estella.

Let us take a look at how an illiterate servant, Gangu, is being prolix in the story *The Child* by Premchand in an anthology edited by S. Batra and P.S. Sidhu. The conversation between the narrator and his servant Gangu proceeds as under:

> "I do not want an advance," said Gangu. "I have never asked you for one".
>
> "Then you must be wanting to complain against someone," I said. "You know I hate backbiting."
>
> "No, Sir," said Gangu, "I have no complaint against anyone."
>
> "What have you come to bother me about them?" I said impatiently.
>
> Gangu made another attempt to disclose his secret. I could see from his face that he was trying to muster up strength to do it.
>
> At last he said, "I wish to be relieved of my duties, Sir. I shall not be able to serve you any longer."
>
> This was the first request of its kind and I felt hurt. I was considered an ideal employer and the servants thought it

their great fortune to stay on with me. "Why do you want to leave? I asked."

"You are the image of kindness, Sir," said Gangu. "Who would want to leave you unless there was a very good reason? I find myself in a situation which leaves me with no other alternative. I do not want people to raise their fingers at you on my account." This was most intriguing. I forgot all about morning walk and sitting myself in a chair said, "Why do you talk in riddles? Why don't you say clearly what is on your mind?", Gangu replied haltingly again: "Sir, the thing is that—the woman who has been just been turned out of the Widows' Home Gomti Devi" and he stopped without finishing the sentence. I asked impatiently, "What has she to do with your job?"

"I want to marry her, Sir", said Gangu. (155-56)

Gangu is an illiterate servant of the narrator who belongs to the middle-class. Gangu has decided to marry Gomti Devi. She is a widow and has created a stir in the placid atmosphere in her *mohalla*. She had been sent to the Widows' Home and married off twice by the authorities of the Home. But she had run away from the Widows' Home. Finally she had been expelled. Now she has taken a room in the *mohalla* of the narrator and is an object of interest to all the love-lorn young men. In a nutshell, she is a woman of loose character. Gangu has decided to marry her. But before that he wants to leave his job as a servant of the narrator. He wants to tell the narrator why he wants to leave the job. In conversation between the two Gangu delays to articulate that he wants to marry Gomti Devi. He should have cut short his tale. He relates that he does not want an advance, he does not want to complain against any one of his fellow-servants and that he wants to leave the job. He also praises the narrator by saying "You are the image of kindness, Sir." It is only when the narrator asks him what leaving his job has to do with Gomti Devi that he musters up the strength to articulate that he wants to marry Gomti. He does not want people to point their fingers at his Master due to his marriage with a woman of loose character and bad reputation.

In Gricean parlance Gangu is being indirect or circumlocutory. He is being indirect or circumlocutory along the social dimension of 'power'. In view of 'power' one uses a greater degree of indirectness with people who have authority or power over him. One knows that his employer/authority can influence his career either in a positive way or in a negative manner. This happens in the hierarchical settings like working place, court or the military. In this situation, Gangu is a servant and the narrator is his employer. The narrator has power over Gangu. Therefore, Gangu is supposed to be prolix or roundabout in saying what he intends to. He cannot be brief and direct and say "I want to marry Gomti Devi and I do not want to remain as your servant." He needs to seek his employer's permission to leave the job. Moreover he is certain that marring Gomti and continuing to work as the narrator's servant would bring social disgrace for his master. Considering Gangu's role as servant it would have been impolite or rude on his part to be direct and brief. In short, Gangu suspends the Manner maxim to be polite to his employer via being modest-maximizing the praise of the narrator. He achieves this by saying "You are the image of kindness, Sir." And "Who would want to leave you unless there was a very good reason."

The two conversations analysed above can be compared in respect of the breach of the Manner maxim. It is striking to note that in the former it is Mr. Jaggers who flouts the maxim. He is senior in age and status to Pip. His departure from the maxim implicates his nature—sagacious and shrewd. Perhaps he also intends to increase the interest of the information he conveys about Estella's parentage by being oblique and prolix. In the latter illustration it is Gangu who suspends the maxim by delaying to convey what he wants to convey. He is a servant of the narrator and hence is junior in status and also age. His role as a servant and his concern for saving his employer's image force him to suspend the maxim of brevity and clarity. He has suspended the maxim to be polite to his master via being modest. In the next section our concern is with the considerations behind the deviation from being brief, clear and orderly by the characters in the five novels.

5.2. Manner Maxim in the Five Novels

The novelist can carry forward the story in two distinct ways. First, he can devote major portions of a novel to description or explanation. Second, he can carry the story forward through characters. It follows that conversation between characters acquires a great significance in accomplishing this task. The conversation in the novel has dual functions: it reveals the characters and it also carries the story forward. The conversation between characters in a novel reveals such facts about characters as their age, class, education and sex. From conversation one comes to know whether a character is cultured, polite, educated, articulate or reserved. As Boulton (1975: 120) comments "It is full of clues to character." Above all, conversation also reveals the intention of a character—social or conversational intentions as the character engages in conversation. This is strikingly revealed when we analyse the conversation in novel by applying the Gricean maxims—particularly their non-observance. In this section, we would analyse why and how the characters in the five novels deviate from maxim of Manner, the maxim about being brief, clear and orderly.

Let us begin with Jai Nimbkar's *Temporary Answers*. This novel delineates the characters: Vineeta, Abhijit Gokhale, Vilas, Madhuri, Kishori, Madhu, Mrs. Kibe, her daughter Shobha, Mrs. Bhingare and her son Madan. Of these the first three are the cynosure in the novel. The heroine Vineeta is linked to Abhijit Gokhale—a Professor of Geography and a playwright and Vilas—Vineeta's childhood friend and now a doctor settled in Pune. Vilas is being vague in his following conversation with Vineeta:

> "So you came back. What were the other things you were fed up with?"
>
> "Oh, various things," he said vaguely. (19)

Vilas is Vineeta's childhood friend. After completing his medical education in Bombay he went to England for a job and stayed there for a few years. He has now come back to India. One afternoon he visits Vineeta who is living with her parents in

Pune. Vineeta asks him why he came back to Pune. Vilas replies that racial prejudice is one thing he was fed up with. On being asked what the other things were he was fed up with, Vilas replies "Oh, various things." He does not explain or relate what those various things are. Thus, his use of a phrase 'various things' makes him blatantly vague. He takes a cigarette out of his pack and asks her if she does not mind his smoking. His vagueness implicates that—'he does not want to tell the other things that he was fed up with.' Perhaps the various things he was fed up with are not worth-mentioning. His use of 'various things' is a deliberate move to skip the topic and talk on the subject he has come for. He has come to persuade Vineeta to be a partner in his clinic he is planning to set up in Pune. He is an ENT specialist and she will be a paediatrician. By employing a vague phrase 'various things' Vilas intends to come to the point in his visit.

Madhuri is Vineeta's younger sister. She is about twenty. She has constant bickerings with her mother. She is fed up with her mother's nagging and lecturing too. Once she runs away with a boy Ram Sawant—the Cycle-stand in-charge at the College. Two days later Vilas brings Madhuri home. Then follows this exchange between Vineeta and Madhuri:

> "You wanted to marry him?"
>
> She gave a short laugh. "Why else do you think I went with him? Just to get back at mother?"
>
> "Madhuri, you are not married, are you?"
>
> "Don't worry. He had more sense than I did. Marriage had never been part of his plans. He was just out for a good time with a girl. When he found out that marriage was the price he might have to play for the good time, he kicked me out." (58-59)

Vineeta asks her sister Madhuri if she wanted to marry Ram Sawant. Madhuri replies not by making a straightforward assertion but by employing a rhetorical question. Rhetorical questions are as Frank (1990: 737) states "Questions asked without intention of receiving a reply." In the terminology of

Speech Act Theory by Searle (1969, 1975) they are an indirect way to imply more than what is said.

Rhetorical questions are a strategy employed by conversers to perform some valuable function in the ongoing conversation. As Frank (1990: 726) remarks "They enable speakers to use indirectness to soften, rather than to strengthen their statement." Madhuri employs the strategy of rhetorical question "Why else do you think I went with him? Just to get back at mother?" to soften her statement that "it is with the very purpose of marrying Ram Sawant that she ran away with him and not to get back at mother." This is not an information-seeking question. Her intention is not to obtain an answer from Vineeta. She is being indirect to excuse herself of her behaviour (running away with Ram). Had she answered Vineeta's question directly and in a straightforward manner, it would have meant a shameless acceptance of bringing a social disgrace for her 'respectable family' (her father is a professor) by her act of running away with Ram. To avoid this she is being indirect and has suspended the maxim of directness and brevity.

Abhijit Gokhale intends to propose to Vineeta. He knows that Vineeta is busy at the Charity Clinic till night. Hence, he visits her at her house at ten o'clock at night. He is rather circumlocutory in his following conversation with Vineeta:

> "You just happened to be passing by?"
>
> "No, I came to see you, but I would have gone away if your house was dark. I have finished a scene I was writing. I didn't want to start on another and I felt too restless to sleep. So I thought I would come and see you."
>
> "At ten o'clock at night? Have you thought of my reputation?" He clapped his hand to his forehead. "Oh, my God, I forgot all about. What shall we do now? Do you suppose you could marry me? That would make it all right, wouldn't it?" (91)

Vineeta asks Abhijit if he just happened to pass by her house and what people would say about his meeting with her at ten o'clock at night. His reply to the first question includes the clauses 'I came to see you', 'I felt too restless to sleep', and 'I thought I would come and see you'. These provide the clues to gather that his visit is not unintentional. To the second question he replies 'What shall we do now?' "Do you suppose you could marry me? That would make it all right, wouldn't it?" It emerges that his intention is to propose to her. It also emerges that he is being circumlocutory in saying what he wants to. He proposes to her in an indirect way by asking 'Do you suppose you could marry me?' and 'That would make it all right, wouldn't it?' It would have been blunt on his part to say directly—'I want to marry you, Vineeta.' He avoids to be direct not to hurt her. One observes that his assertion 'that would make it all right' is his attempt to persuade her to accept the proposal. In brief, his direct proposal 'I want to marry you' would have been an imposition on her. The direct imposition might have hurt her because she is still confused and has not given a thought to the matter of her remarriage. Abhijit deviates from being direct and brief by way of opting out of the maxim.

A week later he visits her again at her house. She is angry with him because during his stay at Ahmedabad he has not bothered to write to her or even call her. Knowing that she has being hurt he sits beside her on the sofa. He takes her in his arms and his arms tighten her around her. Her anger subsides. She has a feeling of comfort and security in this delicate touch of his. He compliments her that she is so slim and looks so beautiful all the time. She is glad that he has been pleased too. Then follows the conversation between them given below:

> "You do. I don't want to leave you and go away, but I have to. Vineeta, don't you see how untenable this situation is? All right, let's assume we don't marry. What alternatives do we have? We can't live in the same city and stop seeing each other. So we have practically only one alternative—to continue as we are what guarantee is there that even this won't develop into the kind of relationship you are afraid of?"
>
> "No guarantee at all. In fact I think you have received proof that it can very well develop into that sort of relationship." (108)

Abhijit makes another attempt to propose to her. She squarely tells him that it is better he gives her up and leaves her alone. To persuade her to accept the marriage proposal he compliments that she is very beautiful. He convinces her that they can't avoid seeing each other. As they will continue to see each other without marrying, it is possible that frequent meetings will develop into the kind of relationship she is afraid of. She supplements that their meetings will develop into that sort of relationship. Abhijit and Vineeta are matured people. They know that the relationship they are talking about is a physical relationship. They are being indirect through the phrases 'the kind of relationship' and 'that sort of relationship.' The socio-cultural background in which they are living forces them to avoid mentioning the unmentionable. In the Indian socio-cultural context it is generally observed that talking about sexual or physical relationship is a taboo, even if the participants are married. Abhijit realizes that Vineeta is unwilling to accept to marry. Had he used the phrase 'sexual or physical relationship' directly, it would have hurt her. She, too, realizes that if she uses the phrase directly, it will excite him to be intimate with her which she does not want at the moment. In brief, it is for the socio-cultural and ethical reasons that they are being indirect. They deviate from being direct by way of opting out of the maxim.

One of the themes in *Heat and Dust* is the inter-racial union of sexual passion. This is exhibited in such relationship as the Nawab and Olivia, the narrator and Inderlal and the Nawab and Harry. The era when Olivia came to India with her husband Douglas Rivers was the era when adultery was considered a sin and extra-marital relationship was condemned by both the Indian and the British society. The English—the colonizers—found the Indians to be irrational, people and sexually perverted. It is this attitude of the then Englishmen that makes Mrs. Saunders to exhort and warn Olivia about Indians. She does this by being circumlocutory and ambiguous in the following exhortation to Olivia:

> "You hear a lot of stories," Mrs. Saunders said. "There was one lady in Muzzafarabad or one of those places—she

> was a lady form Somerset." She sighed (thinking of the fate of this lady, or of distant Somerset). "Her *dhobi*", Mrs. Saunders whispered, leaning closer to Olivia. "He was ironing her undies and it must have been too much for him. They're very excitable, it's their constitution. I've heard their spicy food's got something to do with it—I wouldn't know if there is any truth in that but of this I am sure, Mrs. Rivers: they've got only one thought in their heads and that's to you-know-what with a white woman." (119)

One morning Olivia goes to the Saunders' house in the Civil Lines with the purpose of consulting Dr. Saunders. Unfortunately he has left for the hospital. She finds Mrs. Saunders out of her bed. Mrs. Saunders begins to tell Olivia about the Indians—the Indian servants. She tells Olivia a story of one English lady (from Somerset) living in India. Her *dhobi* was excited when he ironed the undies of that lady. Mrs. Saunders goes on telling Olivia that the spicy food that the Indian eat makes them highly sexual. This leads them to commit immoral action of seduction. She implies this by using the deictical term—'it' thus—being vague or ambiguous. Her exhortation to Olivia implicates that 'Indians are sexually perverted, beware of them.' Mrs. Saunders implicates this by being circumlocutory and vague and thus deviates from being clear by way of flouting the maxim.

Proverbs and idioms are important aspects of all languages. Proverbs are short statements with supposed truth or moral lesson. Proverbial expressions perform a variety of functions like complimenting, criticizing, warning, advising, persuading and accusing someone. Like proverbial expressions idiomatic expressions are used by almost all normal speakers irrespective of their education, culture, profession and social class as well as status. Idioms are expressions peculiar to the language. Idioms are typically characterized by long usage and non-permissibility of change of their order of words. One could say that to speak or write idiomatically is to speak or write vigorously, graphically and naturally. The use of idioms either enhances or softens the intended force of one's utterance.

If an idiom is taken word by word in terms of their meaning, the meaning of the idiom will not be clear from the meaning of its parts (words). For Grant and Nation (2006: 2) an idiom to be interpreted needs two criteria: "compositionality—taking all the words in the idiom together, not in parts and the context in which the idiom occurs." If someone says—'his mother kicked the bucket,' the listener will miss what the speaker says if he takes the words—'kicked' and 'the bucket' as individual words having their usual sense. By using this idiom, therefore, the speaker is being ambiguous or unclear—deviates from Grice's Manner maxim. The Nawab in *Heat and Dust* employs an idiom—'hit the nail on the head' in the following encounter with Dr. Saunders:

> "You did quite right, Doctor. Quite right. You set a good example."
>
> "It's the only way to deal with them, Nawab Saheb. It's no use arguing with them, they're not amenable to reason. They haven't got it here, you see, up here, the way we have."
>
> "Exactly, Doctor. You have hit the—what is it Harry?"
>
> "Nail on the head."
>
> "Quite right. The nail on the head." The Nawab nodded gravely. (121)

The Nawab's British counterpart Dr. Saunders is flushed with the Nawab's food and drink. He freely expresses his considered opinion of India and Indians from his hospital experiences. He tells the Nawab about an Indian whom he called to his office. Having no argument with the fellow Dr. Saunders slapped his ears. For him Indians have no reasons/intellect and it is useless arguing with them. The Nawab compliments Dr. Saunders on his act and to do so remarks—'You have hit the nail on the head.' Taken literally the idiom means—'strike a blow at an object exactly.' Taken in the context the Nawab intends to convey that Dr. Saunders has rightly dealt with the Indian fellow by slapping/boxing his ears. Put it briefly the Nawab is being indirect in his plausible compliment to Dr. Saunders. By being idiomatic the Nawab deviates from being clear and implicates the compliment on Dr. Saunders' art of treating the Indian fellow as an animal and manhandling him without an argument.

The following is an interesting occasion when the Nawab is being roundabout or circumlocutory in answering Olivia's simple and innocent question:

> "Who were those men?"
>
> He didn't answer at once, and when he did, it was with another question: "Who do you think they were?" He gave her one of his shrewd looks, then, laughed: "I suppose you think they were bad men. You must have heard many stories I think, isn't it and you believe they are true." Again she felt she did not have to defend herself or answer him.
>
> "But if they are bad men," he went on, "I think they can't be so very bad because look what they have come here for." He pointed to the mound in the shrine on which some fresh garlands had just been led and sticks of incense were still smouldering. "You see, they did not come for any bad purpose but to pay their devotions." (133-34)

Observing the rough men's humility and look of adoration for the Nawab, Olivia asks the Nawab who those rough and armed men were. A simple and innocent question it appeared but it was very perplexing for the Nawab to answer in brief and clear manner. He might have answered straightforwardly—"they are holy men and have come to pray and tell their wishes to Baba Firdaus." But he wanted to test her reaction about those men—the bandits—the outlaws. Olivia had watched them falling at Nawab's feet and he talking to them in an easy and familiar way. She was curious to know what connection there was between the Nawab and the rough men. As readers we know that he had nexus with them. He was hand in glove with them—helped them loot the nearby villages. He protected them from being arrested by the policemen. Olivia wanted to know why those men were humble to him and touched his feet. The Nawab intended to exonerate himself from having nexus with the dacoits and this forced him to be roundabout/ circumlocutory in answering her question. To make her feel the truth of his words he even showed her the mound in the shrine with fresh garlands and incense-sticks burning. To remove the trace of suspicion from Olivia's mind the Nawab suspends the maxim of brevity and clarity.

Maji, one of the Indian mythological figures and the potent Indian Goddesses—is being ambiguous in employing a pronoun 'It' in her following response to the narrator:

> "When I spoke to her about the woman who had so mysteriously followed me, she said, "You see, it has started." (163)

The young narrator was going all the way to the hospital. A woman followed her mysteriously. The narrator did not like to be followed and hence turned her way to Maji's hut. She told Maji about the mysterious woman. Maji reacted—"You see, it has started." The pronoun "It" she uses here generates two meanings: "It" means—the hunt of a midwife for the narrator as a prospective client for abortion. "It" also means—'the narrator's pregnancy.' Together "It" means—the hunt has started and the narrator's pregnancy has started. In the previous meeting Maji has warned the narrator to be careful of Indian midwives who would come to her to offer their services for abortion. Maji had herself been a midwife. She could know whether a woman was pregnant by the way she walked and held herself. Now in this meeting Maji gathers that the narrator has come to her hut to get aborted. Just by looking at the narrator's abdomen Maji understands that the narrator is 8 or 9 weeks' pregnant and this is a good time to get the foetus aborted. Maji does not speak in clear terms possibly because she thinks she thinks she and the narrator share what meaning "It" conveys here. Her use of the pronoun "It" might be a part and parcel of the midwifery jargon. In brief, Maji opts out of being clear to take the narrator in confidence and to persuade her to get the foetus aborted.

In *Cry, the Peacock* too the characters like Gautama, Maya, Harbans Singh and Nila's mother are being vague, circumlocutory and indirect in their conversational contributions to their interlocutors. One observes that they deviate from being brief and clear by way of flouting, suspending and infringing the Manner maxim. What significance their being vague, circumlocutory and indirect has in negotiating their relationship with their interlocutor will be clear from the illustration that follows. In the following encounter with Maya Gautama is being circumlocutory:

> "You know what I really wish to do Gautama? I should like to go south—to Travancore, Cochin, Mysure, Malabar, all those places."
>
> "In summer? In the heat? Why?" he asked surprised.
>
> "I want, I want," I stammered swiftly, "to see the Kathakali dances." I have heard of the ballets they have in their villages. They say they go on for days and days! And the dancers are all men, and they were such fantastic marks. And the drums..."
>
> "Well, well," Gautama was amused. "I thought I could never underestimate your appetite for the curious. But I was wrong—I had underestimated it."
>
> "But Gautama, I thought you would be interested in that, too—more that in the hills pony rides and things. It must be such marvellous sight, so violent and bizarre." I groped for words painfully. The vision was excruciating in its vividness to me and here was one who did not even glimpse it, no matter what I said. "The masks they wear—you must have seen them? And their costumes. And the special kind of music and it is all out in the open, at night, by starlight—and perhaps they have torches.
>
> "Yes, I suppose they dance by torchlight...." Gautama got abruptly, having finished hid cigarette and stretched. "If that is your only reason for wanting to go all that way South, I suggest you wait till a Kathakali troupe comes to give a performance in Delhi, as it is bound to sometime—perhaps in Winter. It will be less expensive." (42-43)

Maya wants to get away with Gautama for a short holiday. When he asks her where she would like to go, Maya replies that she would like to go South to enjoy the Kathakali dances. She goes on to describe the ballets, the fantastic masks, costumes, drums and the Kathakali men-dancers. Thus, she tries to persuade him to join and enjoy the marvelous sight. He suggests her to wait for the Kathakali troupe coming to Delhi for performance. His suggestion serves as an indirect refusal to go to South. His deviation from being straightforward implicates—"I will not accompany you to South. You will definitely not go to South." At a deeper level his indirect refusal serves as an illustration of his philosophy of 'detachment' as contrasted with Maya's philosophy of 'attachment.' Her wish to see the Kathakali dances suggests her attachment to the art—to the world. His refusal to go to South suggests his detachment from such things as music, dance and drums.

At a party hosted by Mr. and Mrs. Lal there are guests like Gautama, Maya, a Prim lady and her Sikh Husband Harbans Singh. As they enjoy the food, they talk on a variety of topics. Their talk veers to astrology and palmistry. These two words were the taboos in the family of Maya's father and Maya's in-laws. The Prim lady's husband claimed to have a good knowledge of palmistry. Maya is disgusted by hearing the word palmistry. Then follows this talk between Maya and Herbans Singh:

> I questioned, "You believe in palmistry? Have you found the lines in your hand dictating *your* life? You are convinced?"....
>
> He laughed jovially. So jovially that an alliance with the albino of the black and oil stick temple gate was discounted immediately. "You see", he said, "How interested women always become in this! As soon as I mentioned I am a palmist-even if I add that I am only an amateur palmist—they gather around me like bees. Shall I read your palm then and tell your future?" (77-78)

The Prim lady tells Maya that she believes in 'destiny' or 'fate.' She had been told by an astrologer that she would marry a man from West of Jhelum and was to bear two sons and she did. She knows nothing of palmistry. Maya then turns to Harbans Singh and asks whether he believes in palmistry and if he is convinced of his life in future. Instead of answering in one word "yes" he tells that he is an amateur palmist. The circumlocution he employs is geared to ridicule the 'fatalism' that women believe in. To underline that he is a palmist he advances to ask Maya if he should tell her about her future.

Replying that he is a palmist is less important to him than ridiculing women who gather around a palmist like bees. In brief he flouts the maxim of brevity and this reveals his cynical attitude to women.

Three days after Gautama's death his mother and Nila—his sister accompany Maya to the Lucknow house. Nila and her mother sit in the semi-darkness at the window. Nila engages with a Pomeranian and her mother sits knitting for a small orphan who has just been admitted to her crèche. The mother has tiredness on her face. Nila looks at her mother and this dialogue follows between them:

> "Yes", Nila said, "I suppose so." She pursed her lips, then, exploded again. "It means we won't be able to leave for at least another week. It'll take him that long to get back."
>
> "Oh, Yes."
>
> "But I saw the servants opening up another bedroom this morning."
>
> A hint of vagueness overcame the harsh, steady voice of her mother. "There are so many rooms," she said vaguely. "This old house, it is full of rooms." (211-12)

By referring to the Lucknow house having several rooms Nila's mother is being vague. We know that to make the ongoing conversation successful it is expected that the one who produces vague or ambiguous expression detects the vagueness and tries to avoid it in the following of his/her contribution. This can be done by employing ambiguity-avoidance-strategy suggested by Ferreira, Sleven and Roggers (2005: 279) "Speakers might clarify or correct already articulated description." Why Nila's mother speaks about the house full of many rooms remains vague. She does not employ the strategy to clarify her expression—'there are so many rooms' and this old house, it is full of rooms'. From Nila's utterance which follows—"how did they manage to live here—just the two of them," we may gather that Nila and her mother are expressing their sympathy for Maya who might have tolerated and managed to live in such a big house with her father. It could be put that Nila's mother's suspension from being clear underlines her sympathetic concern for Maya who has lost her mental equilibrium holding herself responsible for her husband's death.

Once at about eleven o'clock in the night Maya is in distress after having a debate with Gautama about love and life. Unable to stand this argument that 'love does not last long, death cuts it short' she succumbs to temperature and falls asleep. She begins to mumble in her sleep. This is what happens:

> "But to perish? Who? Tell me who?"
>
> Gautama woke up. "What is it?" he said and held me in his arms. "What is it, Maya? What are you dreaming of?"
>
> After I had let myself be soothed by his fleshy presence, I turned away from him. He was hot, unbearably hot. So was my bed. The sprinkled earth had dried even in the moonlight. My tongue was thick with thirst. It seemed to me that death was after all very real, very probable. "Terrible," I sighed pushing and pushing my hair from my face. "Not to know, it is terrible Gautama." (125)

As Maya begins to mumble in the bed, Gautama wakes up and asks her what she is dreaming of. In the state of temperature Maya only utters "Terrible, it is terrible." She is unable to tell him plainly what terrible she is dreaming of. Her head is hot. Her tongue is thick with thirst. Her skin is burning with heat. This physical state of Maya makes her utter—"Terrible, it is terrible" and she is unable to explain what terrible dream she is having. Her purpose is not to generate any implicature as such.

In *Socialite Evenings*, Shobha De presents a gallery of socialites: actors, actresses, film-producers, directors, ad-men, reporters, journalists and rich businessmen connected with the Bollywood. The conversations of these socialites are on a variety of topics like love, marriage, family, sex, film production, eating, drinking and cosmetics. One of the things that strikes us is that these people engage in free and frank talk about extra-marital relationships, love-making and seduction. Talking about this style of characters and about the novelist Patil, S.R. (2007: 62) comments "Nothing is behind curtain. She calls a spade a spade." Even though the characters and the writer Shobha De are direct and free in talking about such sensitive issues, there are occasions and situations in this novel in which the characters are indirect and circumlocutory. In other words, they do not adhere to the norms of being clear, brief and straightforward. Let's illustrate why and how they deal with the maxim in this novel. A few such situations are analysed below:

> Karuna hailed from a typical Indian Middle-class family. Her father was a disciplinarian. He had set norms for his family: "Lights off at 10 pm. Up at 5.30. No eating between meals. No idle talk over the telephone. And no unnecessary laughter." He wanted his three daughter to be a lawyer, a teacher and an IAS officer respectively. Ironically nothing of this mattered for Karuna. She wanted to be in the charmed circle of rich girls. She longed to be a night club crooner and very often rehearsed her songs in the bathroom using the plastic mobile shower as a mike. She wanted to be noticed. At this juncture of time she found a schoolmate in Charlie. Charlie introduced Karuna to adult movie, smoking and fleshy cloths (stretch pants). About the age of fifteen Charlie had sex with one Anglo boy. She wanted to share this excitement with Karuna and straight comes to the house to tell her. This is how the dialogue followed between the teenagers in *Socialite Evenings*:
>
> Charlie was looking even more triumphant than unusual.
>
> "I did it!" she announced.
>
> "What?"
>
> "Don't be dumb—IT!!"
>
> "You mean—THAT?"
>
> "Yes!" (21-22)

Karuna lied to her father that she had to get some notes for the test and thus ran out of the house. Charley had signaled that she wanted to share something very important with Karuna. As Karuna came down to the landing, Charlie announced that she has done it. The second time she made the pronoun 'IT' the nucleus of her utterance. When Karuna asked if she had done 'THAT', Charlie replied positively. The background knowledge about Charlie helps Karuna gather that Charlie meant 'sex' by

'IT'. Charlie uses the pronoun "IT" as a substitute for 'sex' and Karuna uses "THAT" as its substitute. Karuna's use of 'THAT' is according to Levinson (1983: 90) 'anaphoric' referring to the same activity (sex) as a prior linguistic expression "IT" refers to. Both Karuna and Charlie are oblique in referring to Charlie's sexual act. This is because of the setting of the talk. Karuna's father is on his bed upstairs. He has just berated and asked her to be back in five minutes. To hide from him that she is talking with a detestable girl Charlie Karuna is being oblique. Charlie's obliquity serves as Barat (2000: 122) says to make Karuna "aware of her sexual identity and needs." It serves as an introductory lesson for Karuna about the sexual life of the charmed circle of rich girls.

In the following conversation, too, the topic is sex. But this time it is not Charlie's but Anjali's. Both the conversational partners—Karuna and Anjali—avoid using the three-letter-word directly. This is how they deal with the topic:

> Anjali finally phoned nearly a month after her wedding.
>
> "Hi," she said but, there was no cheer in her voice.
>
> "Sort of."
>
> "What do you mean 'sort of'?"
>
> "What are doing?"
>
> "Nothing special". (123)

Anjali has married Punjabi businessman Kumar Bhandari. She is his third wife. The other two are at Madras and Juhu respectively. Kumar has not divorced them yet. A month after her wedding Anjali contacted Karuna telephonically. The first thing Karuna asked Anjali was whether she had been to bed with Kumar. Karuna used the euphemistic verb 'deflowered' as a substitute for 'having sex.' Anjali gave a vague reply 'sort of'. When asked about what she meant by 'sort of', instead of clarifying 'sort of' Anjali enquires what Karuna was doing. Karuna is indirect in using the verb 'deflowered' and Anjali is vague in employing the phrase 'sort of'. They suspend the maxim of clarity and are not straightforward because of the medium of their conversation—telephone. They do not intend to share such sensitive thing on telephone—which they think might be tapped. Anjali thinks that the secret about her husband Kumar would be exposed. The secret about him is that he is a homo. He prefers boys. He has picked up an orphan Murty as his bedmate. To keep up his image Anjali suspends the maxim of clarity. Karuna sarcastically employs the word 'deflowered' as she feels that Anjali has been a fool in marrying Kumar. It is in the next face-to-face encounter that Anjali shares this aspect of Kumar's personality with Karuna.

In the later phase of her life Karuna landed a job in the Prithvi theatre. She got a small role in the Hindi version of O'Neill's *Desire Under the Elms*. This was a play being directed by a Delhi woman named Swapna. After the first performance of the play the following dialogue takes place between Swapna and Karuna:

> "Well?" She demanded in her usual aggressive way.
>
> "Well, What?" I asked, though I knew perfectly what she was after.
>
> "Well, you know—what happened last night?"
>
> "Nothing."
>
> "What do you mean by nothing? You were talking to him. He must have dropped you back. What did he say? Did he like the play?"
>
> "I don't know. We didn't discuss it."
>
> "Then what did you discuss?"
>
> "Other things." (247)

The last reply "other things" by Karuna is vague. After the performance of the play the art-film maker Mr. Girish Sridhar and Karuna have discussed the direction and performance of the play. For him the play is badly directed but Karuna came through the role very good. Swapna wanted to be close to him but he was not interested in her. It was Karuna he wanted to talk to. He asked Swapna to leave them and she did. During their talk Sridhar offered Karuna a key-role in his modern version '*Shakuntala*.' When she refused, he requested her to at least audition for the movie. He then dropped Karuna at her PG accommodation kept by a Parsee woman Mrs. Jeroo Mehta. Swapna is dying to know if he (Girish) has expressed any interest in her play. Karuna wants to avoid telling her about his reaction about the play and his offer to Karuna of the role in *'Shakuntala'*. Taken as a whole in the context of the novel Karuna's attempt to be vague and to avoid telling Swapna what passed between her and Girish is highly suggestive.

It suggests a transition phase in Karuna's life. She is happy with the odd and small roles she is getting and more than that she is not interested in the movie world. Somewhere she wants to keep at bay from working in the films and feels obliged to care for her aged parents as they are quite alone. She suspends the maxim of clarity while talking to Swapna about what she discussed with Girish. This she does to save herself from being involved in some scandal or gossip invented by film reporters.

Despite her refusal Girish persuades her to help him in writing the draft/script of '*Shakuntala*'. She is able to manage this particularly on weekends. Karuna and Girish thus become an item for a film magazine. Girish has promised another second rung star named Anjana the role in his movie. He ditches Anjana for Karuna. This has bitterly stung Anjana. She gives a film magazine reporter an interview and lashes out Girish. In her excitement and onslaught on Girish she flouts the maxim of brevity. We quote below a question from the reporter and a reply from Anjana:

> "Will there be any nude scenes in your films?"
>
> "Look Baba. Don't ask me such questions. But simply I have read '*Amar Chitra Katha*.' In fact, Shakuntala is shown in the forest with animals. Now you tell me, where can a woman get clothes in a forest? She is natural, no? She can wear leaves and animal skins, but she can't get silks and chiffons. Our nudity will be dignified and classy. I am ready to strip if the role demands it. In this case I am convinced it is in keeping with the character of Shakuntala. I have already started going to the health club to work out for those important scenes. Like the one in the river, when she uses the drink given to her by that king—what's

> his name?" The reporter did not know. "Never mind. That is a very beautiful scene. It has to be well presented, but it must also look sexy." (266)

Rejected for the role by Girish Anjana is not going to sit back and only cry. Her brother Babu tells her that he will launch his own '*Shakuntala*' and Anjana will play the key-role in it. The reporter asks her if there will be nude scenes of Shakuntala in their film. This is 'yes/no' question and Anjana should have replied 'Yes'. But it is crystal clear that she is circumlocutory in her reply. It implicates "Come what may, I will act in the film." She circumlocutes to justify acting nude scenes in the films. It reflects what Nayar (2000: 115) calls her "dual interest." She wants to tell Girishji—"*Main bhi kuch kam nahi hoon,* Mr. Sridhar." Her other interest is to avenge Sridhar for stringing her along for two years by dangling this role in front of her.

In the four novels: *Temporary Answers*, *Heat and Dust*, *Cry, the Peacock* and *Socialite Evenings*—we have discussed how the characters are vague/ambiguous, indirect and circumlocutory. Deviations from the maxim of being clear and brief are very motivated and intentional. The departures from being clear and brief reveal the character—traits, communicative intentions and the concern for saving self and others from disgrace or defame.

Shashi Deshpande's *The Binding Vine* deals with a very delicate issue in the Indian socio-cultural context and the issue is rape. There are two types of rape dealt with–pre-marital and marital. The former relates to Kalpana and the latter happens to the heroine's mother-in-law, Mira. The axis of the novel mainly revolves around Kalpana—a victim of pre-marital rape. The major characters like Urmi, Shakutai and the minor ones like Vanaa and Dr. Bhaskar Jain try avoiding to refer to Kalpana being raped. Let us see how they manoeuvre in doing this. Look at the following interaction in *The Binding Vine*:

> "Tell her it's the truth."
>
> "What is he saying, tai? Tell him my daughter is not that kind of girl."
>
> "Nobody is accusing your daughter...."
>
> "Your daughter hasn't done anything, he hasn't saying that."

> "It was an accident, a car knocked her down."
>
> "This doctor has examined your daughter."
>
> "She was raped," she says still speaking in English.
>
> "Your daughter has been...." Vanaa hesitates, searching for the Marathi word, gives up. "Someone has wronged her." (58)

Urmila happens to visit a hospital where her sister-in-law Vanaa works. As she enters Vanaa's room, she finds Vanaa and Dr. Bhaskar Jain consoling a woman. The woman is Shakuntala. Her daughter Kalpana has been hospitalized. Dr. Bhaskar Jain has carried out the medical examination and tells Vanaa that Kalpana has been raped and also has a head injury. He speaks in English thinking that Shakuntala should not understand what has happened to Kalpana. He asks Vanaa and Urmila to tell Shakuntala what the truth is. Vanaa avoids telling her and says—"It was an accident, a car knocked her down." Urmila says—"Your daughter hasn't done anything." Vanaa hesitates to speak the truth directly and couches the truth in an utterance—"Someone has wronged her." For Bhaskar Jain there is no harm in telling the mother what has happened to her daughter. Urmila and Vanaa know what 'being raped' means in the Indian society and culture. They know what Guttal (2003: 59) observes "Rape disgraces the victim rather than the culprit." Hence, Vanaa employs the verb 'wronged' as a substitute for 'raped.'

Shakuntala, the mother, is torn and shattered psychologically by this traumatic incident. Urmila asks her whether her sister Sulu can come to hospital to look after Kalpana. The following exchange takes place between the two:

> "What about your sister?"
>
> "Sulu?" she hesitates. "She never goes out. And she is looking after my home. She cooks, gets things from the shops—she does everything." She sighs. "I'm managing but God knows how long I can continue like this. The nurse was telling me this may go on and on." Her eyes go blank, visionary, perhaps, a future of unending misery.

> "What will I do? What will *we* do?" Her tone is not helpless. She's trying to imagine what it will be like. "For a few days, everyone was sympathetic. But now.... They all know about it, Tai." I realize she's referring to Kalpana's being raped. "People in our *chawl* are talking about it. Even in my school—I sent Sandhya with a leave letter and she said they were trying to get it out of her, what happened to Kalpana. That's why I do not want anyone to come here. I don't want their pity. What's the time, tai?" (91)

In India illegitimate pregnancy, rape and illicit relationship are the things about which murmurs spread fast. The same thing has happened with Kalpana's rape. This is what haunts and horrifies Shakutai. She uses the pronoun "It" repeatedly and also a phrase—"What happened to Kalpana" to refer to rape. She knows that rape to Kalpana means trouble for everyone—the girl, her family and the relatives. This is more traumatic for a woman like Shakutai whose husband has left her for another woman. She avoids being straightforward to save herself, her daughter Kalpana and her younger daughter Sandhya.

As and when the topic surfaces in their encounter, Shakutai continues to be oblique as one observes in her following ruminations:

> "Sometimes I think, Urmila, I've had enough. What have I had all my life but trouble? I should die, I've had enough. The kinds of things they are saying, the police people, about Kalpana. Such dirt. Her father cried like a child when he read it." (177)
>
> "I brought her up with so much love, I wanted so much for her," she murmurs.
>
> "But Why Shakutai, why did she do it?"
>
> "Her husband Prabhakar, he did it to my Kalpana, my Sulu's husband—it was he...." (188)

Shakutai's sister Sulu commits suicide. Sulu has a sense of guilt as S. Indira (1995: 26) observes "Her barrenness and fear of her husband have paved the way for the ghastly crime committed on Kalpana." Kalpana's rape has already shattered Shakutai.

The revelation that Prabhakar—her sister's husband—is the culprit gives her more terrible blow and unsettles her. The silence and the gaps in her last utterance suggest how unable she still is to articulate the terrible truth.

Shakutai repents that a daughter (Kalpana) was born to her instead of a son. A girl or a woman in Indian society has a typical status. Lokhandwala (2007: 99) remarks "The girl child especially in the rural context is considered unimportant and has more rights and privileges and even considered a burden to the parents. This is obviously reflected in the use of language."

Mira's story and Kalpana's tragedy have led Shakutai to the realization of woman's or girl's place in our society. She is being oblique and elusive when she tells Urmila about her sex with her husband, her pregnancy and her womb. This is what and how she relates to Urmila:

> "I, a woman had, who sleep there, in public, with strange men walking up and down. And my husband...," the voice drops low, "You know what men are, he wanted to.... We're not animals I told him." As if he cared. And I got pregnant. It was the worst thing that could happen to us then. I'd just begun working in a grocer's shop, just started earning some money, and this happened. I didn't want the child, I didn't want Kalpana, I wanted her to die."
>
> She sees my face and flashes out me.
>
> "You can't understand, you won't understand, how will you? I took things. I used to hit myself hard—hear with the rolling pin when making chapaties but nothing happened. She was born." (110-11)

Even though the conversation takes place in the same sex and informal setting, Shakutai avoids to articulate freely and straightforwardly what she wants to. "He wanted to" means "he wanted to have sex" with her. "This happened" means "she got pregnant" and "here" means "her womb." Shakutai is being oblique and illusive perhaps because this is an aspect of Indian women when they name the unnamable acts and parts of their body. There is another aspect to this—the woman who names the acts and the parts of the body straightforwardly is supposed to be an immodest, indecent, obscene and rude woman in Indian context. Shakutai's obliquity results from the fear of being named such an indecent and obscene woman.

Dr. Bhaskar Jain is also at times indirect in his encounters with Urmila. He expresses his love for Urmila and his proposal to marry her in the following exchange:

> "It leaves out the girls. Girls are not going to neatly accept any man their parents choose for them—not anymore. What if the girls your mother chooses for you refuses you? Has she thought of that?"
>
> "My mother—think of any girl refusing me! Ha! He is smiling now, but there is a kind of self-mockery in it." "I am the only son of rich parents, a highly qualified man—how can any girl refuse me? No, no, it can't happen, it's impossible. My mother wants a 'sweet, homely, fair, convent-educated girl' for me, and she'll get her, never fear."
>
> "So there are no problems."
>
> "None. Except that I've gone and fallen in love with a dark, sharp-tongued, married woman." (160-61)

Bhaskar Jain's mother wants her son to get married and has even got a list of eligible girls from their community. She has also got their photographs. This enrages Urmila because she thinks that girls are treated like objects in a catalogue. Bhaskar tells her that it is quite sensible and there is nothing wrong in it on the part of his mother. Urmila realizes him that girls nowadays are free to refuse the boys their parents choose as their husbands. It comes as shock to Bhaskar. He wonders how a girl could refuse such highly qualified man as he. Urmila asks him to go and marry a sweet, homely and fair girl his mother wants for him. It is now that Bhaskar tells her his problem—he has fallen in love with Urmila and wants to marry her. This he does in an oblique/indirect manner by describing Urmila as a dark, sharp-tongued and married woman. He dares not to be plain and straightforward in his love and marriage proposal because he is aware of 'a new woman' in Urmila who chastises him. He also knows that Urmila is a married woman with a six-year-old son Kartik. Her assertion of modern girls' attitude and her being married constrained him to be direct in his proposal. He probably thinks if he says—"I love you and I want to marry you," it would hurt Urmila. He opts out of being clear and direct to avoid to hurt her. His obliquity/indirectness is his testing-strategy—he intends to test what her reaction to his proposal would be.

Thus, in this section we have discussed why and how the characters deviate from the Manner maxim by being vague, ambiguous, oblique/indirect, idiomatic and employing rhetorical question. It emerges that the interrelationship between the interlocutors, their social status, role, setting, power and concern for saving their image and that of the other force them to be oblique, circumlocutory, indirect and vague. Despite this ambiguity and circumlocution the flow of conversation goes on and as Ferreira, Sleven and Roggers (2005: 28) comment "Communication ultimately succeeds, this is because speakers (and their grammars) balance the threat of ambiguity." In the section that follows the concern is with how the characters in the novel face the clash between being informative, truthful, relevant and being brief and clear. It illustrates how the characters deal with the Manner maxim and its clash with the other maxims of the Cooperative Principle.

5.3. Manner Maxim and the Other Maxims of Cooperative Principle

The conversational principle by Grice introduces the communicative values such as relevance, brevity, truthfulness and clarity into the study of languages. Such values are operative differently in different societies and cultures. For example in Israeli culture naturalness, sincerity, truthfulness and clarity are very important values in various types of relationships. As Shoshana Blum-Kulka (2005: 270-71) reports "In Israelis an emphasis on sincerity and truthfulness in interpersonal relations overrides the importance of avoiding infringement on the other." It follows that the Israeli communicators care more for adhering to the Gricean maxim of being truthful than for avoiding imposition on the interlocutor. In Indian culture, on the other hand, people adopt a prolix, circumlocutory and roundabout way of talking thereby breaking the Manner maxim when it comes to preserving the face of the other. Various social factors like social status, power, distance, age, shared knowledge and interrelationship between the conversational partners constrain the adherence to and deviation from a maxim in a given situation. Linguistic communication becomes a kind of juggling act balancing one value against another. One finds in a situation in which one has to decide whether to be informative or truthful, to be relevant or direct and brief. In pragmatic terms—one faces a situation of "maxim-confluence". In the present section our concern is to investigate how the characters in the novels under study deal with the maxim-clash and why they do so.

Jai Nimbkar's *Temporary Answers* presents the complex strands that weave through human relationships. It presents the relationships like—parents-daughter, husband-wife, sister-sister, colleague-colleague and friend-friend. Such relationships force oneself to define oneself a new. Vineeta's younger sister Madhuri faces the situation between being informative and being brief and direct. Let's see how she deals with the situation in the following encounter with Vineeta:

> "You wanted to marry him?"
>
> She gave a short laugh. "Why else do you think I went with him? Just to get back at mother?"
>
> "Madhuri, you are not married, are you?"
>
> "Don't worry. He had more sense than I did. Marriage had never been a part of his plans. He was just out for a good time with a girl. When he found out that marriage was the price he might have to pay for the good time, he kicked out." (58-59)

Madhuri returns home after her elopement with Ram Savant—a Cycle-stand boy at her College. Taking her in confidence Vineeta asks her two questions: "Did you want to marry him?" and "Are you married with Ram?" To the first Madhuri could have replied "Yes" and to the second "No". She is being more informative to the question and thereby intends to assert that she wanted to get rid of her nagging mother and hence eloped with Ram to marry him. To the second question too, a word, "No" would have been enough. But the information she provides and the indirectness she employs seems to be her strategy to justify her act of running away with a Cycle-stand boy. In a nutshell, Madhuri faces the clash between being informative and being brief as required by Vineeta. By suspending the maxim of being informative and that of brevity Madhuri wishes to insinuate her relationship with both—her mother and Ram Sawant. What is striking about Madhuri is that she does not hide anything from Vineeta and meets the demand of the maxim of Quality (of being truthful).

Abhijit Gokhale also faces the situation of being informative and being direct in his following conversation with Vineeta:

> "You just happened to be passing by?"
>
> "No, I came to see you, but I would have gone if your house was dark. I have finished a scene I was writing. I didn't want to start on another and I felt too restless to sleep.
>
> So I thought I would come and see you".
>
> "At ten o'clock at night? Have you thought of my reputation?" he clasped his hand to his forehead. "Oh, my God, I forgot all about that. What shall we do now? Do you suppose you could marry me? That would make it all right, wouldn't it?" (91)

As is clear that Abhijit visits Vineeta—a lonely widow—at her flat at ten o'clock at night. When she asks him if he just happened to pass by her flat, he first replies 'no' and then pours in unasked information about his writing and his restlessness. By being more informative Abhijit suggests her that his visit is not casual and unintentional. When she asks him what would happen to her reputation if people see him with her at her flat, he expresses that he is sorry having not thought of it. Then the questions he poses are his indirect way of putting a marriage proposal to her and persuade her to accept it—"that would make it all right, wouldn't it?" His tag question is employed to assure her obliquely that marriage not meeting like this would set the things right between him and her. He is a bachelor and she is a widow. He opts out of being informative and direct because he is to solicit her opinion about such a delicate and demanding issue as marriage (her remarriage). He has experienced that Vineeta is ambivalent in her response to him and she is in the state of indecision and mental confusion. This background knowledge he has about her makes him to be more informative to suggest that he has come to her intentionally. It also makes him to be indirect in his proposal of marriage to her. Here, one is reminded of a bachelor—Dr. Bhaskar Jain in *The Binding Vine* who is also being indirect in expressing his love for and marriage proposal to Urmila—a married woman with a six-year-old son Kartik.

Our reading of *Heat and Dust* proves beyond doubt that the Nawab of Khatm—a principal character in the novel–has many evil sides to his character. His wife Sandy (Zahira is her real name) is not with him. He is bankrupt—constantly in need of money. He has nexus with the dacoits who loot around the town of Satipur. The topic of his liaison with the dacoits surfaces time and again in the course of the novel. But the Nawab himself and his guest Harry manoeuvre to camouflage these dark sides from Olivia. In so doing the Nawab breaks the norm of being informative, truthful and brief and clear. When Olivia suspects of his association with the dacoits, the Nawab deviates from the Gricean maxim as can be seen in his following encounter with Olivia:

> "Who were those men?"
>
> He didn't answer at once and when he did it was with another question: "Who do you think they were?" He gave her one of the shrewd looks, then, laughed: "I suppose you think they are bad men. You must have heard many stories I think, isn't it? and you believe they are true." Again she felt she did not have to defend herself or answer him.
>
> "But if they are bad men," he went on, "I think they can't be so very bad because look what they have come for." He pointed to the mound in the shrine on which some fresh garlands had just been laid and sticks of incense were still

smouldering. "You see, they did not come for any bad purpose but to pay their devotions." (133-34)

When the Nawab takes Olivia to Baba Firdaus' shrine, some rough and armed men emerge from the shrine and touch the Nawab's feet and stand before him with an attitude of humility. As the Nawab dismisses them, Olivia asks him who those men were. She suspects from their desperado faces that they are like the bandits. The Nawab could have told her straightforwardly that they are holy men and have come to pray to Baba Firdaus. But shrewd as the Nawab is, he is sure that it would not have removed Olivia's suspicion about his association with them. He is being wordy and circumlocutory in his reply to her question. This move of his doubly-motivated: he wants to remove the trace of suspicion from Olivia's mind about his nexus with the dacoits and also wants to save himself and the third party—the dacoits—from being exposed and disgraced. By his wordiness he also produces the plausible impression in Olivia's mind that the men are holy men as the Nawab and Olivia are. In his attempt to protect his image and also that of the dacoits the Nawab suspends the maxim of being informative as required, the maxim of brevity and that of truthfulness in his replies to Olivia. To prove the truthfulness of his reply he takes recourse to using repeatedly the verbs of inner perception—'I suppose', 'You think', 'I think', 'You believe', 'I think', and 'You see'. While considering how the characters deal with the maxims of being informative, truthful and relevant we have already discussed how on the other occasions also the Nawab and Harry do not hesitate to deviate from these conversational norms.

Anita Desai's *Cry, the Peacock* presents how a mismatched marriage brings misfortune to both—husband and wife. The novel is an interesting and exciting study in character-contrast. Maya is emotional. Gautama is not very sensitive. She loves life, art, nature and poetry. For Gautama these things are not important. He has been brought up in the family in which there are discussions about parliament debates, bribery, corruption and money. They would talk on everything under the sun but love. We know that Maya loves her pet-dog Toto deeply. When Toto dies, she wants the corpse to be buried in a befitting manner. When Gautama comes home in the evening, he acts in a very indifferent manner. He rings up to the Public Works Department which takes away the corpse. This cold and formal behavior of Gautama lacerates Maya's feelings within her.

After this Maya feels suffocated within the four walls of her house. She sees in retrospect her Princess-like life in her father's house. She yearns for going out in Summer. She tries to persuade Gautama to find time and get away just for a short holiday. This is how she proposes and he disposes:

> "I want—I want," I stammered swiftly, "to see the Kathakali dances. I have heard of the ballets they have in their villages. They say they go on for days and days! And the dancers are all men, and they wear such fantastic masks. And the drums...." "Well, well," Gautama was amused. "I thought I could never underestimate you appetite for the curious. But I was wrong—I had underestimated it."
>
> "But Gautama, I thought you would be interested in that, too—more than in the hills and pony rides and things. It must be such a—marvelous sight, so—violent and bizarre." I groped for words painfully. The vision was excruciating in its vividness to me, and was one who did not even glimpse it, no matter what I said. "The masks they wear—you must have seen them? And their costumes. And the special kind of music.
>
> And is all out in the open, at night by starlight—and perhaps they have torches. Yes, I suppose they dance by torchlight...." Gautama got up abruptly, having finished his cigarette and stretched. "If that is your only reason for wanting to go all that way South, I suggest you wait till a Kathakali troupe comes to give a performance in Delhi, as it is bound to sometime—perhaps in Winter. It will be less expensive." (42-43)

Maya expresses her desire to see the Kathakali dances. The Kathakali dancer's costumes, their masks, their drums and their music—all fascinate her. She is interested in seeing the marvelous sight of the dancers. She tries to persuade him by telling him that he would also be interested in the Kathakali dances—more than in the hills and pony rides. Temperamentally Gautama is averse to music, art and dance. He could have dismissed Maya's proposal in a straightforward manner—'we would not go to the South.' He does it in an oblique way suggesting her to wait for the troupe coming to Delhi—perhaps in Winter. He puts his dismissal in a conditional way—"if that is the reason for going to South, then don't go to South. You can see the dance in our home town—Delhi." It is his lack of love for art and music and further his love for money that make him to be more informative and oblique in his dismissing the issue and rejecting her proposal. He is a man of logic. Perhaps he thinks that dismissing her proposal directly and briefly in a sentence would not have driven his point home. To underestimate her appetite for the curious and the fantastic, he is being more informative and circumlocutory in his response to her proposal.

Once Gautama takes Maya to a party hosted by Mr. and Mrs. Lal. The other two guests at the party are Prim lady and her husband Harbans Singh. When the subject of palmistry surfaces during the dinner, Harbans Singh boasts of having a good knowledge of palmistry. He was a collegemate of Gautama. He prides on having prophesied that Gautama would stand first in B.A. examination and that one day would be a great lawyer. Maya is scared of the words—'fate' and 'destiny.' To challenge his claim of being a palmist she asks him if he believes in palmistry. This is how he replies:

> "Excited I turned now to the husband who was still protesting at the accusation of pretence. "And you?" I questioned. "You believe in palmistry?" Have you the lines in your hand dictating *your* life? You are convinced?"
>
> He laughed jovially. So jovially that an alliance with the albino of the black and oil slick temple gate was discounted immediately. "You see," he said, "how interested women become in this! As soon as I mention I am a palmist—even if I add that I am only an amateur palmist—they gather around me like bees. Shall I read your palm then and tell you your future?" (77-78)

The Prim lady tells Maya that her husband pretends to have good knowledge of palmistry. Things in life happen not according to palmist's prophecies but according what is written in our destiny. Maya wants to know what Harbans Singh's reaction to his wife's remark is. All the four questions Maya asks are 'yes/no' questions. Harbans Singh could have asserted by saying 'yes'. Of course, he does not respond to Maya's questions positively but by being more informative and in an indirect way. It is his cynical attitude to women that he wants to assert. He even goes to the extent of comparing women to bees—thus belittling them. In the context of the ongoing conversation Harbans Singh faces the situation of being brief and informative as required by Maya's question. To assert that he is a palmist and to make fun of women as fatalists he sacrifices both the maxims—being informative and being brief and clear.

Shobha De's *Socialite Evenings* defines the institutions of family and marriage afresh. In the Indian context family is the smallest sociological unit. Family implies marriage which in turn lends stability and togetherness to family. Family and marriage are, thus, interrelated units. For a variety of reasons the family in India is in the state of disintegration. One can point out the reasons like promiscuity in sexual relations, excessive leisure among the women in the rich classes and economic independence. Economic security is a cornerstone that holds the husband and wife together. This is the picture that emerges in Shobha De's *Socialite Evenings*. Karuna's friend and mentor Anjali divorces Abe. Anjali is on the lookout for a rich 'available' man. She gets one rich man in Kumar Bhandari—a Punjabi businessman. Anjali is his third wife. The first lives with two daughters in Madras. The second lives with one son at Juhu. He has not divorced them yet. A month after Anjali's marriage with Kumar she telephones Karuna. This is how the telephonic talk proceeds:

"Hi!" she said, but there was no cheer in his voice.

"Have you been deflowered yet?"

"Sort of...?"

"What do you mean 'sort of'?"

"What are you doing?"

"Nothing special". (123)

When Karuna asks Anjali if she has been to bed with Kumar, Anjali vaguely mutters—'sort of' and withholds to release the information she possesses. When asked what she means by 'sort of'. She avoids to answer the question. The fact is that she wants to share the realities about Kumar with Karuna. It has turned out that Kumar is 'gay'. He is a 'homo'. He has his workouts with a boy Murty. He has married Anjali only as a matter of social prestige. The marriage between Anjali and Kumar lacks emotional and sexual relationship. It is a deal, a contract. He gives her money—economic security. She buys the stuff she likes-bags, saris, shoes, jewellery and so on. Kumar has freedom to cuddle Murty. Anjali would not divulge these things on the telephone for ultimately she has to keep up his image. With this consideration in mind Anjali suspends the maxim of being informative and that of clarity in her reply to Karuna.

Karuna has a small role in the Hindi version of *Desire Under the Elms* directed by Swapna. When the play is performed at the Prithvi theatre, an art-film maker Girish Sridhar is in the audience. After the performance he avoids talking to Swapna and instead concentrates on Karuna. Swapna has noticed that Girish, too, is interested in the play. She is eager to know what is in his mind and what has passed between Girish and Karuna. The next morning, she rings up Karuna. Let us see how Karuna deals with her in the following exchange:

"Well, you know—what happened last night?"

"Nothing."

"What do you mean nothing? You were talking to him. He must have dropped you back. What did he say? Did he like the play?"

"I don't know. We didn't discuss it."

"Then what did you discuss?"

"Other things." (247)

As readers we know that Girish himself is working on a modern-day adaptation of "*Shakuntala*" and has offered the key-role to Karuna in the film. According to him Karuna belongs to classical mould of artists and fits into the classical framework of his film. He also asks her to meet him later for lunch. Karuna has also understood that there is 'something beyond his beard' and 'his voice' (247).

Karuna is not enthusiastic about entering into the cinema life. She is content with the money she is getting presently for modeling for suitings and dresses. Moreover she is aware of the eminent gossip about her relationship/affair with Girish. Her desire not to divulge what happened between Girish and her and to protect herself from the possible gossip in the columns of film magazines run by notorious reporters—lead Karuna to be untruthful and vague to Swapna who is a hysterical woman from Delhi trying to set her foot in the Bollywood.

In *The Binding Vine*, the novelist places the protagonist—Urmila between her dead mother-in-law Mira who was subjected to marital rape and Kalpana a victim of pre-marital rape. In Indian society rape is a horrible indignity for the victim. As Nityanandam (1995: 61) records "The dividing line between criminal and the victim, the attacker and the prey becomes blurred." Even Shakutai—the mother of rape victim—adopts an ambivalent attitude towards her daughter. There is no doubt that she worried about Kalpana but she mutters to Urmila—"Here boys are like—they're like dogs panting after bitches. And you paint and flaunt yourself, do you think they'll leave you alone?" (146). The male counterparts like Dr. Bhaskar Jain and the police take rape of Kalpana in a very casual way. It is the mother, Urmila and Vanaa who try to camouflage the horrible happening to Kalpana. It is a question of choosing between life and death for them—the question whether to speak the truth to Shakutai and be direct or not. This is the dilemma they face when Bhaskar Jain asks Urmila and Vanaa to tell Shakutai that Kalpana has been raped. The following interesting piece of exchange illustrates what is on their mind:

> "Tell her it's the truth."
>
> "What is he saying, Tai? Tell him my daughter is not that kind of girl."
>
> "Nobody is accusing your daughter...."
>
> "Your daughter hasn't done anything, he isn't saying that."
>
> "It was an accident, a car knocked her down."
>
> "This doctor has examined your daughter."
>
> "She was raped," he says still speaking in English.
>
> "Your daughter has been...." Vanaa hesitates, searching for the Marathi words, gives up. "Someone has wronged her." (58)

Vanaa consoles Shakutai by telling her that Kalpana has been injured in a car accident—a sheer falsehood. When Dr. Bhaskar Jain repeats that Kalpana has been raped, Urmila hesitates to reveal the truth to Shakutai. Vanaa's mother tongue fails her for revealing it. Finally, she relates in an oblique manner that someone has wronged Kalpana. Considering the intensity of the moment and the condition of Shakutai it would have been rude on the part of Vanaa and Urmila to be truthful and to be direct. Vanaa's and Urmila's untruthfulness and obliquity are the strategies employed to save Shakutai from shock. Their first duty is to console and commiserate the victim's mother. Hence, they do not hesitate to sacrifice being truthful and direct. In a couple of other situations in the novel one observes that the characters face the clash between being informative, truthful and brief and direct. Socio-cultural considerations force them to deviate from being so. In the section that follows we would discuss the relation between maxim of Manner and the concern for being linguistically polite to others.

5.4. Manner Maxim and the Politeness Concern in the Five Novels

The Manner maxim demands that the conversational partners avoid vagueness and ambiguity in their verbal contributions. At the beginning of the twentieth century philosophers like Moore and Russell viewed ambiguity as a defect in language. They advocated for removal of ambiguities in language and creation of an ideal language devoid of imprecision, ambiguities and contradictions. It was with the advent of Austin and the like-minded philosophers that it was recognized that people manage to communicate effectively despite ambiguities and imprecision in language. It was claimed that people are ambiguous and indirect and ambiguity and indirectness are deliberate and intentional in most of the circumstances. The context of situation in which people are ambiguous, indirect and circumlocutory help one to arrive at why people are ambiguous and roundabout in their conversation. Experts in the Pragmatic field claim that to be ambiguous and indirect is perfectly rational because behaving so brings people advantage, helps them avoid hurting someone, and avoiding a taboo word or topic helps them achieve their goal. Being ambiguous and indirect are the instances of departure from the Gricean maxim of Manner we have been discussing. One of the motivations for being oblique, ambiguous and indirect is to show the concern for the other. That is one is vague and circumlocutory and one's vagueness and circumlocution are 'other-centered'. In the five novels under investigation one comes across a few such conversational exchanges in which the characters do not hesitate to break the maxim to save the others' 'face'—positive face—one's desire to be liked and appreciated by others.

In *Temporary Answers*, one comes across a couple of situations in which characters are indirect and their indirectness is alter-centered. Abhijit Gokhale is expectedly and understandably indirect in his marriage proposal to Vineeta. This is how he behaves linguistically with Vineeta:

> "At ten o'clock? Have you thought of my reputation?" He clapped his hand to his forehead. "Oh, my God, I forgot all about that. What shall we do now? Do you suppose you could marry me? That would make it all right, wouldn't it?" (91)

Abhijit is a bachelor. Vineeta is a widow in her thirties. She has been staying alone in a flat away from her parents and her younger sister Madhuri. Abhijit's visit to her flat at ten o'clock at night is by no means unintentional. He has come with a marriage proposal—proposal to marry Vineeta. The setting of the conversation—Vineeta's flat and the time of the conversation—ten o'clock at night—together his desire not to hurt her make Abhijit to be indirect in his proposal. As yet he has no any right over Vineeta though he has been in love with her for quite sometime now. It would have been rude on his part had he been direct and blunt in his proposal. He is being polite to her in the Lakoffian sense—by not imposing the proposal on her and by giving her the option to accept or reject his proposal. He opts out of being clear and the motivation is—'alter-centered.' He considers her reputation as a doctor.

It is Vineeta who is being indirect in answering Abhijit's last question in the following encounter:

> He said, "Where were you yesterday?"
>
> "I came home very late."
>
> He said with a laugh, "Don't tell me what I know already. Why were you back so late?" "Had to work late, then, a couple of house calls, then I ate out. Sitabai had the day off and didn't feel like cooking."
>
> "Vineeta?"
>
> "What?"
>
> "Oh, Nothing I love you."
>
> "That is nice to know, so early in the morning."
>
> I didn't say I love him. I had never been able to say it easily. Once he had asked me why I was so afraid of using the word love and I had told him I didn't like to use it until I was sure we meant the same thing by it.
>
> "I'll see you in the evening. Will you be home early?"
>
> "It's difficult to say. You'd better not count on it."
>
> "Are you avoiding me?"
>
> "Whatever gave you that idea?" (165)

It is more than obvious that Abhijit is trying to reciprocate with Vineeta. He rings her early in the morning the day he is to leave alone for his spiritual renewal. He is very covert in telling her that he loves her. He desires to see her in the evening and wants to know whether she would be home early. As the practice at her clinic is unpredictable, she tells him not to count on it. He has an inkling that Vineeta is avoiding him. When asked, she replies, "Whatever gave you that idea". By this she indirectly wants to state that she is not avoiding him.

There seem to be three motivations for her to be indirect in her reply. One is—her resentment at Abhijit leaving alone—not allowing her to accompany him in his going out. But she cannot be straightforward and direct to articulate her resentment. The other is—a flicker of hope she cherishes about her relationship about Abhijit. Vineeta is not firm about marrying Abhijit. The last one is—her consideration for him. She knows that Abhijit needs to restore his mental balance and his faith in himself so that he can continue writing the play. Her indirect assertion that she is not avoiding him is geared to contribute to his regaining his faith in himself and achieving his spiritual renewal. As at the moment she does not want to break up her relationship with him. Apart from her flicker of hope about her relationship with him her attempt to be indirect is a sign of her concern for Abhijit. Comparing these two instances it emerges that in the former it is Abhijit who opts out of being direct and is linguistically being polite to her. In the latter it is Vineeta who is being indirect in her reply and it is due to her consideration for Abhijit. One gathers that Abhijit and Vineeta intend to get their relationship going.

We have already stated elsewhere in this study that a central theme in *Heat and Dust* is the East-West encounter. We have the Indian characters—the Nawab, Inder Lal, Ritu and Maji and their British counterparts—Douglas Rivers, Olivia, Harry, Mr. and Mrs. Saunders, Mr. and Mrs. Crawford, Major Minnies, the young narrator and Chid (Chidanand). One observes that apart from the exception of the Crawfords and Major Minnies the British and the Indians do not have a healthy and positive attitude to one another. They do express their hatred for one another as and when the issue comes up. Mrs. Saunders views the Indians as sexually pervert. On one occasion she tells Olivia "it is not good to let them see you in bed—the servants" (119). She tells Olivia that they have only one thought in their heads and that is sex. The Nawab tells Harry and Olivia that you "all are the same" (obnoxious) (120). Dr. Saunders views the Indians to be irrational, fickle and reckless. He has many anecdotes to relate about India and Indians from his hospital experiences.

Dr. Saunders is invited by the Nawab to a dinner. Pleased by the food and drink he is led to express his so-called opinion about Indians. Let's see how he expresses it and how the Nawab deals with him in the exchange:

> "Then Nawab Sahib, I had the fellow to my office and no further argument, smartly boxed his ears for him, one-two, one-two."
>
> "You did quite right, Doctor. Quite right. You set an example."
>
> "It is the only way to deal with them, Nawab Sahib. It is no use arguing with them, they're not amenable to reason. They haven't got it here, you see, up here the way we have."
>
> "Exactly, Doctor. You have hit the—What is it Harry?"
>
> "Nail on the head."
>
> "Quite right. The nail on the head." (121)

Dr. Saunders tells the Nawab that the Indians are irrational—they are not amenable to reason. It is no use arguing with them. You can smartly deal with them by boxing them. The Nawab compliments Dr. Saunders—"You did quite right. You set a good example. You hit the nail on the head."

By employing the idiom—'hit the nail on the head' the Nawab drives home his point that Dr. Saunders has struck the blow at an object exactly—rightly dealt with the Indian whom Dr. Saunders refers to. If one could doubt the sincerity of the Nawab's compliment, one could say that the Nawab is indirectly criticizing Dr. Saunders for being blatantly so stupid in expressing his opinion about the Indians and that too in the presence of his Indian royalty and host—the Nawab. However, excited and hurt the Nawab may be, he avoids to be direct and blunt in his attack on Dr. Saunders. This he accomplishes by way of complimenting and by being idiomatic. Ultimately, Dr. Saunders is the Nawab's guest and he is being called into humour the Nawab's intimates—Olivia and Harry.

Towards the end of the novel the young narrator involuntarily makes her way to Maji's hut. By the way the narrator walks and holds herself down as a client for getting an abortion. While checking up the narrator Maji is being ambiguous in using the pronoun "It" and mutters incomplete utterances. She deals with the narrator in the following manner:

> She said, "You see, it has started." Apparently it wasn't mysterious at all—the woman has a midwife marking me down as a potential client. She must have noticed me before and followed me today to check up her suspicion. My condition would be perfectly obvious to her by the way I walked and held myself. In a day or two she would probably offer me her services. And Maji offered me her own again: "This would be a good time," she said. "8 or 9 weeks—it would not be too difficult." (163-64)

For the narrator Maji was one of the Indian dark mythological figures—the potent Indian Goddess. As Maji easily recognizes that the narrator is crying, Maji is being ambiguous/vague. She wants the narrator to be taken into confidence and to be persuaded to get aborted. To make the narrator feel easy and comfortable she tells the narrator that the narrator is 8 or 9 years pregnant and hence this is a good time for her to get the foetus aborted. Maji's vagueness is, thus, other-centered. By being linguistically polite to the narrator Maji emerges to be a seasoned midwife and as a motherly figure for the narrator.

In *Cry, the Peacock*, the protagonist—Maya and her husband Gautama are a star-crossed couple. Their very attitude to life differs from each other's. She believes in attachment and he in detachment. Naturally one very rarely comes across their verbal exchanges showing concern for each other. On an occasion Maya is being vague in uttering "It's evening" in response to his question. This is how he questions and replies:

> He looked so startled; so like an antic owl from whose beak its prey has been snatched that whooped with laughter.

> "What is it?" he asked, slightly put off, rather grumpy and stirred his tea briefly.
>
> "It's evening," I told him, almost singing. "You're home and work's over for the day, you know." (194)

Maya witnesses a horrible dust storm during the day. She rushes from window to window and hears the trees creaking and screaming in the wind. After the storm declines, she settles luxuriously in her chair utterly in peace. As Gautama arrives, she forgets to jump up and greet him. Gautama is unmoved by this strange behaviour of Maya. This makes her laugh. As she whoops with laughter, he asks what it is. Her reply, "It's evening" seems to be rather vague. She camouflages a lot of explanation behind uttering "It's evening." The storm has given her a sense of flying, of being lifted off the earth and into the sunset and of release from bondage. Maya realizes that Gautama has some pain of headache visible on his face. She goes on adding "You're home and the work is over for the day." This she does to give him a sense of relaxation and comfort. This expresses her warmth of love for Gautama coming back not to his house but to his home. She may not have welcomed him by jumping up but she does welcome him by serving a cup of tea. Through her reply "It's evening. You're home" Maya is being linguistically polite to him.

Maya's mother-in-law also shows her sympathetic concern for Maya by being a little vague in her conversation with Nila:

> "But I saw the servants, opening up another bed-room this morning."
>
> A hint of vagueness overcame the harsh steady voice of her mother, "There are so many rooms," she said vaguely. (211-12)

After the tragic end of Gautama Maya goes mad. She is brought to Lucknow house by her mother-in-law and Nila—her sister-in-law. Nila engages herself in playing with a Pomeranian dog and the mother sits knitting for an orphan just admitted to her crèche. Nila tells her mother that the servants were opening up another bed-room and the house was being tidied up. Her mother vaguely utters—"there are so many rooms." This vague utterance of her expresses the concern for Maya—"how a young girl, Maya, might have tolerated and managed to live with her father in such a big house." Tidying up such a big house makes one itch to bring out a broom and a bucket. Briefly put, Nila's mother's suspension from being clear serves to express her sympathetic attitude to Maya—the one who has lost her mental equilibrium.

In *Socialite Evenings* every one is in his world. Almost every one is selfish and self-centered. Everyone struggles to rise in his carrier by hook or by crook. They are career-hungry, money-hungry and sex-hungry. Despite being married they do not hesitate to have an extra-marital affair. These observations could very well apply to the key figures like Anjali, Karuna and Ritu. One could also add a nympho starlet Nisha to the list. Each of these women represents what R. Mala (1991: 58) calls "The typical Laurencian woman who holds the sexual autonomy in her hands." There is a sexual power politics. In this game of sexual power politics the woman is assigned a superior position and man is regarded as 'a conditioned dog.' In this lust-laced world of sexual promiscuity the female characters speak freely of their sex and their affairs. On one occasion or two one observes that they are being vague or ambiguous when it comes to sex and their vagueness and indirectness serves as a face-saving strategy.

Let us take the first example in which Anjali's verbal contribution is vague. She suspends the maxim of clarity and straightforwardness:

"Have you been deflowered yet?"

"Sort of."

"What do you mean sort of?"

"What are you doing?"

"Nothing special." (123)

A month after Anjali's marriage with Kumar Bhandari Karuna asks her whether she has been to bed with Kumar. She replies vaguely and incompletely saying 'sort of.' When asked again Anjali avoids to explain what she means by 'sort of.' Her attempt is to hide from Karuna how her marriage with Kumar has not worked and would not work. This is because Kumar is a homo and indulges in vile acts with a boy Murty. Her marriage with Kumar is a deal. He would give her financial security and she would not mind Kumar having the boy Murty. Anjali's vagueness is motivated. She wants to save her 'positive face' and also that of Kumar. She suspends the maxim of clarity to save herself from being ridiculed and Kumar being exposed and disgraced.

In the other instance it is Karuna who lies to Swapna and suspends the maxim of clarity in the following exchange:

> "What happened last night?"
>
> "Nothing".
>
> "What do you mean nothing? You were talking to him. He must have dropped you back. What did he say? Did he like the play?"
>
> "I don't know. We didn't discuss it."
>
> "Then what did you discuss?"
>
> "Other things." (247)

The 'he' in this exchange is Girish Sridhar—an art-film maker who was present in the audience during the performance of Swapna's Hindi version of *Desire Under the Elms*. After the performance he dismisses Swapna—the director of the performance and talks to Karuna. He has offered Karuna a key-role in his modern adaptation of "*Shakuntala*." He has explicitly told Karuna that the direction by Swapna was bad but he complimented that Karuna came through the role very good. Swapna is dying to know what has passed between Karuna and Girish during their meeting. Karuna lies to Swapna twice and finally tells vaguely that Girish and she discussed 'other things'. Karuna's vague reply is doubly motivated. She, like Anjali in the previous example, intends to save herself as well as Girish—a widower living with his son Kunal. Karuna realizes that not revealing anything about Girish ultimately eliminates the possibility of any gossip about her and Girish. To save herself and Girish from impending disgrace in the form of film-magazine gossip Karuna suspends the maxim of clarity in telling Swapna about what she discussed with Girish.

The Binding Vine mirrors the society governed by patriarchal norms. There are codes of conduct for girls and women in such a society. A girl is expected to behave herself so that her speech and behavior do not attract men's attention. If she takes liberty, she is at fault. "Here boys are like—they are like dogs panting after bitches. And if you paint and flaunt yourself, do you think they will leave you alone?" (146). This is what Shakutai relates to Urmi expressing her rage and despair at Kalpana. According to Shakutai, a married woman's prior duty is to please her husband whether she likes it or not. She has to put up with physical assault by her husband. Women in the Indian society are expected to be secretive about the sensitive things like rape, sex and pregnancy. The stories of Mira, Shakutai, Kalpana and Sulu testify to these harrowing facts.

While discussing the deviations from being informative, truthful and relevant we have observed that it is the socio-cultural norms and considerations that force Vanaa, Urmi and Shakutai to be over-informative or under-informative, untruthful and irrelevant. These observations apply also to their being vague or ambiguous and indirect in their interaction with their conversational partners. It has been repeatedly stated that rape and sex are very sensitive issues in Indian social set up. The factors like social distance or intimacy and relative status do not seem to result in their being vague or ambiguous. One comes across a number of situations in which Vanaa, Shakutai and even Urmi suspend the maxim of clarity and brevity when it comes to Kalpana being raped, Shakutai's pregnancy and her concern for keeping her and her daughter's honour in tact. This is why Shakutai appeals to Dr. Bhaskar Jain—"Even if it is true, keep it to yourself, don't let anyone know of it" (59). It has already been discussed how these women are vague and indirect for showing their concern for the other—to save the other's 'face'. Such instances occur several times in the novel.

It is the factor of relative 'right' between Bhaskar Jain and Urmi which seems to govern his being indirect in expression of his love and his proposal to Urmi:

"So there are no problems."

"None. Except that I've gone and fallen in love with a dark, sharp-tongued, married woman." (160-61)

Bhaskar is a bachelor and Urmi is a married woman having a six-year-old son Kartik. It is glaring that Bhaskar does not want to marry a sweet, fair and convent-educated girl to be chosen by his mother. He has cherished the desire to marry Urmi. He has as yet no any right over Urmi. Considering her status and the family background she hails from Bhaskar hesitates to be straightforward in expressing his love. His concern is not to hurt and shock her by being direct and clear. He opts out of being clear and it is to make her feel easy and comfortable. His departure from being clear is, thus, alter-centered.

5.5. Conclusion

Grammarians, linguists, purists and some philosophers view ambiguity, vagueness and prolixity as deficiencies in language. For them clarity, brevity and economy are the precepts of good and effective linguistic behavior—both spoken and written. Crystal (2004: 129) appeals for the survival of language saying "Language has to be clear, care has to be taken to avoid ambiguity and subtleties of expression have to be carefully managed." To be brief and clear means to speak only what is necessary and speak to the point. Clarity and brevity are the imperatives of good communication. That linguistic behavior is good which obeys these precepts or principles. Any deviations from these lead to bad communication or bad style. Despite these claims one observes that not even a casual conversation is free of vagueness, ambiguity and prolixity. This is more so about fictional conversation which abounds in vagueness and indirectness on the part of characters. In this chapter, we have observed how the demands of the maxim of clarity and brevity subsumed in Grice's maxim of Manner remain unfulfilled by characters.

The characters in the novels under study deviate from the demands of this maxim on a number of occasions. Their vagueness, ambiguity, indirectness and circumlocution are unavoidable and integral parts of their linguistic resources.

These strategies serve their personal as well as social purposes. They reveal and indicate their attitude to their interlocutors. The characters are deliberately indirect and vague in negotiating their relationship with each other. Their deliberate ambiguity and indirectness depends according to Nerlich and Clarke (2001: 15). "On social factors: preverbal: age, sex, social status and interactional factors: purpose of conversation, topic, medium/ mode and the register of conversation".

The deviations from Manner maxim by these characters express a lot of socio-cultural and interracial reality. One observes that the characters are indirect and circumlocutory when it comes to taboo topics like sex, rape and pregnancy in the Indian social set up. One of the motivations of being vague and indirect is to show the concern for the other's 'face': a self-esteem that one possesses about himself or herself. The deviations from the maxim we have analysed are geared to preserving both the aspects of face: positive face—a desire to be liked and appreciated by others and negative face-freedom from imposition. One could state that vagueness and indirectness result from the need to protect the face of the self and of the other. Thus, linguistic ambiguities, vagueness and indirectness have their bearing on character revelation, theme elaboration and on a number of occasions serve the purposes of creating intimacy and cementing social bonds between characters.

6

Conclusion

The first chapter of this study is a theoretical framework. It has attempted to discuss the relationship between language and social norms, the Gricean Principle of verbal cooperation and the models of Politeness. It has pointed out the simultaneity of occurrence of pragmatic principles—the Cooperative Principle and the Politeness Principle in conversation. The second, third, fourth and fifth chapters are the piecemeal and threadbare study of the deviations from the maxims of Cooperative Principle in five Indian novels in English under investigation.

The in-depth and piecemeal analysis of the deviations from the Cooperative Principle maxims by the characters in the five novels brings forth certain observations about the language used by these characters. In this chapter these deviations from the maxims have been clubbed and their significance has been pointed out in the light of following dimensions:

1. Taxonomy of non-fulfillment of the Cooperative Principle—its four maxims—Quantity, Quality, Relation, and Manner.
2. Maxim-deviations and social implications.
3. Maxim-deviations and socio-cultural realities.
4. Maxim-deviations and ideological (re)construction.
5. Maxim-deviations and the concern for politeness.
6. Maxim-deviations and suggested meaning.
7. Implicatures and the study of novel.

In his seminal paper "Logic and Conversation" (1975), Grice argues that talking or conversation is a cooperative endeavour between speaker and hearer. It is conducted by the conversational partners to the achievement of their mutual ends. It follows then that they conduct their conversation according to a set of principles or maxims. One of such principles is a pragmatic principle called Cooperative Principle. In simplest terms it means that the conversational partners should conduct their conversation as required by the purpose or direction of their talk-exchange. In so doing they make their conversational contributions informative, truthful, relevant to the ongoing context and brief, clear and orderly. In Gricean terminology the partners conduct their conversation adhering to the maxims of Quantity, Quality, Relation and Manner. This proposal of conversation as a cooperative effort and a team work between speaker and hearer exhibits the following features:

1. The participants conduct their conversation on the basis of tacit assumption of cooperation.
2. The participants have a common immediate aim or purpose behind carrying the conversation.
3. Their conversational contributions are dovetailed—neatly joined or structured.

Thus, conversation is a purposive and rational activity on the part of the conversational partners.

A very crucial and significant observation Grice makes in the paper is that "A participant in a talk-exchange may fail to fulfill a maxim in various ways" (49). All that this means is that there are many an occasion on which the conversational partners deviate from behaving as required by the maxims. For analysis of conversation it is the deviation rather than the observance of the maxims that counts. This is because the deviations from maxims generate additional or unstated meanings called 'implicatures.' These implicatures are as Syal and Jindal (1999: 131) put "Possible through the deliberate violation of the conversational maxims." In simplest terms implicature is the difference between what is literally stated and what is meant or implicated by a speaker. Deviations are paramountly significant also because they give the analyst the insights into the two social factors: (1) Preverbal—age, sex, geographical region and social, economic status of the partner and (2) Interactional factors—the purpose, field or topic, medium or mode and the register (formal or informal) of conversation.

Perhaps the most systematic categorization of deviations from Gricean maxims has been given by Jenny Thomas (1995). She proposes and amply illustrates the taxonomy of non-fulfillment of the maxims as follows (1995: 64-78):

1. "Flouting a maxim.
2. Violating a maxim.
3. Infringing a maxim.
4. Opting out of a maxim.
5. Suspending a maxim."

Grice's chief interest is in the blatancy of non-observing a maxim—flouting of a maxim. A speaker ostentatiously or blatantly fails to fulfill a maxim and does so to trigger his interlocutor to look for an additional or unstated meaning—implicature. This concept of implicature is the centerpiece of Gricean pragmatics. To generate an implicature a speaker is blatantly over or under-informative, is untruthful, is irrelevant and is vague, ambiguous and indirect. When an implicature is generated, Grice (1975: 49) says "A maxim is being EXPLOITED."

The process of calculating and working out an implicature takes place along the following lines:

(a) The interlocutor relies on the conventional meaning of the words/utterances used.

(b) The interlocutor thinks that there is no reason to suppose that the speaker is not observing a maxim of CP.

(c) The interlocutor takes into account the context—the preceding utterances or socio-cultural context of the utterances.

(d) The interlocutor thinks that the speaker has produced the utterance/s—'U' with 'I' = implicature, supposing that 'I' is required.

(e) The interlocutor also thinks that the speaker of the utterance/s allows him to think of 'I' = implicature.

All this is a set of very informal procedures for getting at the meaning implicated by the speaker. This procedure helps one explain how the interlocutor gets to the level of implied meaning from the level of stated meaning or expressed meaning. To state briefly, a flout is one type of Grice's taxonomy of non-fulfillment of maxims. The other type of this taxonomy includes the rest of the categories—violation, infringement, suspension and opting out of a maxim. The difference between a flout as a non-observance of a maxim and infringement, violation, suspension and opting out as non-observance of a maxim is that the former is intended to convey implicature whereas the latter produce what Mooney (2004: 907) calls "Social implication." Social implication is the implication about the speaker and the relationship between the interlocutors. Such social implication is the effect or result of non-fulfilling a maxim by way of infringing, violating, suspending and opting out a maxim. The necessary condition for producing social implication is that both the interlocutors share items of background knowledge, beliefs, information and socio-cultural codes. The suspension of a maxim in particular is conditioned by social and cultural norms. It reflects one's affiliation to his group, his society or community and his knowledge of socio-cultural codes or norms. This knowledge of socio/communal and cultural codes may be called after Mooney (2004: 911) "Cultural literacy". It is cultural literacy that may be said to force one to suspend a maxim.

In the present study our focus has been on both the categories of non-fulfillment of maxim. It has been observed that the characters in the five novels flout the maxims on a number of occasions and their flout generates implicated meanings—implicatures to be recuperated by their interlocutors. This is what happens between Ritu and Karuna in *Socialite Evenings*. Ritu tells Karuna that her husband has an affair with tartlet who is a secretary somewhere. As he comes back home, Ritu gets red, grabs a huge vase and flings it at him.

Karuna asks her a simple yes-no question and Ritu gives her almost a page-long reply:

> "Did you aim for his crotch or his head?"
>
> "I would have missed either—but what happened later was awful. He came at me like a maniac. First he pulled out his leather belt from the trouser and then he stood over me with his eyes blazing. *Phatak*—I felt the leather on my arm and I was so stunned I couldn't even scream. Before I could open my mouth, it landed on my arm again. I lost my balance—I was sitting on the edge of a carpet. He was still standing at the same spot with his arms raised. Suddenly I felt a sharp kick in my side. And another one. Then I heard him say "Shit! There goes my Bally shoe." "Can you believe it?" Then he threw his belt away and started to slap me around. One heard hit cracked against my nose. Before I knew it, my favourite Anokhi *dupatta* was drenched in blood—my nose was like a geyser with blood gushing for it. May be it was the sight of all that blood that made him panic. He stopped and yanked my face up by the hair. "Shit! I'd better get a doctor. Is there any ice in the fridge?" I was still on the floor with the *dupatta* stuck to my nose. Some of the blood fell on the carpet—the stains are still there. I walked to the kitchen slowly to get some ice. It was so unreal, the whole thing. When I went to the bathroom to wash my face, I was shocked out with my wits. The whole thing was swollen—twice its size. My eyes were beginning to puff and one side of the face was turning purple where it had got badly bruised. There was a thick well across my arms. But do you know something—I quite enjoyed the whole thing. You must think I'm crazy. But it was thrilling in its own way. Not the pain—but the experience. He didn't look like a pipsqueak anymore. I thought of Marlon Brando in "*A Streetcar Named Desire*", have you seen the film? You must." (129)

It is more than obvious that Ritu's reply has more information—more than what is required by Karuna's question. Karuna recuperates the implicature generated that "Ritu is shameless as for her thrashing from her husband is thrilling. She takes delight in being beaten and she as a whore-like wife steeped with carnal desire like Brando is a sadomasochist." Karuna relies on the utterances produced by Ritu and reasons that Ritu has produced the utterances with this implicature generated. All the same Karuna assumes that there is no reason to suppose that Ritu is not being cooperative. This procedure assists Karuna to calculate the implicature conveyed by Ritu through being blatantly over-informative. The already existing explicit information in Ritu's utterances helps Karuna take the above implicated meaning out of her utterances. Mey (1999: 236) argues "My utterance in its final analysis, receives its meaning not only from what I put into it, but to an equally high degree from what the other can get out of it."

Ritu and Karuna engage in this process of meaning-making. One produces it through a flout and the other recovers it through the procedure outlined above. This is how the study of the flouts from the maxims enriches the reading of fictional conversation and the study of novel in general. We have seen the characters in the five novels doing this at times in their verbal encounters. Implicatures are, thus, embedded in their utterances having explicit or overt meanings. Such implicatures are generated by the characters' flagrant deviations from being truthful, relevant and brief and clear. Olivia in *Heat and Dust* tells Harry a blatant lie in the following conversation:

> Harry said, "Have you noticed something? That you are never taken to Begum and her ladies?"
>
> "I *have* met them, thank you." She gave a forced laugh. It was hard going. (102)

Despite Olivia's frequent visits to the palace the Nawab has been discourteous to Olivia by not taking and introducing Olivia to the Begum—his mother and her ladies. Olivia tells Harry a blatant lie that she has met the Begum and her ladies. This is to implicate to Harry that "The Nawab has been courteous to take and introduce Olivia to his mother and her ladies and that she has been intimate enough now to have made the Nawab do so." In the circumstances Olivia is led to implicate this because if she admits that she has really not been introduced to the Begum, it will signal that Olivia is not received into the palace on the footing of intimacy. In the other novels *Temporary Answers*, *Cry, the Peacock* and *The Binding Vine* too, Kishori, Vineeta, Abhijit Gokhale, Maya, Gautama, Shakutai, Vanaa and Urmila flagrantly deviate from the maxims. This leads to convey implicatures for their interlocutors to recover.

The other types of non-fulfillment are infringement, violation, suspension and opting out of a maxim. These non-fulfillments do not generate implicatures embedded in utterances. They tell us about characters—their nature, attitude to and relationship with interlocutors and their traits. Such deviations are conditioned by social/communal and cultural norms about linguistic behavior. In other words such non-fulfillments produce what Mooney (2004: 909) calls "Social implications." Traditionally we learn about a character through what the character says about himself/herself, what other character says about the character, through what the character does—through his actions and through representation of what passes through mind of the character—his inner thoughts and flux of emotions. By applying the yardsticks of Gricean maxims we arrive at the social implications—we learn about a character through how and why the character infringes, violates, suspends and opts out of a maxim in a given context. In simple words social implications result from how characters say what they say to their interlocutors.

Characters in a novel are the agents of action of the novel and they carry the story forward. The non-fulfilments mentioned above produce the truck load of implications. These implications—social implications—have a crucial bearing on the theme of the novel concerned. In the five novels selected for this study we come across a number of such non-fulfilments conveying social implications. A few examples from these novels would help to validate the observation about how implications about characters are produced. One readily recalls the Nawab in *Heat and Dust* who time and again tries to evade the topic of his nexus with the dacoits and exonerate himself from having the liaison with the bandits. In his attempts to do so he is over-informative, untruthful, irrelevant, and at times roundabout in his replies. When Olivia sees the rough men emerging from the Shrine of Baba Firdaus and falling at the feet of the Nawab, she asks him who these men are. Laughingly he replies, "I suppose you think they are bad men. You must have heard many stories I think, isn't it and you believe they're true. But they are bad men," he went on, "I think they can't be so very bad because look what they have come here for." He pointed to the mount in the shrine on which some fresh garlands had just been laid and sticks of incense were still smouldering. "You see they didn't come for any bad purpose but to pay their devotions" (133-34). The Nawab employs the verbal and the non-verbal strategy to camouflage the truth from her. It emerges that the Nawab is a shrewd person. His guest and friend Harry also emerges as the Nawab's protector—an image-saver for the Nawab when he replies to Olivia's question about the dacoits—"Honestly I don't know Olivia. A lot of things go on and I'd just as soon not know about them" (103).

In *Cry, the Peacock*, Maya's mother-in-law reveals her sympathetic concern for Maya by being vague. Nila—her daughter—tells that the servants were opening up another bed-room in the Lucknow house. Her mother vaguely utters —"There are so many rooms. This old house, it is full of rooms" (211-12). The vague response is geared to sympathise Maya who must have tolerated and managed to live in such a big house with her father. In *Temporary Answers*, Kishori unconsciously projects herself as an inveterate liar and a selfish woman by violating the maxim of truthfulness on a couple of occasions. When she comes to leave her children Hemant and Smriti with Vineeta, she tells Vineeta "If we leave Saturday evening, we should be back by Wednesday morning" (73). It is already planned that Kishori and her husband Madhu will not be back from Hyderabad until Saturday. When they return on Saturday morning, it is in the afternoon that she turns up to collect her children from Vineeta. This is how she pleads for her delayed comeback: "Well, we thought of telephoning, but it would have meant wasting hours waiting for a call to get through. And telegrams are mostly useless. They are so slow that you would probably have not got a telegram before we arrived here" (76). This further produces that Kishori is a 'user' and 'a happy-go-lucky' sort of woman. Her own need is the guiding principle of her life. All other considerations are minor and negligible for her.

The bachelors like Abhijit Gokhale and Dr. Bhaskar Jain in *Temporary Answers* and *The Binding Vine* respectively adopt a roundabout manner of expressing their love and proposal of marriage. Abhijit in *Temporary Answers* has been in love with Vineeta for quite some time now. He has already proposed to her and promised to keep her happy. But once again he visits Vineeta's flat at night. She is a widow in her early thirties living away from her parents. The sudden visit by him to her flat surprises her and she blames him for not thinking of her reputation. Abhijit is rather indirect and roundabout in proposing to her: "Oh, my God, I forgot all about that. What shall we do now? Do you suppose you could marry me? That would make it all right, wouldn't it?" (91). His being indirect in saying what he wants to say reflects that he wants to persuade her to accept the proposal and marry him because marriage would end her apprehension about her reputation and set all the things right between her and him. Bhaskar Jain is a bachelor and highly qualified person—a doctor. He can easily marry a sweet, fair and Convent-educated girl. But he desires to marry Urmila. He opts out of being direct and uses obliquity as a strategy. He proposes: "None. Except that I've gone and falling in love with a dark sharp-tongued, married woman" (160-61). This perfectly describes and matches to Urmila. She is a married woman having a six-year-old son Kartik and whose daughter Anu has recently died. Both these instances reveal that bachelors like Abhijit and Bhaskar in the Indian social set up lack courage to be plain and straightforward in expressing their love when they fall in love with a widow and married woman with children.

The characters in the novels are ironic at times. Their use of ironical and metaphorical language performs various functions. Irony and metaphor are rhetorical devices. For Gloria, Fein and

Schwarz (1988) irony functions as a muted form of negation. For Dews and Winners (1997) it functions as a muted form of criticism or a muted form of praise. Karuna in *Socialite Evenings* is being critical of Nisha—a nympho starlet and Anjali's friend after Anjali's divorce from Abe. Anjali is eager to show Karuna Nisha's perfect body. She invites Karuna in her house. When Karuna reaches there Nisha is very much there with an enormous red *bindi* on her forhead and in a white saree. Anjali tells that Nisha's husband likes her in this Indian Marilyn Monroe style. He imagines he is screwing a '*devi*' and not a 'pros.' He even recommends her to his producers. Nisha gets five thousands and an odd role in a film too. Karuna passes a calculated ironical remark: "Oh, great. She sounds real classy" (103). Karuna's ironical remark is employed to criticize Nisha—'a foul-mouthed slut' (102).

Ritu and Karuna's violation of being truthful in the encounter with Mataji produces the implication that 'Ritu and Karuna are the practical-minded and wise wives from the socialite class. Mataji is an assistant to Babaji—a sadhu, a rajyogi, one of the Indian sexy Sanyasis'. Mataji is the Godly mother. She leads the evening *bhajans* and makes our *kundalini* rise. It is Babaji that they are interested to meet and not Mataji. Babaji is being given an almond oil massage in a suite of the Taj Mahal. Mataji entertains Ritu and Karuna and Karuna outside. When she asks them if their husbands are doing '*naukri*', they falsely tell: "Yes—both officers" (158). Their strategy of lying implicates how practical-minded and wise wives they are. They are well-versed at putting off people like Mataji. Both of them have a mutual end and that is to meet Babaji. They are not interested in Mataji at all. Their non-fulfillment of the maxim of truthfulness underlines their practical-mindedness and knack of handling people like Mataji.

The social implications are also the implications that tell us something about the relationship between the interlocutors. The non-fulfilments of the Gricean maxims by the characters in the five novels throw light on the relationship between the characters involved in verbal interactions. A perusal of these non-fulfilments assists one in an attempt at character-study. We have a number of situations in the novels where the departures for the maxims reflect the interrelationship between the characters. Take for example Vineeta and Kishori in *Temporary Answers*. Vineeta is sickened by Kishori's slick lying on a couple of occasions. She has realized that Kishori has used her to look after her children. When the next time Kishori entreats Vineeta to look after her children for a couple of hours, Vineeta tells her falsely: "I am going out. I have an appointment" (77). Her violation from being truthful throws light on her determination to resist Kishori's appeal.

In *Heat and Dust*, the Nawab is being irrelevant to Olivia when she sincerely assures him that she will not tell anyone in Satipur that the Nawab is bad person having nexus with the outlaws and dacoits. He irrelevantly points out the need for all of us to become noble souls: "It is necessary for all of us to strive for this—but also I know how far I am from such a goal. Yes, very far indeed" (135). His suspension from being relevant hints that he is disheartened and rather panicky that he is being exposed to Olivia. He rumbles his talk by digressing from the topic of ongoing conversation. It hints that the relationship between the Nawab and Olivia is being shaky at this juncture of time in the novel. In *Cry, the Peacock* one comes across encounters between the protagonist Maya and Gautama that throw light on the fragile relationship between the two. One recalls that one evening Maya and Gautama are in their study. Inwardly she is haunted by the astrologer's prophecy that one of them would die within four years of their marriage. As Gautama is busy and absorbed in his book, she asks him if he will work late this night. She looks at his long, set face with the frown. She also switches on the light. But she notices that—'he did not reply' (165). He withholds from answering her question—opts out from replying to her. It reveals that she is trying to interact with him but he is cold and unresponsive. She is passing through a crisis but he is concerned with his professional work and absorbed in his studies. She desires for his love but he is insensitive to her desire. His strategy of withholding his response is one of the occasions that implies that there is lack of love, care and companionship in the relationship between the two. One feels that a mismatched marriage between these two will only fail.

In *The Binding Vine*, Bhasker Jain changes the topic of his conversation with Urmi when once she serves him a cup of tea. She tells him that she has added lemon grass to the tea. He remarks that the tea smells good. After some silence he drifts the topic and says, "I wish I'd known you before your Anusha died" (86). One gathers that he wants to commiserate her for the death of her daughter Anu. But his strategy of shifting the topic—suspending from being relevant—is employed to establish and consolidate his relationship with her. This is evident from the contextual clue that he has driven her to her house despite her unwillingness to be driven in his car. Towards the end of the novel *Socialite Evenings* one observes that Karuna is fatigued after she breaks from Krish. She gets odd job in advertising and gets money too. Even though Girish Sridhar insinuates that he wants to be close to her, she does not wish to be involved with him. She is aware of the imminent gossip of her relationship with him that might be published in the notorious film magazine. Hence when Swapna repeatedly asks her what has passed between her and Girish, Karuna suspends from revealing the truth and also is vague in replying to Swapna's questions. Karuna replies—"Nothing" and "Other things" (247). Her untruthfulness and vagueness suggest that Karuna is rather reluctant to be related to any man at this stage of her life.

Anjali-Karuna's one time mentor—is also being irrelevant and ambiguous when it comes to the relationship between her and her husband Kumar Bhandari. When Karuna asks her to send Murty to collect her chappals from the shoe-shop, Anjali irrelevantly mutters—"You're horrid! But useful. Bye for now" (150). When asked about her married life with Kumar, she is being vague—"Sort of" and "Nothing special" (123). Her attempt is to camouflage the secrets about her husband so that her marriage with him sustains. Ultimately he has given her the financial independence and security though he refuses to have sexual relation with her.

Literature is a mirror of life. It reflects the society of which it is the product. A literary work concentrates in it the social, cultural, economic and religious facts of the period in which it is written. Iyer (2004: 43) observes "Literature is the storehouse of the cultural and sociological aspect of its people." It follows that reading and appreciation of a literary work calls for social, cultural, economic and religious knowledge on the part of a reader who has to accomplish these tasks. There are a variety of aspects of society and culture which are useful in reading literary text. Lazar (1993: 65-66) mentions thirteen such aspects like:

> Objects and products existing in a society, proverbs, idioms and formulaic expressions which embody cultural value, social structures, roles and relationships, customs, traditions and festivals, beliefs and superstitions, political and economic background, institutions, taboos, metaphorical or connotative language, humour, representative (who will represent and when and how), genre and lastly the status of the written language.

These observations implicate that there is a lot between literature and socio-cultural aspects of a country. One gets glimpses of the above socio-cultural realities through the study of literature of a country or a society. In this study we have focused on how Cooperative Principle operates in the five Indian novels in English. The way the characters in the novels deal with the conversational maxims reflects the Indian socio-cultural realities like marriage, rape, sex, pregnancy, relative status and power of the interactions and the structure of human relationships. Madhuri—Vineeta's younger sister—elopes with Ram Sawant—in-charge of the Bicycle stand at her College. When she returns after two days, Vineeta asks her if she has married Ram. Madhuri suspends the maxim of clarity and brevity and in her devious way states that it is with the very purpose of marrying him that she ran away with him and not to get back mother. Her devious manner of reply reflects how the constant bickerings between young and old generations lead to the asocial act of elopement on the part of adolescent and college-going girls like Madhuri in a reformative city like Pune in mid 1980s. The middle-class people like Vanaa, Shakutai and Urmi still shy away from talking freely of sex, rape and pregnancy. Time and again they are untruthful and rather indirect when it comes to such sensitive and delicate issues in the Indian set-up. The bachelors like Abhijit and Bhaskar Jain are forced to be indirect in expressing their love and proposal of marriage to a widow like Vineeta and a married woman like Urmi with a sixty-year-old son Kartik. It reflects that they are held back by the feeling that they have yet no right or power over Vineeta and Urmi respectively.

One also observes that the doting father brings his daughter up like a princess and pampers her. In *Cry, the Peacock*, Maya marries Gautama. Her marriage with Gautama is based on the friendship between her father and Gautama rather than upon anything else. In their encounters with each other they are over or under—informative, untruthful, irrelevant and vague or indirect. These deviations from the conversational maxims reflect how Maya is lacerated from within and how Gautama is a believer in the philosophy of detachment. He refuses to go out for a short holiday with Maya and reasons falsely—"There is a lot of work" (41). Instead of being brief and direct he indirectly refuses her proposal to go South and see the Kathakali dance. He thwarts her by saying—"If that is your reason for wanting to go all that way south, I suggest you wait till a Kathakali troupe comes to give a performance in Delhi, as it is bound to come some time—perhaps in winter. It will be less expensive" (43). It reveals that the marriage between the two lacks love and care and hence is doomed to fail. The marriage that lacks the foundation of love cannot last long and cannot succeed.

Parties seem to be a fashion among the middle-class people too. But they are no more a source of entertainment. They are hollow parties and suggest how these people try to show off their wealth and highlight the loopholes in the family life of others. The Prim lady in *Cry, the Peacock* tries to degrade Mrs. Lal by pointing out that Mrs. Lal has no *ayah*. To save her husband from this degradation Mrs. Lal suspends the maxim of truthfulness in telling the Prim lady—"She does not stay here at night" (70). It gives one a glimpse into the superficiality exhibited by these people—an important stratum of Indian social structure.

Socialization is a process of educating one as a social member. One is acculturated into a social role as a male or female. This entails one's plain roles like that of a son, husband, father and a daughter, a wife and a mother. This process of socialization in a way imposes a role on one. This culturally imposed role constructs one's gender. One is indoctrinated in being and behaving as a son, husband, father, daughter, wife and mother. Gender is, thus, a social and cultural construct. In this process of socialization and gender construction the literature of a country or a society plays a crucial role. One could also study the deviations from the maxims from the point of view of their contribution in construction of ideology and gender. An ideology is a mental representation that forms the basis of social cognition—a basis of shared knowledge and attitudes of a group. The deviations we have studied in the present study function in (re) constructing the ideologies of love, marriage, sex, family and gender in the Indian socio-cultural set up of 80s and 90s.

In *Socialite Evenings*, Anjali deviates from being truthful, relevant and direct on a number of occasions. When asked whether she has been 'deflowered' after her marriage with Kumar, she is being vague and untruthful—"Sort of" and "Nothing special" (123). When asked if she uses a vibrator, she evades the topic by saying—"Let's have lunch" (135). Karuna asks her to send Murty to collect her chappals from the shoe-shop. Anjali suspends the maxim of carrying on the topic of Murty—"You're horrid! But useful. Bye for now" (150). These replies by Anjali project that in this glittering world of Bombay socialites marriage is a deal, a contract. It is a matter of convenience for both the husband and the wife. They can continue living together as husband and wife without having sex at all. It is the money and financial security that keeps the husband and the wife bound together. Fidelity to each other is conveniently neglected—perhaps it is not a matter of consideration at all. This projection of the ideology of marriage exposes what Prasad (2001: 15) comments "The moral and spiritual breakdown in modern society in which a hapless and forsaken woman longs for pleasure and wants to fly freely in the sky of freedom."

In this world of socialites one is indoctrinated directly or indirectly in his or her role as a male or a female. In her school days the protagonist Karuna finds herself in a charmed circle of rich girls like Charlie, Kiran and Manju. One finds how excited Charlie tells Karuna that she was deflowered by an Anglo boy in a car. Her indirectness and Karuna's untruthful remarks in her encounter with her father give one insights into how young girls in this world are charmingly vicious and the middle-class like Karuna are socialized by them and how their role as female is constructed. It is very difficult for a girl or woman in this miserable world of cinema to adhere to moral principle such as chastity. It has the power as Manavar (2001: 117) opines "To shatter the moral values of any human being."

In *The Binding Vine*, on the other hand, we get different facets of the ideologies of sex, marriage and family in the lower middle class women like Shakutai and Sulu. In this section of the Indian patriarchal society marriage seems to be the sole goal of the existence of a young girl like Kalpana. Her chances of getting married are bright as long as she has 'honour.' As long as she does not do anything wrong or anything wrong does not happen to her, she is 'honoured' in society. Once she goes wrong or is wronged by someone, her 'honour' is lost. This is what happens to Kalpana. She is brutally raped by Prabhakar—the husband of her mother's sister Sulu. The sky falls on Shakutai. As a member of the Indian male-dominated society she realizes that pre-marital rape of Kalpana equals to loss of 'honour' for the whole family—her father (who has deserted her mother for another woman), her mother and her younger sister Sandhya. It has undetermined not only the chance of Kalpana's marriage but also that of Sandhya. It is this thought that forces Shakutai to be over-informative when asked how many children she has. Pat comes her reply—"Three. Kalpana is the eldest" (59). She grieves to Urmi and Vanaa—"You people are trying to blacken my daughter's name" (58). "I have another daughter, what will become of her?" (59). It is this very thought that makes Urmi and Vanaa to be untruthful and roundabout in relating to Shakutai that Kalpana has been raped.

The ideology of family as projected in the novel is far from satisfactory. Shakutai's husband left her for another woman and she now shoulders an enormous burden of rearing and marrying off her three children—Kalpana, Sandhya and Prakash. Urmila's husband is a naval officer and has long absences from home and wife Urmi. She reacts to Vanaa—"Marriage with a man who flits into my life a few months in a year and flits out again" (164). Her mother-in-law Mira's marriage was not a happy affair either. A sprightly college girl Mira was persuaded to marry a man who had lustful obsession for her. Then in marriage she was subjected to forced sexual activity under the name of 'love'. Another impression one gathers is that 'sex' is a taboo for these middle-class women. They have apprehensions of talking about 'sex' and 'pregnancy.' This makes Mira suffer the sexual assaults in silence. This also makes Shakutai to be indirect and elliptical while telling Urmi about her sex with her husband and about her pregnancy. She confides to Urmi —"You know what men are, he wanted to." "This happened" (she got pregnant) and "here" (her womb) (111).

One gets a peep into the constructing of contrasting ideologies of sex, marriage, family, love and gender through the study of deviations from the maxims by the urban middle-class section in *Temporary Answers*, *Cry, the Peacock*, *The Binding Vine* and the rich upper-class society in *Socialite Evenings*. Those who follow the traditional codes of conduct for girls and women view marriage as a "bringer of security in such social set up as Indian." In spite of incompatibility between husband and wife women marry for this very reason. This is the view held by Vineeta's mother, by Shakutai who is so much worried about the marriage of her children and even by the protagonist Urmi as she tells Bhaskar that marriage provides security. In *Socialite Evenings*, on the other hand, women view marriage as a matter of convenience. It is not faithfulness to husband or wife that binds them in their marriage but money and financial security that are paramountly significant. In this Bollywood world as Ningthoujam (2006: 100) observes: "Marriages are mere games of catching rich grooms who can be discarded once they become non-functional." Anjali—Karuna's one time mentor—divorces Abbas and has a series of affairs—with an Income-Tax Officer, Pierre-French teacher at Alliance, Karan and finally marries Kumar. Although she realizes that he is a homo, Anjali decides to continue her marriage with him. She gloats in thinking that Kumar is a golden-eggs laying goose. Whenever the topic of her conjugal life with Kumar and that of the boy Murty he has kept comes up, Anjali evades the topic and is at times irrelevant and vague in her replies. Because of the considerations of money, power and fame the institution of family seems to have disintegrated in this Muppyland.

There are codes of conduct for girls and widows and women belonging to the urban middle-class. Vineeta is irritated to find that Abhijit visits her at her flat at ten o'clock at night. He forgets her reputation as a doctor and her position as a widow in her early thirties living alone and away from her parents. It is this irritated mood of Vineeta that makes Abhijit to be indirect in proposing to marry her and persuading her to accept the proposal. Shakutai—a wife deserted by her husband and a mother of three children—prescribes the codes of conduct for Kalpana when she tells Urmi—"Here boys are like—they're like dogs panting after bitches. And if you paint and flaunt yourself, do you think they'll leave you alone? Ever since Kalpana grew up, I have had to live with this fear. But Kalpana does not understand. Once she started earning, she thought she could do anything what she wanted" (146). This is how Shakutai is blatantly irrelevant to Urmi's question about using lipstick. It hints at how a girl is indoctrinated in playing her role as a daughter.

In *Heat and Dust*, one gets insights into the private life of an Indian prince—the Nawab at Khatm. On occasions he is being over-informative, untruthful, irrelevant and circumlocutory whenever Olivia asks him about the arm and rough men. He deviates from the maxims to camouflage the dark sides of his sides of his life. Even Harry—his guest—becomes an accomplice in this task. The Nawab's wife Sandy (Zahira is her real name) is from Cabobpur and the Cabobpurians are threatening to lodge a case of dowry against him. The Nawab's Khatm is bankrupt. He has nexus with the dacoits who pay him the rake—the commission for protecting them. One gets a picture of his sexual, domestic and married life from his deviations from the maxims of Cooperative Principle. His encounters with Olivia expose the dark and the fractured life of his. Put in a sentence—the non-fulfillments of the Gricean maxims by the characters in the five Indian novels in English project or construct various facets of the ideology of sex, love, marriage, family and gender existing among the urban middle-class and the rich upper-class sections of the Indian society. They serve as indicators of how ideologies are communicated and constructed through fictional conversation.

After discussing the significance of the maxim-deviations in producing social implications, reflecting the socio-cultural realities and constructing ideologies of love, sex, marriage, family and gender we would like to record how the Cooperative Principle and the Politeness Principle conflict in human verbal interactions. The present study leads one to state that the Cooperative Principle is sacrificed for the sake of social function of language—being polite to others and saving their "face" a self-esteem that all human beings possess. There are various models of Politeness in pragmatic literature. We have attempted to study deviations from the Gricean maxims for sake of politeness as proposed by Lakoff (1973), Brown and Levinson (1978/1987) and Leech (1983). Philosophers of language and pragmaticists claim that there is a goal/purpose in conducting communication, (i) the goal of being cooperative and (ii) that of being polite to the others. While studying the non-fulfillments of the Gricean maxims we have observed that the characters in the five Indian novels in English sacrifice the maxims of giving required information, truthfulness, relevance and brevity, clarity and orderliness to show their considersation for others. The two types of non-fulfillments in particular—suspension and opting out of maxims function for being polite to the others.

The characters in these novels at times suspend and opt out of being informative, truthful, relevant and brief and clear and the motivation is to save their interlocutor or the third party from social disgrace and from being hurt. Shobha—a daughter of Mrs. Kibe—who was supposed to be with Madhuri—suspends the maxim of truthfulness in her reply to Vineeta that Madhuri was friendly with Ram Sawant with whom Madhuri has eloped. When asked if she thinks of any one Madhuri was friendly with, Shobha hesitatingly says, "No" (55). In the circumstances Shobha and Mrs. Kibe realize that admitting Madhuri's friendliness with Ram would amount to passing on gossip about Madhuri. This in turn would threaten the 'face' of not only Madhuri but also that of her family as a whole. To save them all from disgrace and from being hurt Shobha tells a lie to Vineeta. This is because as Michell (1984: 376) observes "Women more often simply lie to protect themselves from verbal and physical abuse in a misogynist culture." Here, Shobha lies to protect another woman from being hurt and being disgraced socially.

The lies told by Harry to Olivia in connection with the Nawab's nexus with the dacoits—"Honestly, I don't know Olivia" (103). About the Nawab's domestic and financial troubles—"Oh, I don't know Olivia." (142) are 'alter-centred'. Harry employs the strategy of lying to protect the Nawab's positive face –desire to be liked by others. In *Cry, the Peacock*, Mrs. Lal suspends the maxim of truthfulness when asked if she has no *ayah* by replying—"She does not stay here at night" (70) and the reason is to save not only herself but also her husband from being degraded. On the same occasion it is to make her guests feel easy and comfortable that she tells falsely that she has not been hurt by hitting against her husband's chin. It is obvious that her collision with her husband has hurt her head and perhaps her eye that gets red and weeping. It is for the guests' comfort that with surprising decisiveness she says, "No" (72).

Anjali in *Socialite Evenings* suspends the maxim of relevance on a couple of occasions and this seems to be her move to avoid bringing her husband Kumar and the boy Murty in focus. When Karuna asks her to send the boy Murty to collect her chappals from the shoe-shop, she mutters—"You're horrid! But useful.

Bye for now" (150). When asked about the things between her and husband, she irrelevantly spits on Si in reply—"I can feel her bad vibrations everywhere. She spreads *paap* wherever she goes. She is so morally corrupt" (141). As reader one gathers that this is her move to save her husband from being vilely talked about by Si. Earlier too when Karuna asks her if she has been 'deflowered' by Kumar, Anjali is being vague and rather elliptical in her reply—"Sort of" (123). The motivation for sustaining her marriage and relationship with Kumar is an important factor behind her being elliptical and vague in her reply. It is necessary that Anjali saves Kumar from being exposed. Her suspension from being clear or straightforward is, therefore, alter-centred.

In *The Binding Vine* which deals with a sensitive issue—pre-marital and marital rape, the characters like Vanaa, Urmi and Shakutai are over-informative, untruthful, irrelevant and indirect in their verbal interactions. Talking about Kalpana being raped Shakutai says—"They all know about it, *tai*," "they were trying to get it out of her, what happened to Kalpana" (91). "The kind of things they are saying, the police, the people about Kalpana. Such dirt" (177) and "Prabhakar, he-he did it to my Kalpana, my Sulu's husband" (188). She is being indirect and her indirectness is indicative of her worries about not only Kalpana but also about Sandhya. Vanaa and Urmi face the clash between being truthful and direct in telling Shakutai about Kalpana's rape. To be considerate to her—not to hurt her—they suspend and opt out of the maxim of truthfulness and directness—"Your daughter hasn't done anything" (58) "It was an accident, a car knocked her down," "Someone has wronged her" (58). Their deviations from the maxim of truthfulness and directness attempt what West, Lazar and Kramarae (1997: 124) say "To suppress the question of why so many men assault women in the first place." Bhaskar Jain opts out of being direct in expressing his love and desire to marry Urmi—"None. Except that I've gone and fallen in love a dark, sharp-tongued, married woman" (161). One recalls here how Abhijit Gokhale avoids imposing marriage proposal on Vineeta—"What shall we do now? Do you suppose you could marry me? That would make it all right, wouldn't it?" (91). He is being polite to her by not imposing and by giving her the freedom to accept or reject his proposal.

These instances of non-fulfillments of the maxims by the characters in the five novels under study support the observation that one of the motivations for sacrificing the Cooperative Principle is to be polite to the others. In pragmatic terminology these deviations from the maxims of Cooperative Principle are the off-record strategies of being polite. Employing the off-record strategies of politeness means being polite in such a way as to hide it. In simplest terms it would mean being polite through sacrificing the maxims of Cooperative Principle. The off-record strategies of politeness employed by the characters in the five novels could diagrammatically be shown as under:

Cooperative Principle maxims-deviations	Quantity	– being over-informative – being under informative
	Quality	– telling lies – being ironical
	Relation	– changing the topic (without hedging)
	Manner	– being vague/ambiguous – being idiomatic – being indirect/oblique

Broadly speaking these strategies of politeness are the deviations from the Gricean maxims that perform the social or phatic function of language-strengthening relationship and promoting comity with fellow-beings.

The deviations from the Gricean maxims produce implicatures and social implications. Social implications are something that tell us about the character/speaker and about the relationship between the speaker and hearer. Implicatures are, on the other hand, the implicated meanings which are calculated by the hearer on the basis of conventional/literal meaning of utterance and the assumption of verbal cooperation. These are produced when a speaker flouts a maxim. The implicatures and social implications are suggested meanings/

suggestions—meanings other than the literal meanings of utterances. K.K. Raja (1963: 279) uses the term '*Vyanjana*' or 'suggestion' for such meanings. This *Vyanjana,* he claims, is the suggestive power of language. Jespersen (1948: 309) opines "Suggestion is impression through suppression. Expression is what the speaker gives, suppression is what he does not give and impression is what the hearer receives." This suggestion or suggestive meaning is conveyed when a maxim is contravened by characters in the five selected novels.

This brings us to the relation between the suggested meaning and the study of literature—in particular the study of novel. We arrive at the suggested meanings in novel via the study of how characters deviate from the maxims—the norms that guide our reading and study of novel. Thorat (2007: 67) believes that "Literature can be looked at as socio-linguistic fact recognized by a culture as possessing certain institutional values and performing certain socio-cultural functions." He looks at innovations and deviations made by Indian writers in English. One can look at deviations from the Gricean maxims, as he says, as an adaptable resource for making meaning. It is necessary that one seriously considers how and why the character deviates from or non-fulfils a maxim in a given context.

A perusal of the deviations from the maxims in a novel leads one to the meanings hinted or suggested. Talking of the novel *The Portrait of a Lady* by Henry James, Peck (1995: 50) comments, "The novel consists of hints rather than statements." This observation applies well to the present study of deviations and the study of novels selected. The novel *Pride and Prejudice* by Jane Austen opens with a statement—"It is a truth universally acknowledged that a single man in possession of a good fortune must be in want of a wife." If the ironic significance of this statement is not taken cognizance of, it is likely that the interpretation of the novel will be missed. The point is that one needs to view and evaluate the statement in terms of violation from the maxim of Quality. The characters, the context, the utterances and their literal meaning are all the crucial factors and aspects of interpretation of novel. Hence, Rajimwale (1998: 225) pertinently remarks "Interpretation strategies are, therefore, devised to unfold the process and mechanism of these factors lending significance to the actual written text."

The present study undertaken has applied the Cooperative Principle as an interpretative strategy. The implicatures and the social implications embedded in novelistic utterances can be unearthed with the application of the interpretative strategy of this principle—its non-fulfillment by characters in the novel. This study has attempted to do this. This has led to interesting, significant and illuminating revelations about the language used in novel. The process of interpreting a novel is like winnowing away the chaff from the grain. The chaff is the *Abhidha*—the primary or literal meaning of novelistic utterances and the grain is the *Vyanjana*—the suggested meaning of the utterances. Maxim-deviations are the devices that assist one in this process of winnowing.

Communicators employ different ways of conveying what they want to convey. Much of what they intend to convey is done in an indirect or an implicit manner. If one intends to criticize someone, one is generally indirect. One may accomplish this task by being ironical. Irony is a device that helps one in causing offence in an indirect way. In fact, the Irony principle demands that if you intend to cause offence, do it in such a way that it does not conflict with the Politeness Principle. In pragmatic terms—be ironical if you want to offend or criticize your addressee. This, in other words, means that you sacrifice being truthful in order to be polite to your addressee. This is what Karuna in *Socialite Evenings* does when she remarks about Nisha to Anjali—"Oh, great! She sounds real classy" (103). Philosophers of language call such acts as criticizing, requesting, advising, complimenting, congratulating, threatening and offering speech acts. Austin (1962: 6) claims "The issuing of the utterance is the performing of an action." These actions performed by producing utterances are speech acts. These are variously called 'language acts', 'linguistic acts' 'communicative acts' or 'illocutionary forces.'

Austin classifies the speech acts into three categories: (i) Locutionary act—an act of uttering speech sounds, morphemes, words and phrases, (ii) Illocutionary act—an act performed by a speaker in producing an utterance and (iii) Perlocutionary act—an act of producing some effect on the action, thought, attitude and feeling of an addressee. In the above illustration Karuna's act of producing the utterance—'Oh, great! She sounds real classy' is a locutionary act. Her intention to be critical of Nisha is her illocutionary act—speech act of criticizing. Anjali takes Karuna's utterance literally and goes on adding the pluses of Nisha. This is the perlocutionary act. What is striking about Karuna's criticism of Nisha is that she is criticizing without using the verb-'criticise.'

Speech act theorists divide the speech acts into two broad categories: direct speech act and indirect speech act. A direct speech act is an act which uses an explicit performative verb to perform the act such as—'I *order* you to get out' and 'I *warn* you to abstain from wine.' An indirect speech act is as Watts (2003: 190) states "One in which the illocutionary force of the speaker's utterance does not correspond in a one-to-one fashion with the illocutionary act." Hence Downes (1984: 317) suggests "We must infer the indirect act." A direct speech act is an act which is directly cooperative in nature in that the utterance which performs the act is sufficiently informative, not misleading, relevant and is brief and orderly and overtly uses the performative verb intended for that act. An indirect speech act is indirectly cooperative in that it involves deviations from a maxim of cooperation. In *Temporary Answers* Abhijit's intention is to persuade Vineeta to marry him but he performs the act by being indirect—by opting out of the maxim of Manner. Vineeta infers Abhijit's indirect act of persuasion and refuses the proposal by saying—"You are utterly mad" (91). With these illustrations one can state that deviations from the Cooperative Principle can be looked at as performing indirect speech acts. It would be a fascinating study to examine the deviations in terms of indirect speech acts. Speech acts are realized differently in different cultures. Hence, Patil Z.N. (1997: 47) asserts "Literary sources can provide valuable data for identifying culture-specific speech act effects." There are immense possibilities of viewing deviations from the cooperative maxims as performing indirect acts.

Another possibility of future exploration is the perlocutionary effect—the effect that the deviation from a maxim has on the hearer. It is interesting to see how the hearer recovers the semantic uptake/the implicated meaning of the speaker. It is also important to see how the hearer reacts or responds to the speaker's utterance—which is a deviation from the maxim of Cooperative Principle. Attardo (1997: 756) proposes "locutionary cooperation" (LC) and "perlocutionary cooperation" (PC). Locutionary cooperation is the cooperation that the speaker and the hearer put into the text to encode and decode its meaning. Perlocutionary cooperation is the cooperation that two speakers must put into the text/situation to achieve the goal that the speaker wants to achieve with the utterance. There is relation between the maxims and the purpose of the talk. Grice (1989: 28) states "The conversational maxims are especially connected with the particular purposes which talk (so talk exchange) is adapted to serve." Certainly the transmission of information is too narrow a goal of conversation. Conversation as a purposive behaviour and has to account for purposes such as influencing or directing the actions of others. Once a character deviates from a maxim, it is possible that it is meant to affect the hearer—his attitude, belief, action or thought. The present study could be extended to the examination of deviations and the perlocutionary effect.

While examining deviations and reconstruction of ideologies of love, sex, marriage, family and gender in the five novels we observed that the deviations in *Temporary Answers* and *The Binding Vine* and those in *Socialite Evenings* project contrasting ideologies of sex, marriage, family and gender. A comparative approach could be adopted to examine deviations by characters belonging to urban middle-class as in the former two novels and those belonging to the rich upper-class in the latter novel. Different facets of these ideologies emerge as we saw in an example or two. It could be examined how people from different sections of the Indian socio-cultural set up exploit the Gricean maxims of verbal cooperation. We have not done this in the present study.

Despite the empiricist and rationalist justifications of the Gricean Principle of conversational cooperation its application is language-specific and culture-dependent. As Horn (1988: 131) notes "The principles of Grice and others might well be universal but their relative strength in a given context might well vary across languages and cultures." The same is true of the so-called theories of Politeness by Goffman, Lakoff and Brown and Levinson. The pragmaticists from the Non-Western cultures claim that the Western scholars' claim to universality of their theories is invalid. Ming-Chung Yu (2003) and Yuegono Gu (1990) argue that the maxims of politeness in Chinese are moral maxims and the Western concept of negative face which shows concerns for individual's privacy and autonomy is irrelevant in Chinese and Japanese cultures which value collective orientation. In fact, Gu (1990) proposes four maxims of politeness: (i) The Self-denigration maxim: This maxim absorbs the element of respectfulness—self's positive appreciation or admiration of other concerning other's face and social status. (ii) The Address maxim: In Chinese a proper name is arranged in the order—surname + middle name + given name. The middle name cannot be used alone. In Chinese the given name is an address term to be used by lovers and occasionally by parents. English culture, on the other hand, has reverse order. (iii) The Generosity maxim and (iv) Tact maxim: In Chinese culture invitation involves talk-exchanges like invitation, decline-invitation again, decline again and insisting invitee's presence and acceptance of invitation. It may be realized in a single utterance as in English culture. Matsumoto (1988) argues that in Japanese the concept of preserving individual's territories seems alien. One must acknowledge one's dependence on the others and one's acceptance by other members of the group.

These arguments suggest that there is a need for development of pragmatic theories to be applied to interaction in multilingual speech communities. As Janney (2007: 36) claims the so-called Western theories rely "On assumptions rooted in monolingual Western communities and cultures." As novels and other literary works are socio-linguistic facts, the applications of so-called pragmatic theories to Non-Western literature such as Indian novel in English would provide valid data about how these principles operate in this culture. The present study would make a substantial contribution as data for developing pragmatic theories for such Non-Western multilingual culture as Indian.

The Gricean framework of maxims and their non-fulfillments equips one to process meaning in fictional conversation. The maxims which are the guidelines for conducting conversation serve as Blum-Kulka Shoshana (1997: 39) puts "To systematize the process of inferencing and ensure its success." They add to the enrichment of interpretation of texts and assist one to make sense out of apparent non-sense—apparently unrelated, literally false, ironical and ambiguous verbal contributions by communicators. Specifically the deviations from the maxims serve as windows through which one peeps into the characters' personality, their relationship with interlocutor, their social status and role and their communicative intention. They assist one to go beneath the mask of the characters and see the latent individual, social and cultural reality. It would be no exaggeration to state that in the study of deviations from the Gricean maxims lies God's plenty.

Bibliography

Primary Sources

De, S. (1989) *Socialite Evenings*. New Delhi: Penguin Books.

Desai, A. (1980) *Cry, the Peacock*. Delhi: Orient Paperbacks.

Deshpande, S. (1993) *The Binding Vine*. New Delhi: Penguin Books India Pvt. Ltd.

Jhabvala, R.P. (1975/1994) *Heat and Dust*. London: Penguin Books Ltd.

Nimbkar, J. (1974) *Temporary Answers*. Mumbai: Orient Longman Ltd.

Secondary Sources

Akmajian *et al.* (2001) *Linguistics: An Introduction to Language and Communication*. Delhi: Prentice Hall of India Pvt. Ltd.

Attardo, S. (1997) "Locutionary and Perlocutionary Cooperation: The Perlocutionary Cooperative Principle." *Journal of Pragmatics*, Vol. 27, (6), 753-79.

Austin, J.L. (1962*) How To Do Things With Words*. Cambridge, Mass.: Harvard University Press.

Barat, Urbashi (2000) "From Victim to Non-Victim: Socialite Evenings as a version of Kunstlerroman." Jaydipsinh Dodiya ed. *The Fiction of Shobha De*. New Delhi: Prestige Books, 119-28.

Batra, S. and P.S. Sidhu eds. (1980) *A Choice of Short Stories*. Delhi: Oxford University Press.

Besnier, N. (1986) "Information Withholding as a Manipulative and Collasive Strategy in Nukalaelae Gossip." *Language in Society*, 18, 315-41.

Bijawat, R. (1997) *The Evolving Image of India In The Novels of Mrs. Ruth P. Jhabvala*. New Delhi: Classical Publishing Company.

Black, E. (2006) *Pragmatic Stylistics*. Edinburgh: Edinburgh University Press.

Blum-Kulka, S. (1997) "Discourse Pragmatics." Teun A. Van Dijk ed. *Discourse as Social Interaction: Discourse Studies: A Multidisciplinary Introduction,* Vol. 2, London: Sage Publications, 38-63.

——. (2005) "The Metapragmatics of Politeness in Israeli Culture." Richard J. Watts, Sachiko Ide and Konrad Ehlich eds. *Politeness in Language: Studies in its History, Theory and Practice*. Berlin: Walter de Gruyter Gmbh and Co., 255-80.

Board of Editors (1998/2006) *Popular Short Stories*. New Delhi: Oxford University Press.

Borate, T.S. (1993) "Love and Marriage Versus Individual Freedom: Temporary Answers." R.K. Dhawan ed. *Indian Women Novelists*, Set II Vol. I, New Delhi: Prestige Books, 221-35.

Boulton, M. (1975) *The Anatomy of the Novel*. London: Routledge and Kegan Paul Ltd.

Brown, P. and G. Yule (1983) *Discourse Analysis*. Cambridge: Cambridge University Press.

Brown, P. and S. Levinson (1978) "Universals in Language Usage: Politeness Phenomena." E.N. Goody ed. *Questions and Politeness: Strategies in Social Interaction*. Cambridge: Cambridge University Press, 56-311.

——. (1987) *Politeness: Some Universals in Language Usage*. Cambridge: Cambridge University Press.

Burt, S.M. (2002) "Maxim Confluence." *Journal of Pragmatics*, Vol. 34, 993-1001.

Chandra, S. (2000) "Family and Marriage in Socialite Evenings." Jaydipsinh Dodiya ed. *The Fiction of Shobha De*. New Delhi: Prestige Books, 142-48.

Chilton, P. (1987) "Cooperation and Non-Cooperation: Ethical and Political Aspects of Pragmatics." *Language and Communication: An Interdisciplinary Journal*, Vol. 3, (3), 221-39.

Choudhary, B. (1995) *Women and Society in the Novels of Anita Desai*. Delhi: Creative Books.

Coates, J. (1986) *Women, Men and Language*. Essex: Longman Group Ltd.

Cook, G. (1994) *Discourse and Literature*. Oxford: Oxford University Press.

Crystal, D. (1997) *The Cambridge Encyclopaedia of Language*. Cambridge: Cambridge University Press.

——. (2004) *The Language Revolution*. Malden: Polity Press.

Cutting, J. (2000) *Pragmatics and Discourse*. London: Routledge.

Desai, A. (1982/1988) *The Village By* The *Sea*. London: Penguin Books.

——. (1985) *Bye Bye Blackbird*. New Delhi: Orient Paperbacks.

Dews, S. and E. Winner (1997) "Attributing Meaning to deliberately false utterances: The Case of Irony." C. Mandell and A. McCabe eds. *The Problem of Meaning: Behavourial and Cognitive Perspectives*. Amsterdam: Elsevier, 377-414.

Dickens, C. (1860/1965) *Great Expectations*. Harmondsworth: Penguin Books Ltd.

——. (1996) *Hard Times*. Mumbai: Orient Longman Ltd.

Downes, W. (1984) *Language and Society*. London: Fontana Paperbacks.

Ferreira, V.S., L.R. Sleven and E.S. Roggers (2005) "How do speakers avoid ambiguous linguistic expressions?" *Cognition: International Journal of Cognitive Science*, Vol. 96, (3), 263-84.

Fielding, H. (1742, Reprint 2002) *Joseph Andrews*. New Delhi: UBS Publishers Distributors Ltd.

Finegan, E. and N. Besnier (1989) *Language: Its Structure and Use*. New York: Harcourt Brace Jovanovich Publishers.

Forrester, M.A. (1996) *Psychology of Language*. London: Sage Publications Ltd.

Forster, E.M. (1995) *Aspects of the Novel*. New Delhi: Atlantic Publishers and Distributors.

Fowler, R. (1977) *Linguistics and the Novel*. London: Methuen and Co. Ltd.

Frank, J. (1990) "You Call That A Rhetorical Question?" *Journal of Pragmatics*, Vol. 14, (5), 723-38.

Fraser, B. (1990) "Perspectives on Politeness." *Journal of Pragmatics*, Vol. 14, (2), 219-36.

Fraser, B. and W. Nolen (1981) "The Association of Deference with Linguistic Form."

International Journal of the Sociology of Language, Vol. 27, 93-109.

Gibbs, R.W.Jr. (1987) "Mutual Knowledge and the Psychology of Inference." *Journal of Pragmatics*, Vol. 11, 561-88.

Giddens, A. (1989/ 1993) *Sociology*. Oxford: Blackwell.

Giora, R., O. Fein and T. Schwarz (1998) "Irony: Graded Salience and Indirect Negation." *Metaphor and Symbol,* 13, 83-101.

Goffman, E. (1967) *Interaction Rituals: Essays on Face to Face Behaviour*. New York: Doubleday.

Grant, I. and Paul Nation (2006) "How Many Idioms Are There in English?" *International Journal of Applied Linguistics,* Vol. 151, 1-14.

Grice, H.P. (1971) "Meaning." Steinberg, D.D. and I.A. Jokobovits eds. *Semantics: An Interdisciplinary Reader in Philosophy, Linguistics and Psychology.* Cambridge: Cambridge University Press, 53-65.

——. (1975) "Logic and Conversation." P. Cole and J.L. Morgan eds. *Syntax and Semantics,* Vol. 3: Speech Acts, New York: Academic Press, 41-58.

——. (1982) "Meaning Revisited." N. Smith ed. *Mutual Knowledge*. New York: Academic Press Inc., 223-43.

——. (1989) *Studies in the Way of Words*. London: Harvard University Press.

——. (1997) "Utterer's Meaning and Intentions." P. Ludlow ed. *Readings in the Philosophy of Language*. Massachusetts: MIT Press, 59-88.

Grundy, P. (2000) *Doing Pragmatics*. London: Hodder Headline Group.

Gu, Y. (1990) "Politeness Phenomena in Modern Chinese." *Journal of Pragmatics*, Vol. 14, (2), 237-57.

Guttal, V. (2003) "Shashi Deshpande's The Binding Vine and A Matter of Time: A Reading in Post-Colonial Context." *Littcrit: An Indian Response to Literature*, Vol. 29, (1), 55-63.

Halliday, M.A.K. (1973) *Explorations in the Functions of Language*. London: Edward Arnold.

Holmes, J. (1988) "Paying Compliments: A Sex-Preferential Politeness Strategy." *Journal of Pragmatics,* Vol. 12, 445-65.

——. (1992) *An Introduction to Sociolinguistics*. London: Longman.

Horn, H.R. (1988) "Pragmatic Theory." Newmeyer, F.J. ed. *Linguistics: The Cambridge Survey I*. Cambridge: Cambridge University Press, 113-45.

Hudson, R.A. (1980) *Sociolinguistics*. Cambridge: Cambridge University Press.

Indira, S. (1995) "A Bond or a Burden? A Study of Shashi Deshpande's The Binding Vine." R.K. Dhawan ed. *Indian Women Novelists*, Set III, Vol. VI, New Delhi: Prestige Books, 21-27.

Iyer, S.S. (2004) "Socialisation and Gender Construction in Shashi Deshpande's Novels." T.M.J. Indra Mohan ed. *Shashi Deshpande: A Critical Spectrum*. New Delhi: Atlantic Publishers and Distributors, 42-48.

Janney, R.W. (2007) "Post-Colonial Pragmatics." *Asian Quarterly: An International Journal of Contemporary Issues*, Vol. 5, (1), 27-42.

Jawale, V.G., G.B. Moharir, V.A. Patil, R.T. Bavaskar, A.A. Sutar and A.S. Bagul eds. (2002) *English For Students of Arts*. Jalgaon: Prashant Publications.

Jesperson, O. (1948) *The Philosophy of Grammar*. London: Allen and Unwin.

Jhabvala, R.P. (1971) *An Experience of India*. London: John Murray.

——. (1972) *A New Dominion*. London: John Murray.

Kasper, G. (1990) "Linguistic Politeness: Current Research Issues." *Journal of Pragmatics*, Vol. 14, (2), 193-218.

Katz, J.J. (1972) *Semantic Theory*. New York: Harper and Row.

Keenan, E. (1976) "The Universality of Conversational Postulates." *Language in Society*, Vol. 5, 67-80.

Kelkar, A. (1999) "Language as Empowerment." *South Asian Language Review*, Vol. 9, (1 and 2), 1-16.

Krishnaswamy, N., S.K. Verma and M. Nagarajan (1992) *Modern Applied Linguistics*. Madras: Macmillan India Press.

Lakoff, R. (1973) "The Logic of Politeness or Minding Your P's and Q's." *Papers from the Ninth Regional Meeting of Chicago Linguistic Society*. Chicago: Chicago Linguistic Society, 292-305.

Lawrence, D.H. (1992/2004) *Sons and Lovers*. New Delhi: Fortune Books.

Lazar, G. (1993) *Literature and Language Teaching*. Cambridge: Cambridge University Press.

Leech, G.N. (1983) *Principles of Politeness*. London: Longman.

Leech, G.N. and M. Short (1981/1986) *Style in Fiction: A Linguistic Introduction to English Fictional Prose*. Essex: Longman Group Ltd.

Levinson, S.C. (1983) *Pragmatics*. London: Cambridge University Press.

Lokhandwala, M. (2007) "The Cultural Nuances of English in Non-Native Contexts." *Asian Quarterly: An International Journal of Contemporary Issues,* Vol. 5, (3), 86-104.

Lyons, J. (2002) *Language and Linguistics: An Introduction.* Cambridge: Cambridge University Press.

Mala, R. (1991) "Sexual Predicament and Shashi Deshpande's Women." R.K. Dhawan ed. *Indian Women Novelists*, Set I, Vol. V, New Delhi: Prestige Books, 50-59.

Manawar, Twinkle B. (2001) "A Film Star's Struggle of life in Shobha De's Starry Nights." A.N. Prasad ed. *Indian Women Novelists in English*, New Delhi: Atlantic Publishers and Distributors, 112-17.

Matsumoto, Y. (1988) "Reexamination of the Universality of face: Politeness Phenomena in Japanese." *Journal of Pragmatics*, Vol. 12, 403-26.

Meerabai, K. (1996) *Women's Voices: The Novels of Indian Women Novelists.* New Delhi: Prestige Books.

Mehta, R. (1977) *Inside the Haveli.* New Delhi: Arnold Heinemann.

Mey, J. (1999) *When Voices Clash: A Study in Literary Pragmatics.* Berlin INy: Mouton de Gruyter.

——. (2001) *Pragmatics: An Introduction.* Massachusetts: Blackwell Publishers Ltd.

Michell, G. (1984) "Women and Lying: A Pragmatic and Semantic Analysis of telling it slant." *Women's Studies International Forum,* 7, 375-80.

Mohanty, J. ed. (1983) *Ten Short Stories.* Hyderabad: University Press (India) Ltd.

Monti, A. (2000) "Shakti Unleashed in Muppyland: Shobha De and the Making of Modern India." Jaydipsinh Dodiya ed. *The Fiction of Shobha De.* New Delhi: Prestige Books, 27-33.

Mooney, A. (2004) "Cooperation, Violations and Making Sense." *Journal of Pragmatics*, Vol. 36, (5), 899-920.

Nahal, C. (1975) *Azadi.* Delhi: Orient Paperbacks.

Narayan, R.K. (1958) *The Guide*. Chennai: Indian Thought Publications.

——. (1965) *The Bachelor of Arts*. Chennai: Indian Thought Publications.

——. (1999) *Under The Bunyan Tree and Other Stories*. Chennai: Indian Thought Publications.

Nayar, P.K. (2000) "Socialite Evenings: Towards a Feminist Romance?" Jaydipsinh Dodiya ed. *THE FICTION OF SHOBHA DE*. New Delhi: Prestige Books, 108-18.

Nerlich, B. and David D. Clarke (2001) "Ambiguities We Live By: Towards a Pragmatics of Polysemy." *Journal of Pragmatics*, Vol. 33, (1), 1-20.

Ningthoujam, I.S. (2004) *Image of the New Woman in the Novels of Shobha De*. New Delhi: Prestige Books.

Nityanandam, I. (1995) "Shashi Deshpande's The Bindign Vine: Silent No More." R.K. Dhawan ed. *Indian Women Novelists*, Set III: Vol. IV, New Delhi: Prestige Books, 6-66.

Pandharipande, R. (1992) "Defining Politeness in Indian English." *World Englishes*, Vol. 11, (2 and 3), 241-50.

Patil, S.R. (2007) "Shobha De: Her Command Upon Language: A Critique." *Academic Research*, Vol. 1, (2), 58-64.

Patil, Z.N. (1994) *Style in Indian English Fiction*. New Delhi: Prestige Books.

——. (1999) "A Once-born literature in a twice-born language: Indianness in Indian English Novel." K.V. Tirumalesh ed. *Language Matters: Essays on Language, Literature and Translation*. New Delhi: Allied Publishers, 41-58.

Paul, S. (1993) "Heat and Dust: An Alien Perspective." R.K. Dhawan ed. *Indian Women Novelists,* Set II, Vol. VI, Delhi: prestige Books, 69-82.

Peck, J. (1995) *How To Study a Novel*. New York: Palgrave.

Prabhu, P.H. (1958) *Hindu Social Organization: A Study in Socio-Psychological and Ideological Foundations*. Bombay: Popular.

Prasad, Amar Nath (2001) "A Brief History of Indian Women Novelists in English." A.N. Prasad ed. *Indian Women Novelists in English*, New Delhi: Atlantic Publishers and Distributors, 1-18.

Push Lata (2000) "A Protest Against the Patriarchal in Shobha De's Works." Jaydipsinh Dodiya ed. *The Fiction of Shobha De*. New Delhi: Prestige Books, 62-68.

Rai, U. and S.M. Rai (2003) *Business Communication*. Mumbai: Himalaya Publishing House.

Raja, K.K. (1963) *Indian Theories of Meaning*. Madras: The Adyar Library and Research Centre.

Rajimwale, S. (1998) *Elements of General Linguistics*, Vol. II, New Delhi: Rama Brothers.

Ramanujan, A.K. (1995) *The Collected) Poems*. Oxford: Oxford University Press.

Rao, R. (1974) *Kanthapura*. Oxford: Oxford University Press.

Ryan, M. (2004) *Literary Theory: A Practical Introduction*. Oxford: Blackwell Publishers Ltd.

Sagar, P. (2000) *Anita Desai's 'Cry, The Peacock'*. Agra: Educational Publishers.

Schiffrin, D. (1995) *Approaches to Discourse Analysis*. Oxford: Blackwell Publishers Ltd.

Searle, J. (1969) *Speech Acts: An Essay in the Philosophy of Language*. Cambridge: Cambridge University Press.

——. (1975) "Indirect Speech Acts." P. Cole and J.L. Morgan eds. *Syntax and Semantics, Vol. 3: Speech Acts*, New York: Academic Press, 59-82.

Shahane, V.A. (1976) *Ruth Prawer Jhabvala*. Delhi: Arnold Heinemann.

Sharma, R.K. and R. Sharma (1997) *Social Psychology*. New Delhi: Atlantic Publishers and Distributors.

Sperber, D. and D. Wilson (1986) *Relevance: Communication and Cognition*. Oxford: Blackwell.

Stenstrom, Anna-Brita (1994) *An Introduction to Spoken Interaction*. New York: Longman Group Ltd.

Stockwell, P. (2003) *Sociolinguistics: A Resource Book for Students*. New York: Routledge.

Surendran, C.P. (1992) "Just Another De." *The Illustrated Weekly of India*, 6 Nov., 1992.

Swain, S.P. (2000) "Socialite Evenings: A Feminist Study." Jaydipsinh Dodiya ed. *The Fiction of Shobha De*. New Delhi: Presige Books, 129-41.

Syal, P. and D.V. Jindal (1999) *An Introduction to Linguistics: Language, Grammar and Semantics*. New Delhi: Prentice-Hall of India Pvt. Ltd.

Taylor, T.J. and C. Deborah (1987) *Analysing Conversation: Rules and Units in the Structure of Talk*. Oxford: Pergamon Press.

Thomas, J. (1995) *Meaning in Interaction: An Introduction to Pragmatics*. Harlow: Addison Wesley Longman Ltd.

Thorat, A. (2000) *Five Great Indian Novels: A Discourse Analysis*. New Delhi: Prestige Books.

——. (2007) "Indian English: Acculturation of an Alien Language." *Asian Quarterly: An International Journal of Contemporary Issues*, Vol. 5, (3), 57-66.

Trudgill, P. (1983) *Sociolinguistics: An Introduction to Language and Society*. Harmondsworth: Penguin.

Walker, R.C.S. (19975) "Conversational Implicatures." Blackburn S. ed. *Meaning, Reference and Necessity*. Cambridge: Cambridge University Press, 133-181.

Walter, I. (2000) "Socialite Evenings: An Initiation Tale from Ignorance to Experience." Jaydipsinh Dodiya ed. *The Fiction of Shobha De*. New Delhi: Prestige Books, 149-59.

Wardhough, R. (1986) *An Introduction to Sociolinguistics*. Oxford: Basil Blackwell Ltd.

Watts, R.J. (2003) *Politeness*. Cambridge: Cambridge University Press.

Weisler, S.E. and S. Milekic (2000) *Theory of Language*. Massachusetts: MIT Press.

Weisman, E. (1989) "Requesting Hints." Blum-Kulka S., House J. and Kasper G. eds. *Cross-Cultural Pragmatics: Requests and Apologies*. Ablex, Norwood: New Jersey, 71-95.

West, C.M., M. Lazar and Cheris Kramarae (1997) "Gender in Discourse." Teun A. van Dijk ed. *Discourse as Social Interaction: Discourse Studies: A Multidisciplinary Introduction*. Vol. 2, London: Sage Publications, 119-43.

Weirzbicka, A. (1985) "Different Cultures, Different Languages, Different Speech Acts." *Journal of Pragmatics*, Vol. 9, (2 and 3), 145-78.

Yadugiri, M.A. and B. Naidu eds. (1996) *Understanding Literature*. Mumbai: Orient Longman Ltd.

Yu, Ming-Chung (2003) "On the Universality of face: evidence from Chinese compliment response behavior." *Journal of Pragmatics*, Vol. 35, 1679-1710.

Yule, G. (1996) *Pragmatics*. Oxford: Oxford University Press.

Index